MW00327759

BOTTLENECK

A DRINKING MEMOIR

PAUL FUHR

EAST SHOREWAY RECOVERY SERVICES

ADVANCE PRAISE FOR

BOTTLENECK

"In his first book, Paul Fuhr has created a masterpiece. A tragicomic tale told with the sort of hilarious horror that makes it as addictive as any of the alcohol described, *Bottleneck* is as wise as Mary Karr's *Lit,* as darkly amusing as Jerry Stahl's *Permanent Midnight,* and as profound as Sarah Hepola's *Blackout.* This is the sort of instant classic that leaves you wondering not only how he survived the nearly unsurvivable but also how he's managed to make the story into one of the best recovery memoirs of all time."
—Anna David, *New York Times* bestselling author of *Party Girl*

"Paul Fuhr's *Bottleneck* is a memoir that is honest, terrifying, heartbreaking, invigorating, and inspirational. Yes, it is all these things and more. It is as if Fuhr sliced open his heart and allowed to flow freely what was first the joy and then the pain of that river of plague called alcoholism. This true story of a young man's "lost weekend" is so well-written and engaging that I finished it within twenty-four hours. *Bottleneck* deserves to be a classic. Highly recommended."
—Raymond Benson, *New York Times* bestselling author of 007, *The Black Stiletto* books, and *In the Hush of the Night*

"Reading this book was like experiencing a car crash in slow motion." —Chris Aguirre, *Since Right Now* podcast

"At times hilarious and heart-wrenching, Paul Fuhr's *Bottleneck* is an unflinchingly honest look at the author's descent into alcoholism and his hard-fought, ongoing recovery. Fuhr identifies the insidious seeds of alcoholism that were planted in his childhood and the fallacies that fed its roots as it flourished into a sickly tree casting a shadow over his growth as a husband and father. We watch him navigate the fog of addiction, lamenting how the events of his life play, not like the Hollywood blockbuster flicks that inspired him, but like low-budget, 'low-buffering videos.' And we cheer him on, admiring his forthrightness, into the lucidity of recovery. His journey unfolds like a stunning reboot, a director's cut of the filmmakers he has looked up to, and we're grateful to be there with him for the cinematic telling."

—Chuck Salmons, author of *Patch Job* and *Stargazer Suite*

"*Bottleneck* is an eye-opening and courageous memoir of the dark depths of where alcoholism can go. Paul Fuhr is a masterly storyteller who shares the visceral deep feeling of what it's like to be an alcoholic from morning until night, 24/7. He doesn't take any breaks from his disease. I could taste, sense and feel where he was in each part of his book; whether it was in a dive bar or how he felt towards the end of his drinking, he delivers a compelling story that is told with guts, grace and the final restoration of a man diseased by booze."

—Nancy Carr, author of *Last Call*

"I'm in this."   —Cole Downs, friend/former drinking buddy

This memoir reflects the author's life faithfully rendered to the best of his ability. Some names and identifying details have been changed to protect the privacy of others.

Copyright © 2018 by Paul Fuhr

All rights reserved. In accordance with the U.S. Copyright Act of 1976, the scanning, uploading and electronic sharing of any part of this book without the permission of the publisher is unlawful piracy and theft of the author's intellectual property. If you would like to use material from the book (other than for review purposes), prior written permission must be obtained by contacting the author. Thank you for your support of the author's rights.

Printed in the United States of America

Published by East Shoreway Recovery Services

Cover design & interior graphics by Jason Lichtenberger

ISBN: 978-0-69214-267-7

FOREWORD

NO ALCOHOLIC'S RECOVERY story is truly unique.

That's one of the first very first things I ever heard in an AA meeting, and it stuck with me. The longer I'm sober, the more I agree. It's not cold-hearted cynicism; it's just a fact that the only real differences between two alcoholics' accounts are the details. How old we were when we had that first swig of beer. The consequences that we've faced. The places where we've embarrassed ourselves. The particular brand of booze that finally did us in. The specific relationships we're trying to mend. If you strip away the details, we're all just traveling the same alcoholic arc.

That said, you're holding a recovering alcoholic's memoir. It's important to understand that I don't believe my story is somehow more remarkable or compelling than anyone else's. I didn't resurrect my wrecking-ball past because I wanted to see my details in print. Long before I mustered the courage to step into an AA meeting by myself, I endlessly read other alcoholics' stories. I found truth, comfort and hope in their words. You see, I was 100% convinced that there was no future for me that didn't involve drinking. A sober life just wasn't an option. So I suffered for a long time (and so, too, did my family) because the idea of an alcohol-free life was science fiction.

I'm not an expert. I'm not giving anyone life advice. This is just my story. And I'm putting it out there with the hope that it helps someone in the same way that similar stories helped me.

- PF

ONE

I feel like a quote out of context
Withholding the rest
So I can be for you what you want to see.
I got the gesture and sounds,
Got the timing down,
It's uncanny, yeah, you'd think it was me.
Do you think I should take a class
To lose my Southern accent?
Did I make me up?
Or make the face 'til it stuck?
I do the best imitation of myself.

—Ben Folds Five

1

MY GRANDMOTHER USED to say "Nothing good ever happens after midnight," and I'd just roll my eyes. What the hell did she know? She was just a grandmother. For me, as a professional drinker, "after midnight" was when all the possibilities in life really opened up. That's when the true magic happened—when the rules of rational human beings and the laws of lifelong platonic friendships could be bent like the orbital patterns of planets near black holes. All bets were off.

It was almost three on a Monday morning, those windless doldrums of another alcoholic night. Dead calm, drifting. Too early and too late. I stared at my topless Jeep Wrangler, which I'd just beached at an unfinished train crossing on the outskirts of Phoenix, Arizona. The Jeep's tail end was angled up, presenting itself. I was drunk enough to almost admire what I was seeing, as if the vehicle was on display in a showroom. I circled it and pretended to know what to do, like this happened all the time. The passenger-side tire was plunged halfway in mud, just across a rail.

My passenger, some drunk theater major I'd met just hours earlier, staggered around the dark in heels, freaking out and trying to get cell service. She flailed around in the half-light of the hazards, holding her flip phone up to the sky. She wobbled on her tiptoes with the phone above her head, as if those two inches were going to make the difference.

"This is just fucking perfect," she said.

It wasn't perfect, but I liked girls who cussed.

We were a good twenty miles from where we should be. I often forgot how easy it was to get lost and how fast civilization dissolved in the desert. Then again, drinking had always been about me deliberately getting lost in the middle of nowhere. I was an expert at aimlessness. There were in-progress housing developments all around us: plywood half-shells of cookie-cutter apartments watching two drunk idiots in the dark. Motionless cranes, stacks of drywall, pallets of concrete. This was the great urban sprawl of Phoenix: a city hell-bent on spreading suburbs out in every direction like a swift disease determined to convert every inch of desert into right-angled grids of pre-fab houses, condos, golf courses, and strip malls.

"This isn't anywhere near my apartment," the girl was half-crying.

No shit, I thought.

Around last call, I had offered her a ride home. She had put away so many Sapphire and tonics in two hours that she was starting to repeat her stories and wobble on her barstool. We drove for an hour as I followed the vaguest directions imaginable. She squinted at one road after another, insisting that things were "starting to look familiar." When the palm trees vanished, I wondered if we might be in trouble. When I saw the "Road Closed" sign, I knew we were screwed. I kept driving because I prayed it would all soon be over.

"I can't believe this," Drunk Theater Major slurred, cursing at her phone and stumbling over scattered cinder blocks that marked someone's future driveway. "I can't believe you got us this lost."

This coming from the girl who, mere minutes before, had been telling me about visiting funerals to remember what it felt like to cry. She had apparently been working on that emotion in recent weeks. "It's tricky to cry onstage and have people believe it," she explained, right before I launched the Jeep into the air. She said that it takes hours of practice to authentically cry. And since she was apparently fresh out of dead relatives, she had resorted to inviting herself to friends' families' showings. You know, for research.

The last two shots of Jägermeister weren't sitting well in my stomach, and I could still taste licorice on my tongue. Also, dozens of beers were still kaleidoscoping through my veins from earlier in the day: Miller Lites, Labatt Blues, Fat Tires, Negra Modelos, those cute little jugs of Red Stripe. Maybe a glass of red wine at someone's apartment. I couldn't remember. I just didn't want to think about what they were doing to my insides: scouring everything out, jockeying for domination.

Sundays were designed for drinking. In my mid-twenties, that was what the day was for. Alcohol and Sundays were like rainy mornings and newspapers. Now, the day was gone and I had chased God-knows-what, well into the hours when I should be sleeping. I had to work in four hours on the opposite side of the city. And even though it was essentially a new job, I'd already called in sick enough to ensure that I had to go in. Corporate sick days were cards you had to play smartly, but I was throwing them around like confetti.

It was late July—monsoon season in Arizona—so the air was swollen and thick. There was a faintly electric breeze, smelling of sand and creosote. The desert had been greedy and quickly drank everything it could (much like me on Sundays). The construction site had changed from sand and gravel into something of a slurry pond, which meant my tire had zero chance of getting out.

She stabbed her phone accusingly in my direction.

"This still says 'No Service.'"

I had no idea why I'd offered to take this person home. I should've been passed out in my shitty apartment. It's not like she'd been weirdly charming or that we'd maybe known each other in grade school and were catching up on the last twenty years. We'd simply both been at the same *faux*-ski lodge bar, the Timber Wolf, alone. I think we'd mutually said just enough passably amusing things or had the exact ratio of remembered *Twilight Zone* storylines to connect on some basic human level. And as an alcoholic, that's all I really wanted: connection.

"This is unbelievable," she whimpered.

I was sobering up but not fast enough. I could see all the lights of the valley: Downtown Phoenix shimmering to the west, Tempe and Scottsdale to the south. A series of cell phone towers—tall needles of blinking red lights—taunted Drunk Theater Major from a faraway mountain ridge. She'd not only insisted that this was her street, but that we could jump the railroad tracks, *Dukes of Hazzard*-style.

Neither was true.

"I'm pretty sure we're nowhere near your place," I shook my head.

I was furious, but holding my emotions in check in the same way that Scotch tape doesn't completely mend a broken plastic toy. It was temporary at best. One slight bend and it goes into the trash can.

"I'm sorry," she pouted, her eyes at half-mast.

It wasn't remotely cute. Drunk girls rarely are. They're like the computer Safe Mode versions of themselves—not quite all there. Then again, most drunk girls know their basic way home. This one wasn't aware that she was swaying around like one of those inflatable people-shaped windsocks. In the crimson glow of the Jeep's tail lights, she almost looked demonic.

"I'm so sorry," she kept at it.

I tried to do the drunken math to figure out what angle I'd been playing with her: Nice Guy Offering A Ride Home, or something else.

"It's fine," I lied. "I just need to figure out how to get out of this."[1]

My heart was starting to beat a mile a minute. Reality had caught up with me. She shuffled a few feet forward, pretending

---

[1] I had no idea how often I'd say this sentence over my drinking career.

to size up the situation, and blinked.

"We need to call a cab."

My cell phone was dead, hers clearly wasn't getting service, and I was pretty sure we were hell and gone from the nearest Circle K.

"I just need to think," I said.

She let out a heavy sigh, then collapsed on a sack of concrete. She threw up her hands.

"Maybe we just call the cops."

"We can't *call* anyone," I said, tuning her out. Minutes later, though, her tone changed.

"Hey," she was saying, her voice low.

"Not now."

"Hey."

I circled the Jeep again, this time with panic. I just wanted it—and her—to go away. Most of the problems in my life disappeared if I ignored them them long enough.

"What?"

When I turned, I saw that she was standing. Her eyes were wide, like one of those horror-movie damsels who's seconds away from getting stabbed. She was staring over my shoulder, trying to point. As an actress, she was pretty terrible at basic gestures. For a terrifying second, I feared that she discovered a construction-site hobo shuffling in our direction—someone who'd been sleeping in the kitchen of some quarter-complete condo and, armed with a crowbar, was preparing to defend his territory.

Unfortunately, it was worse than that.

"Train" is all she could manage.

When I saw it, my brain simply shrugged: *Yep. That's a*

train all right. Far down the track, maybe a mile, there it was: the sinister eye of a diesel train's headlamp with twin ditch lights below it.

"Train," she parroted. "That's a train, I think. I think it's on this track. Train. I think it's coming this way. I think that's a train…"

Now, I don't know how it is for you whenever adrenaline kicks in, but for me, everything else vanishes. It flushed through me, carrying the mad mix of alcohol and bad decisions through every cell in my body. I was probably getting drunker by the millisecond, but my focus was getting laser-precise.

"Train," I gritted my teeth. "I *heard* you."

"Well, it's not my fucking fault it's a fucking train!"

She was like a foul-mouthed first-grader, nervously bouncing in her heels.

"How come there's no horn? Shouldn't there be a horn?"

Even shit-faced, I could work out some semblance of logic.

"That's because this train crossing doesn't exist yet."

I was already picturing the train slamming headlong into my Jeep, sending it airborne into one of the apartment complexes as Billy Joel and Bruce Hornsby CDs rained down on everything. I leapt onto the Wrangler, making a misstep on the spare tire. I collapsed into the back seat, smacking my head on the center glove box.

"Train!" she shouted, as if I needed the reminder.

I scrambled into the front seat and turned the key. I slammed the stick into reverse and immediately gave it gas.

Nothing.

I'm not a good judge of distance—especially after an entire day of drinking—but the train was a half-mile away. I could hear it closing in, which told me the one thing that mattered: This Was Really Happening.

"Paul…"

Oh, by the way: it's probably worth noting that I still don't know this girl's name. She remains one of the thousands of background extras in the epic film of my alcoholism. This extra, unfortunately, had speaking lines.

"Get in the back," I instructed.

"But the train."

"I said *get in the back.*"

Something in my eyes yanked her out of her tailspin. She sluggishly swayed toward the Jeep. The heels gave her some trouble and she looked like she was moving underwater. Once she pulled herself into the back seat, I immediately started moving.

"Okay. Now, switch me places."

We did an awkward changing-of-the-guard and she plopped down onto the driver's seat, unsure of what to do. For a split second, I saw it pass through her brain that I was trying to get her killed in a train collision. I slid to the back seat. Just as I'd hoped, I was heavier than her. The rear tire lowered *just* enough to touch the muddy embankment.

"Step on the clutch," I said.

"What's the clutch?"

"It's the *clutch,*" I was losing it. "That pedal. Right there."

Drunk Theater Major was paralyzed. She studied her surroundings like I'd just asked her to launch something from Mission Control. I considered that, after everything, I was going to die at the hands of a drunk actress and a manual transmission.

And that's when the train engineer saw us. A long, shrill horn suddenly cut through the desert night. The girl screamed—and it wasn't an actressy scream, either. It was primal. The train was bearing down on us so quickly that the horn started to have an actual weight on my body. With each decibel, my chest felt heavier. Every molecule in my body caught fire. I couldn't hear myself think.

"*Left one,*" I screamed.

She couldn't hear me, so I jabbed my finger at the clutch.

Amazingly, she depressed it. Reaching forward, I then popped the Jeep into four-wheel drive, making sure the gearshift was in reverse.

"*Now what?*"

"*Gas!*"

"*What?*"

"Gas!"

No matter how loudly we shouted, we were in a silent movie without dialogue cards.

"*Accelerator!*"

"What?"

I wasn't about to spend my last seconds on Earth like this. I stood, swinging my left leg over her body, as if I was trying to straddle my stereo and A/C controls. Without warning, I slammed on the gas pedal while she, out of confusion, eased off the clutch. Before either of us knew what was happening, the Jeep hurtled backward, wrenching free from the mud. The engine protested; the dashboard needles all flipped into the red. I grabbed the top of the windshield with both hands, white-knuckling it for balance. She closed her eyes, keeping her hands off the steering wheel.

Eleven seconds later, a yellow Union Pacific locomotive rocketed past, whisking dozens of freight cars off into the night. The horn continued to blare like a banshee, which I interpreted as the engineer shaking a fist at me. The Jeep also stalled seconds after we'd broken free, so we rolled for a bit before she had the presence of mind to nudge the brake. When we finally stopped, I pulled myself back into the passenger seat.

We said nothing as the train faded away. Minutes later, the absolute silence of the desert had returned. She then calmly stepped out and rounded the vehicle, wordlessly waiting for me to open my door. Her face was streaked with tears. She wore an expression that fell somewhere between spaced-out and withering hate. Once back behind the wheel, I turned the ignition and the Jeep happily rumbled to life, as if it was no different than a puppy who had no idea how lucky he'd been to survive its mad dash through an intersection.

I shakily reached for the shift knob. Even in the arid summer-night heat, I was shivering with low-watt terror over what had just happened. I took us back down the unfinished road, kicking up clouds of gravel. Drunk Theater Major began crying again. I turned onto a main road and watched the development vanish from the rearview.

For the first time that evening, I exhaled, but I wouldn't actually breathe for another fifteen years.

2

I WAS THIRTY-SEVEN when I realized I'd given up on all my dreams. I guess I thought everything would eventually show up on cue, like it was hiding behind some game-show curtain. An extraordinary life was owed to me. There was a great screenplay or novel inside me, just waiting for the right moment to tumble out and deliver me to a better life. What I didn't know was that twenty years of drinking had distanced me so far from reality that I might as well have been a character in one of the many books I hadn't written.

Fantasy is second nature to me. I've always lived with my head somewhere else. There was a real world and then there was mine. I ignored responsibilities and decisions and commitments, which lurked like vague shadows behind frosted glass. I knew those things existed, but I assumed they'd never apply to me. Consequences were for Other People. I grew up thinking I was above the rules. Things would just work out, no matter what. Fate was my friend.

I'm convinced that the key to screwing up children is to constantly tell them how special they are. I know this because I grew up in a generation that was constantly force-fed this sentiment. Everywhere I turned, there was some cartoon, movie, ABC Afterschool Special, or elementary-school "You can do it!" poster, nudging me ever closer to becoming a world-class alcoholic.

Growing up in the Eighties meant a constant barrage of "listen to your heart," "you can be anything," "good things always happen to good people" and "follow your dreams." I'm pretty sure that was the DNA of virtually every slogan and ad campaign of my childhood. I think it was all meant to be empowering, but I just ended up with deliriously high expectations of the future—ones that, later, left me feeling like I'd been shortchanged by the universe. I'd been taught that all I had to do was "reach for the stars" and then something extraordinary would happen—and I don't even know what the hell that was. I just know that it never arrived.

But if every kid was so goddamn special, where did all the ordinary adults come from? I'd been lied to. I wasn't special; I wasn't unique; I wasn't going to see my dreams automatically become reality. All of a sudden, I wasn't comfortable being myself which, naturally, became my default setting in life. I had zero confidence in anything or anyone—especially myself. On a deeply cellular level, I believed everything I'd been told that I was.

I'm a nobody, but it took me forever to be okay with that.

I GREW UP in a small town called Milan, Ohio—a town so small that it's not even a town. Technically, it's a village. Even now, it's a smattering of dusty antique shops, boutiques, family restaurants, and a city hall that surround a modest town square. It's a town with a single stop light. One bank, one barber shop, one flower store. At some point, there was a firearms store right between Milan's two bars.

When I was ten, I remember some asphalt had crumbled to reveal a patch of the cobblestone street beneath. Another era peered back at me. History seemed to be really close to the surface in Milan, always threatening to break through. I could sense it in the decorative wrought-iron fences and hitching posts for horses. Almost everywhere you look is brick, too. Reds, tans, burgundies, browns. Even the occasional cream-colored brick. In fact, one resident loved brick as much as they hated their next-door neighbor: they spitefully bricked up an entire side of their house, windows and all.

Milan also happens to be the birthplace of Thomas Edison, the famous inventor who barely spent any time there. Growing up in a town that fathered the inventor of electricity, though, is to grow up in a very large shadow. Wikipedia "Milan, Ohio" for yourself. Go ahead, I'll wait. It'll take you about thirty seconds to read the whole page. Indians, shipping canal, Thomas Edison. You get the picture. It's a village hemmed in by cornfields in every direction except north: Lake Erie. Milan is home to less than a thousand people. The problem with growing up in a small town is that your barometer gets calibrated wrong. Everything is much smaller and less exotic than you think. The reality is that everyone knows everyone. I mean, you're dealing with a thousand people. That's it. But as a kid, it seemed so much larger and anonymous to me.

When I was in fourth grade, I came across some papers in Computer Lab that had all of my classmates' names on them. Everyone was neatly organized into columns: *Wayne Horvath, Julie Mesenburg, Sarah Koch, Rachel Blakeman, Jeremy McConaughey, Casey Linder, Matt Heid, Chad Springer.* I wasn't looking for anything. I wasn't rooting around for secrets. It was just sitting there out in the open. My teacher, Mr. Paisley, for all his Apple IIGS-programming prowess was also pretty goddamn careless. (And this is coming from a big Mr. Paisley fan.) He reminded me of George Lucas with his beard and sweaters—but whether he knows it or not, Mr. Paisley forever changed my understanding of the world.

Everything tilted on its axis, the day I found those charts. On them were five categories: *Optimal, Upper Basic, Basic, Lower Basic,* and *Remedial.* (Later, I looked up the word "remedial.") Everyone in my grade was sorted into columns per subject. There was one sheet for math, one sheet for language arts, one sheet for social studies, and so on. I expected to see my name in *Optimal* or *Upper Basic,* maybe, but there I was in the *Lower Basic* column with a bunch of kids I didn't feel like I belonged with. I was lumped in with kids who didn't know or didn't care what the capital of Ohio was. (Actual fact.) I saw them as future thugs, sad bus drivers, sullen deliverymen. To this day, I distinctly remember the ice-water shock of discovering that I'd been judged and put into a category. This was what my teachers thought of me.

Still, I don't process things quickly—especially big news—so it was a slow erosion in my head. When my grandmother announced to my parents that she had leukemia, I was in the kitchen, rummaging around for Combos or Little Debbie oatmeal cream pies or something. (I was a heavy, hungry kid.) Even hearing that news didn't bother me right off. It's only the little stuff that immediately gets to me. It's sort of like how, when you hear a 737 overhead, the sound lags a few seconds behind it. That's me. I'm always trailing behind whatever bombshell goes off. I didn't understand my mother's sobbing until much later.

As far I can tell, I had an ordinary childhood. If you organized childhoods into columns like Milan Elementary apparently liked to do, mine would probably be *Upper Basic*. At times, it was pretty *Optimal*. My parents loved each other, rarely fought, and did the best they could with the little money we had. My sister Laura is five years younger and pretty much liked anything that involved horses, princesses or secret gardens. She didn't have time for the James Bond movies I videotaped off network TV.

My family shopped at Big Lots back when it was called Odd Lots. We saw the Blue Light Specials at K-Mart with alarming frequency. We rarely ate out for dinner and when we did, it was at Burger King. My mom cut our hair with electric clippers. My dad had a job at the General Motors ball bearing plant in nearby Sandusky, which my grandfather had hooked up for him. (Working at GM, by the way, meant that we were a "GM Family" and that Ford families could go straight to hell.)

Ball bearing plants dotted the Lake Erie coastline because, back in World War II, military strategists supposedly determined that that was the best place to put them. Why? Depressingly, the constant cloud cover. Since the sky was so frequently gray and butter-knife dull, if the Japanese or the Russians attacked, they wouldn't be able to easily find the country's ball bearing plants and destroy America's ability to build aircraft. In other words, I grew up in certified gloom.

When I went with Dad to work on some Saturday mornings, I was immediately greeted with the bright, unmistakable smells of intelligent work: soldering, epoxy, coffee. There was a black-tiled, soundproof room where they did some kind of testing, which made frequent appearances in my nightmares. I still don't know what Dad did there, but it was like wandering around a space station. There were futuristic tools and lab coats everywhere.

My dad had a number of jobs before the GM one, too. He and his dad opened a TV shop called (wait for it) "Fuhr TV" in an L-shaped strip mall. I basically grew up with an endless stream of strangers walking around the display floor of televisions and VCRs. Mostly, I used to live in the back room, among giant cardboard boxes where I drew the interiors of spaceships. I'd cut out windows with safety scissors and use up every inch of scotch tape, to affix crayoned-cardboard tubes as rockets.

I'm way different than my dad. I don't have the discipline to read instruction manuals nor the patience to follow step-by-step directions. Impatience is a swarming-bees sensation in my brain. I just hope that things will snap together easily or that I can just plug something in and it'll turn on. I'm not wired for anything more than convenience. I don't care how things work; I don't pretend to understand the nuances and principles that keep life afloat, like airflow over aircraft wings. Dad is a methodical, patient man—the sort of person who carefully calculates, measures and considers things before he does them. I don't necessarily wish I was like that, but he puts things together—model airplanes, home PCs, water heaters— whereas I'm fundamentally designed to take things apart. I have the sort of recklessness and self-loathing that helps you become an English major. Still, when my father took that job at GM, he climbed up pretty quickly—mainly because he's fiercely intelligent and understands just about every concept known to man.[2] By contrast, I'm just a great pretender. I'm like one of those ROM emulators for old Nintendo games—I look like the real deal, but if you look closely enough, I'm not fully programmed. The colors and sounds aren't quite the same ones you remember from the arcade version. My code is missing a few lines of script.

So, for a long time, Dad worked while my mom stayed at home with Laura and me. And my mom did what all broke parents do: she took advantage of anything that was free. So we went to museums and parks and lakeside piers. On rare occasions, we'd visit the Sandusky Mall and get a soft pretzel with nuclear-yellow cheese sauce. Mom also took us to the library all the time. And when I say "all the time," I mean *All.*

---

[2] This may seem like a lazy lie, but it's true. There is sincerely nothing my father doesn't know: history, thermodynamics, politics, religion, physics, the mechanical inner workings of an automotive turn signal. He knows everything.

The. Time. I have more memories of the library than I do of any other place from my childhood. Mom joked that we checked out every book when I was young, but there may be some truth to that.[3] I grudgingly brought my teddy bear there for a contest. My bear would be displayed for weeks on a shelf, where it nabbed the "Most Loved Bear" award. I'm still unreasonably proud of that. (In fact, I'm staring at the bear right now, where it's slumped in an acrylic display box.)

Our parents loved my sister and I so much that they created something of a safety bubble around us. Into my senior year, I had a curfew of 10 o'clock. And that was a no-shit curfew, by the way. If you rolled in at 10:10, good luck not getting some passive-aggressiveness from Mom. Sometimes it was so thick, you could drizzle it over pancakes. "Oh, I *bet* no one could drive you home earlier than that," she'd mock-agree with your excuse. It also didn't help that she didn't like or trust anyone in my inner circle. Some were mouthy, some were liars, some seemed shifty, and some were simply too damned loud for her. My parents really just wanted the best for us, but all the curfew accomplished was corrosive curiosity. Parties were always just getting going whenever I'd have to leave. I could feel it percolating as I headed home: the sour emptiness of missing out on something. I'd spend the next few decades trying to get my lost time back.

Very early on, my parents tried to give me a backbone. When I was ten or eleven, my parents made me "hit the town" to look around for a job. They suggested I start with the barber shop: Sipe's. (The guy who owns it isn't even named Sipe.) But I remember going in there, watching two guys get their hair

---

[3] My first word was supposedly "book," but I'm not sure if that's true or a mother's memory.

cut as I sat quietly and patiently in a chair, tossing around what to say to this dude. This was before cell phones so I just sat and stared for a half-hour. I clearly didn't have an appointment. When he was done, I summoned the courage to ask if I could maybe work for him. I'd sweep his clippings or something.

"No," he shook his head. "I do that myself. But best of luck looking for a job."

And that was that.

It was a three-second exchange, but I was flushed with embarrassment and failure. Other kids would've brushed it off. Not me. I gave up. I was angry at my parents for the dumb idea of me asking someone to sweep up hair. It wasn't even practice to prepare for another job: in Milan, not much opportunity existed for a ten-year-old. The experience kicked the lid off this deep, sulfuric well of sadness where all my greatest fears bobbed.

I will never be successful, I suddenly knew. And even if I did achieve some kind of success, I'd be kidding myself that it was real. These are the sorts of things I told myself, full well realizing that all the things I was supposed to be learning while knocking on barbers' doors—brightness of character, self-esteem, integrity—weren't meant for me. Those were things enjoyed by real people.

OUR HOUSE SAT at the edge of the postage stamp of Milan, almost deliberately removed from anyone else my age. There was a burgeoning psychopath named Anthony at whose house I occasionally spent the night when I was twelve or thirteen.

His blank-eyed parents let him watch R-rated movies; he routinely cooked eggs in the microwave until they were weird and rubbery; he hunted cats with rusty knives and pellet guns; he flicked lit cigarettes at me. I pretended to be cool with it all. He not once, but twice, got his hair permed: a thin nest of tiny brown curls. But when you're young, you make friends with whomever is right next to you. Easy connections. I mostly just hung out in his garage and stole his Richard Pryor and Eddie Murphy cassettes. "That shit's for fags," he'd said of them, proudly jamming his Jerky Boys and Fat Boys tapes into his stereo. We tried camping a few times in his backyard, but he was always talking about the girls in his class (he was three years older than me) that he wanted to "bone." It was such an odd, foreign concept to me: to "bone" a girl. I honestly imagined him poking someone with his index finger. I was so confused. Or maybe he would be pointing his finger in their direction, laying claim? *You're mine now,* Anthony would sneer.

"You'll see," he just kept saying. "When you're in high school, you'll see."

A big part of me knew that if he was hanging out with someone like me, his life wasn't working out so well. I sensed early on that me and Anthony weren't destined to be lifelong friends. He was just one of countless people I'd meet along the way who I'd pretend to be okay with, just because they didn't make fun of me. At least, not to my face.

Except for Anthony, our neighborhood was exclusively silver-haired widows. Every house surrounding us held an old woman whose husband had died many years previous. In the summer, I butchered all of their yards with our lawnmower, charging them $10 for the privilege. The neighbor behind us,

Betty, had been the owner of Cedar Point, an amusement park right on the lake.[4] Her house was something of a mausoleum that she solemnly toured me through. I remember how she used to clasp her hands, inverted like the couplings between railcars, as she showed off her china collection and glassware. You know, all the things that a young teenaged boy is obsessed with. There always seemed to be an ancient LP crackling in the background, too.

Donna, another neighbor, kept to herself. She also left all her window blinds open so, from my second-floor bedroom, I'd occasionally see a woman in her late fifties moving from room to room in her oversized, unsexy bra and underwear. I remember the icy chill of the surprise, rushing through me like the scudding wind of a sudden ocean storm. (Please know that I was *never* stationed by my window, flat against the floor, lying in wait like some sort of hormoned-out Army sniper.) It just always caught me off guard. In a pre-Internet age, a model on a shampoo box could do the trick, so she was no different.

Our neighbor Lillian was my favorite, though. Lillian was so batshit insane, she scared me as much as she fascinated me. She spoke in mousy tones, dropping entire syllables and trailing off as if losing interest in what she was saying. From what I could tell, she rarely made contact with the outside world. When she enlisted me to mow her lawn, she stared at me the whole time from her windows. No matter where I was in her yard, she was peering at me through her blinds. And it wasn't full-on staring, either. *That* I could accept. No, it was more like half-spying—as if peering around the corner of her windows made her covert

---

[4] Calling Cedar Point "just an amusement park" really does it a disservice. It's not only the second oldest-running park in the country, but it's sincerely one of the greatest roller-coaster destinations on the planet. I'm also terrified of 90% of its rides.

and unseen. When I went to collect my money, she'd open the door partway, look suspiciously up to the sky, and hand over the money in ones. Always in ones.

It wasn't until later that we discovered she was a ballsy thief. When we could afford to, my mom would spend an afternoon at a nursery and bring home a raft of beautiful flowers to our tiny garden. Azaleas, tulips, hostas. Overnight, lots of them would vanish from our garden and reappear a few dozen paces away in Lillian's garden. Not even hidden behind her house. Right there in front. It was like she was saying "fuck you" with flowers.

Early one morning, when my dad and I were headed to the lake to go fishing for perch, she practically jumped out at us from the bushes. It was like five-thirty in the morning, but there she was—clutching a long rumpled nightgown against her willowy frame, her live-wire eyes terrified of the atmosphere.

"Steven?" she addressed my dad with urgency.

(It's "Steve," by the way. No one called my dad "Steven" except her.)

"Good morning."

If my dad was annoyed, he certainly didn't show it. He was a gentleman.

"The weather," she pointed. "Are they controlling the rain with computering?"

"No, Lillian. I don't think they can actually control the weather with computers."

She stared up at the parade of pink-gray morning clouds. She frowned, unconvinced.

"Are you sure?"

"I'm sure, Lillian. No one's controlling the weather."

"I read things. I read things about computers. I just wonder if it's why there's a drought this summer."

"No, I don't think so."

"Hmmm."

Then she left. If she'd have floated back to her house, several inches off the ground, I sincerely wouldn't have been surprised. But she took her tiny steps back to her door. My dad turned and gave me a high-eyebrowed "What was that?" look, but nothing more. My dad is kind that way. He doesn't say ill words about people—a trait that took me decades to admire and even longer to put into practice. He never put himself first. I remember him once in the basement of our house when the sewer exploded. There he was, down there in that dungeon, sloshing around in six inches of our shit and piss, never once saying a bad word about it. Me? I'd grow up acting exactly how he wouldn't act, doing exactly what he wouldn't do. (Oh, just wait.)

One spring, we took our first family vacation. Someone had offered us their time-share apartment in Myrtle Beach. It was our first real vacation and I was so excited. By Day #1, I had a horrible sunburn, which shouldn't have surprised anyone since I was an Indoors Kid. Within hours, I had tight, warm skin, followed by small pricks of fire along my shoulders, and then a deep, full-on searing pain under my muscles. My mom immediately assumed the worst, angrily proclaiming that we'd have to go to the ER or maybe even go home early. Game over. Trip ruined. Vacation spoiled for everyone. But my dad sat beside me in bed as I cried, whispering to me that nothing was ruined. We wouldn't be going home. He sprayed me down with Solarcane. He sat into the late hours of the night, rubbing my head so I'd fall asleep. Once, I opened my eyes and it was ten o'clock. He was still there.

It remains the greatest kindness I've ever been shown: my father staying awake, helping me to eventually drift asleep, caressing my pain downstream.

ALCOHOLISM KNOTS ITS way through my family in hints and flourishes. It's not something that's often spoken of, but it's not exactly hidden from view either. Sometimes it is maddeningly obvious and, at the same time, completely ignored. I heard about family drinking problems in the same hushed whispers you reserve for a disliked coworker who suddenly enters into a room. Everyone stops talking mid-sentence. I seemed to be constantly living in that unmistakable ellipsis when it came to drinking. Something had always *just* happened; something was always going on, just out of reach.

That's where alcoholism lived in my family: in between the lines. There were flashes of it at family dinners when my grandparents made too-generous pours with wine; get-togethers where the laughter hits a point of hollow absurdity, and no one really remembers why they're laughing; reunions where people have wine-purpled lips and teeth in photographs, like they've been chugging cherry Slurpees all day.

The older I got, the more that Grandpa, my dad's father, became a paradox to me. Carl Fuhr was supposedly a Goodtime Charlie who was also loving, devout, and pious. He had bookshelves lined with Bibles and old hymnals. If you bring up his name today in Sandusky, Ohio, I bet people would still nod.

I like to think a child's first memories of their family are the strongest—they're the most indelible, even though they're the furthest away from where we are now. They're the first etchings. So my first memories of my grandfather are as strong as they are respectful. I never saw the person who often didn't show up for dinner after work, causing my grandmother to throw Dad and his sisters into the car and drive around from bar to bar, looking for him. ("It was just a different time" is the popular rationale/drumbeat.) By the time I knew him, he didn't drink. I remember sitting on Grandpa's lap as he taught me songs about flatulence and peanuts sittin' on a railroad track. ("*Toot toot! Peanut butter!*" remains the best punchline to my inner five-year-old.) I recall he loved jelly beans and had jars of them scattered everywhere; I also recall that he kept a pair of false teeth in a jar beside his bed.

My grandmother, his wife Glenna, was a very gentle soul, though she'd been sick as long as I'd known her. I remember her smile and kind eyes. Her kidneys had given out on her after having one of the few actual known cases of "cat scratch fever." My grandparents lived in a comically small apartment, with one bedroom occupied by an enormous dialysis machine. It wasn't weird to me—it was just something that *should* be in that room. It looked more like a time machine than a life-saving piece of furniture. Apparently, my grandfather had not only purchased the thing, but trained himself how to keep her alive with it. That always struck me as one of the greatest examples of love I've seen.

She passed away one Halloween when I was five and my sister was 0.2. My grandfather seemed to slip off the radar shortly after that. He'd come out of nowhere every so often to stay with us before blustering back off to wherever he came. Grandpa later got re-married to an emotionless wax figure of a woman. I remember both of them being drunk at their wedding reception. It bothered me, seeing how different Grandpa seemed—how the booze made his eyes cartoon-alive yet vacant at the same time. He was a marionette version of my grandfather—a man who'd once been so strong and funny, who now seemed to be animated against his will. I was sad, seeing him surrounded amidst Forced Wedding Fun and a gaggle of of awful new relatives.[5] At the reception, my dad stood and gave an eloquent toast about childhood, love, and second chances. It fell on drunk ears. Grandpa talked through the whole thing, murmuring and joking to people at his table. Others giggled and snorted. I remember tensing up, being angry and protective, and wanting to have Dad start over. It didn't matter.

Years later, I met someone at a bar who'd known my grandfather and called him the sweetest, kindest man he'd ever known. This guy told me my grandfather was apparently something of a patron saint among the local drinking scene, heralded by anyone who'd been within earshot of his barstool. He gave generously, helped people move, picked up random bar tabs, loaned people money he didn't have. He'd managed to keep his alcoholism tamped down for so long that it was soul-crushing to see the tarpaulin eventually come flying off.

On my mom's side, Grammie and Granddad endlessly argued, though. God, I dreaded dinners at their house. Grammie used to put our plates in the oven before we ate

---

[5] If you chew with your mouth open, you're dead to me. These people all chewed and talked with their mouths open.

because she hated how cold they'd get throughout the meal. This is also because she ate with slow, clinical precision which, in turn, made the dinner last as long as the inevitable arguing. Sometimes, I'd mentally take sides with one of them. I had no idea what my grandparents were arguing about, but I'd usually put all my eggs in Granddad's basket. (He never seemed to win, though.) It was like when you're watching a war movie, and you start taking odds on what character is going to survive. I'd put myself in one of the nameless private's boots and wonder how far into the movie I'd make it before I caught a stray bullet to the skull.

When they weren't sniping and criticizing and cursing at one another, I remember wondering how two people who seemingly hated each other that much could live in the same house. Granddad was a mathematician who'd grown up on a West Virginia farm. He served in the Korean War, did radio work on airplanes, then returned as an engineer and had five children. He always kept German beer in the fridge and a glass of Chivas Regal close by at night. I don't remember ever seeing Grammie drink, though my mom has mentioned enough stories about her over the years to suggest otherwise. So maybe Grammie's drinking evaporated with age, but I also don't remember her being particularly warm to me either. She made blunt comments about my weight and loudly refuted me whenever I was clearly making up a story, rolling her eyes and letting out epic sighs. She wasn't a woman to put up with bullshit. Mostly, she held court in her La-Z-Boy, smoking Pall Malls and doing crossword puzzles until dark.

By all accounts, it was my great-grandfather, though, who may have been the genetic wild card and my most kindred spirit.

That man loved the bottle. *Loved* it. Sometimes I wonder if it's him who I feel slithering around inside me. He'd thrown away acres and acres of farmland—priceless now—by selling it off in pieces. In some cases, he just gifted it to random women, no strings attached. These women would just appear in my great-grandmother's life decades after the fact, suddenly owning claim to large swaths of valuable land. My great-grandparents even got divorced, which seems almost inconceivable to me—almost like how the world wasn't actually black-and-white before 1960.

Maybe I was primed to be an alcoholic. It was certainly stitched into my DNA—embroidered into a pattern that I didn't particularly like, though it was comfortable and familiar. It was soothing. It made sense to me. When I was young, I used to take trips to my grandparents' farm in West Virginia up a long, serrated stretch of countryside called Keith Fork Road. The thing I remember most about the farm was the quiet—the sheer nothingness going on. In the morning, I used to walk outside and gaze at the vast hillside dominating everything in view—its CinemaScope greens and yellows staring back at me. The hillside was so large, I remember, that it looked like a still-life painting until I'd see a family of deer move. And the air would be sweet. Literally sweet, redolent with honeysuckle and phlox. At night, we'd "porch." I'd listen to my relatives' stories, watch bats swoop through the security lights, and study the moon as it crawled through the trees, tracking the white eye across each branch. I felt adult there, sipping one Orange Crush after the next.

The only times anyone moved from their patio furniture, rocking through the night, was to go grab another beer or glass of Scotch. I sat there on the metal glider, picking yellow paint flakes from its skin, as I listened to twist-caps coming off with satisfying hisses and ice cubes tinkling in glasses. It was music. This was how life should always be, I thought. I hadn't had a drop of alcohol in my life, but I already loved everything about it. Visiting my grandparents' house on a Sunday afternoon was no different, with TV golf playing serenely in the background. My dad wouldn't even be halfway up the stairs by the time my grandfather would ask him if he "wanted a snort." That's how drinking first emerged to me. It had rules, settings, characters. A vernacular, a mystery.

When I started to drink, I wouldn't have much of a chance against it. It'd just happen. That's what I decided. My alcoholism was a sleeper cell. It'd get activated when I least expected it. When the time came, there'd be no stopping it.

3

I FELT IT grow like ink blossoming in water. My very first drink curled inside me with a delicate, black promise. I was fifteen, sitting on my closet floor in the dark, carefully tracing the thin, stolen bottle of Zima with my fingers. The cold glass was lined with ridges and still beaded with sweat. There was a second bottle sitting next to me. I'd only taken a few swallows, but they were all I needed.

Stop drilling, something told me. *We've hit oil.*

I was sold.

The Zima made my thoughts gauzy and pleasant. More

than that, it suddenly explained all the easy energy I sensed at family parties, like the one that was going on downstairs. All the kinetic thrust of my aunts and uncles, who seemed so fun and so alive and so full of quick jokes, made complete sense. It locked into place. I could hear them getting louder downstairs as glasses were refilled, empty cans were crumpled, bottle caps twisted off. It awakened something distant inside me—a rustling of molecules and music and memories. I felt generations of wit, comebacks, conversations, and joke-telling talent rising up out of the mirth.

You will be a better person, Zima informed me.

As a high school junior, I was the editor of a school newspaper most kids used to carry slices of pizza around on. It was less a prestige job than it was a sign that I was good with words. I tried everything I could to turn that mimeographed rag into *Entertainment Weekly* or *Rolling Stone.* I ran starred album reviews that I wrote about albums no one else in high school would ever listen to.[6] Instead of focusing on my fellow students and their stories and awards and accomplishments, I did two-page spreads on famous historical disasters like the *Hindenburg* and not-so-well researched features about UFOs. No one really said anything because I was pretty good at it. I considered, clutching the Zima, that I could be better. Alcohol could be the passport I needed to get into another world. Truth be told, I knew it wouldn't—I was just a deeply insecure, overweight kid who vaguely resembled a swollen Fred Savage and repeatedly got told I smelled like my parents' cigarette smoke.

No one was missing me downstairs. The music and laughter came in muffled swells, like ocean surf. All the while, I could

---

[6] Among the reviews: Kenny Loggins' *Outside: From the Redwoods;* Michael Bolton's *Time, Love & Tenderness;* Bruce Hornsby's *Hot House;* an album by Traffic I hadn't even listened to.

feel the black bloom of alien confidence, the foreign feeling of being centered and in charge. I'd heard my aunt yammering on about Zima and how "it was better than sex." She was my cool aunt, after all. She routinely used "fuck" like a comma around me. She was a good singer and always knew contemporary music. She insisted we watch *Jaws* together. She was fifteen years older and a bartender, so I officially considered her an expert on booze, bloody movies, and sex. Up to then, the heaviest sexual experience in my life was the time I furiously made out with my pillow, imagining it was Sherilyn Fenn from *Twin Peaks*.

The rush of alcohol through my veins tempered how I felt about myself. It made me feel like I was halfway to something real. Whatever that something was, I didn't know. But I felt like some deep-space pioneer—that brave first pilot who had no family and not a goddamn thing to lose. He could afford to be shot into the cosmos. With a quarter-bottle left of Zima, I could feel myself drifting out on a long-distance mission with no clear destination. Maybe I was the sole survivor of some massive planetary disaster, Kal-El style. I don't know. But with that bottle, maybe I was special. It was the key to unlocking a personality that had been hidden away from me.

In the muted light of my closet—my childhood Clue, Mouse Trap, and Life board games staring back at me—I weighed the bottle, considered how heavy and adult it felt in my hands, then finished it. The electric tang of the Zima was bright on my teeth. It flowed through me like diesel and velvet, making my veins glow. I swallowed back sour guilt.

And it clicked with me right then and there.

This was how I wanted to feel all the time. I'd hear this

phrase decades later in AA rooms: *This is how I wanted to feel the rest of my life.* Yes, I wanted to have the buzz at every second of every day—like Bob Ross was personally accenting my feelings with brushstrokes of happiness here, pretty little dabs of wonder there.

But there was more to it than that.

I wanted to feel as though there was always one more sweaty, full bottle of Zima next to me. Even at fifteen, I could do the math. This was simply how it was going to have to be. A second bottle, always. I wasn't going to drink regularly—yet. I knew that. That wasn't in the cards. For one thing, get-togethers aside, my parents didn't have beer in the fridge, let alone a stocked liquor cabinet. I feel like alcoholism skipped over their generation like how tornadoes sometimes skip over one house but completely flatten the one next door. I wasn't going to let it take root immediately and derail the grand parade of B-'s and C+'s I was pulling down in high school. I was a professional at doing just enough to get by, punctuated with show choir, the newspaper, and being clever enough in class to make the teacher laugh. But I knew that if I ever drank for real, there'd need to be a second drink right behind it. That was going to be the strategy. That's the comfort I had—the security blanket that tempered whatever anxiety I had about stealing two Zimas.

I stood up in the closet, dizzy like I'd been standing on my head for too long, and stuffed two empty Zima bottles into the front of my pants. Everything seemed more dramatic. More weight. I stared at those board games and my scattered action figures. I actually said goodbye to them, out loud. I said goodbye to childhood. I stiffly walked downstairs without anyone noticing, my legs a half-pace ahead of the rest of me, and chucked the bottles into the trash.

I quietly, temporarily belonged somewhere new.

I HAD NO IDENTITY. In that closet with the two Zimas, I sat there and considered how I didn't have an identity or anything to really call my own. I just mirrored comments and personality traits back to people. I was the high schooler Most Likely To Know the Name of a James Bond Villain. "Big Neal" Doerner, my best friend, had Superman. And when I say he "had Superman," I mean that he owned every goddamn Superman comic book, poster, and action figure—before nostalgia was actually trendy. Shawn Daley was the first person I knew who owned a CD player. He was into music like The Dead Kennedys and The Misfits, with some scattered Motown in there. (His dad also had *Playboys* from the 1970s moldering away in their garage, which was doubly awesome.) Most people I knew in high school had cars or band or sports. The sports kids just confounded me. They championed Jose Canseco, Ken Griffey, Jr., and Bernie Kosar. They traded Donruss and Fleer and Upper Deck cards. My parents had tried throwing me into football in seventh grade, which did nothing but make me suddenly hate my parents. I had no clue what I was doing out there on a football field in ninety-degree heat—pushed around by angry coaches who made fun of my striped socks and forced me to run extra miles because I didn't know what pass blocks were or how I'd screwed up some play I didn't know existed.

That wasn't who I was.

I was a James Bond enthusiast—not someone who ran confident miles without wanting to vomit. I knew the schematics of the Zorin blimp as much as I knew that I vastly preferred who I was with Zima running through my veins. I knew the logistics of Operation Grand Slam in *Goldfinger.* All the weird twins in the Bond pantheon: the knife-wielding assassins, Mischka and Grischka; the lithesome Bambi and Thumper; Wint and Kind, holding hands into the sunset. I knew that George Martin scored *Live and Let Die.* Ask me which Bond movie actually has a time bomb that stops at "007 seconds." Better yet, ask me things like what country George Lazenby is from. You see, this is the shit that clutters my brain. But alcohol made it seem okay. Booze hinted at another reality, but I'd have to wait a bit before I could embrace it. In the meantime, I hoped that the world would change overnight and magically meet me at my level.

It never would.

4

I GRADUATED high school with the trajectory of a missile someone had mistakenly pointed at the horizon. I wasn't bound for the atmosphere; I just sort of wobbled on the launch pad, fell, and rolled off into the woods. And even if I'd been pointed upright, I'd have been one of those dummy rockets that space agencies test ahead of the real launch. (They usually explode on the launch pad, by the way.) Deep down, I knew I wasn't ready for the real world. I wasn't designed for it. There was never any intention of me going very far. Lots of my friends had been scrabbling around in their last few semesters for internships, writing personal essays, and dutifully firing off college application after college application. I watched them with an air of puzzlement. Hell, my friend Ken DeChant disappeared for our entire junior year and went into the U.S. Senate Page program, which I still think is amazing. It was like knowing a celebrity or something. I'd done none of that.

Instead of considering how I could do something meaningful for my future, I sat down and wrote page after page after page of imaginary TV shows and treatments for movie screenplays, like one called *Page*—a government thriller about a high school student named Ken DeChant who enters into the U.S. Senate program and discovers that several of his fellow Pages are Russian plants, planning to blow up the U.S. Senate building because, you know, no one thinks to check Pages for security clearance. No one would think twice about it.[7]

No, my future was pretty prescribed. My parents were footing the bill for college—their alma mater, Bowling Green State. Worse, I was heading to its branch campus, Firelands, where my parents met. It was twenty minutes away from my house. I would never achieve the escape velocity I'd long dreamed of, landing me in the desert Southwest—the landscape so fetishized on Boy Scout posters and *Arizona Highways* and the *Roswell Daily Record* from July 8, 1947. I would live at home for two semesters, save money, and then go to main campus. That was the plan. I simply wasn't evolved enough or, maybe, warned enough about the real world to do anything on my own. Everything was taken care of for me in many ways. The edges of reality were dulled and softened to the point where I

---

[7] As everyone knows, *Page* became a huge box office hit and I'm resting on mountains of residuals.

didn't even notice it.

Somewhere in middle school, my dad left the GM plant to start his own company. At the time there was only one major manufacturer of crash-test dummies in the world, so I guess my parents decided it was time for two. The blueprints were public domain, so I remember my dad and his business partner building their first crash-test dummies on the floor of a rented space. I skateboarded between their offices. They connected steel, stitched vinyl, molded rubber. They marveled over what a sewing machine could do. Soon enough, they'd have a full-sized body on the floor of their leased office space. Then there were two more featureless dummies. Then, sitting upright, three. And so on.

My parents eventually employed dozens of people and became the world's leading manufacturer of crash-test dummies, which meant one thing to a teenager: my parents weren't really paying all that much attention. That's not to say they were so out of touch that they didn't give a shit if I was ripping lines of blow and disappearing for days. No, quite the opposite. (Ten o'clock curfew, remember?) That made someone like me toxic to my fellow high schoolers who were off at bonfires and after-football parties.

I was a good kid—I didn't take advantage of the fact that they were looking the other way a lot. I didn't give them any grief: *The X-Files* was on Friday nights, *Saturday Night Live* the next. That's just about the best thing an anxious parent could ask for. It made me pretty lonely, though, sitting in the dark of my room, watching a tiny black-and-white Zenith with rabbit ears. Since Ohio specializes in being gray and cloudy and sometimes kind of bleak, that's how I think of my teenage years. There was an empty place inside me I was constantly trying to fill.

I DIDN'T HAVE any routines; I didn't have sports; I didn't have real extracurricular activities I cared about. Grammie eventually died from her leukemia. Before, there was a sad, liminal time wherein I tried to get closer to her. There was a cruel moment where the cancer went into remission and everyone got super-excited. Maybe I'd seen too many movies, though, because I didn't get my hopes up. I'd seen that third-act twist too many times already. And I was right: it was just around the corner, swift and insidious. Still, my mom was forcing Laura and me to spend time with her. I had her help me with my French homework, which she'd been fluent in at some point in the Forties. She didn't want to do it, and I didn't want to do it. You could just tell. She and I both knew I could easily translate the French 101 verbs myself, but I put up with the charade anyway. Tuesday after Tuesday, though, I watched her just sort of evaporate. We stopped with the French and just sat in matching reclining chairs, staring out into the woods behind her house. We talked a little, but nothing major. She knew she was dying; I knew she was dying. I'd hug her and leave. And every time, there was less to hug. I never got used to it.

She died on my birthday. Family came in from all over. Suddenly, it was time to drink. That's how most everyone got through, it seemed. There wasn't even any question about it. I wasn't old enough to drink, but I was being handed glasses of wine and secret shots of tequila by relatives. It was all accepted, if not expected. I remember the recycling bins were stuffed with alcohol of all varieties. It took two trips for me to drag the empty buckets of beer and half-gallons of whiskey and oversized wine bottles out to the curb. I'd have been embarrassed if I knew any better.

This is what grief looks like, I shrugged.

Shortly after, I offered to move into the house to keep my grandfather company. Everyone thought this was an incredible idea—especially me. It was better than the much-suggested idea of him getting a dog. There would be a 19-year-old in the house now, helping with groceries, dinner, keeping the house clean.

That was the idea, at least.

So I moved in, and nothing good came of it.

AROUND THE SAME TIME, my cousin Matt had married the manager of a movie theater. As far as I was concerned, he may as well have married into royalty. That's how excited I was about it. There were two theaters in Sandusky: the nice one and the shitty one. The Cinema World Plaza 8 was the shitty one: a cinder-block igloo behind a mall. So when I graduated, I immediately went to work there. Still, working at a movie theater felt somehow exotic and glamorous to me. Never mind some of my peers were heading off to schools like Oberlin and USC and William & Mary. I didn't dare to dream. I just wanted to work at the theater.

Margie, my cousin-in-law, was kind-eyed, rocked 80s hair, and always seemed a little beleaguered. When I first met her, I could almost feel the weight of the theater on her shoulders.

She was maybe a year older than me. The theater was a wheezy contraption, barely holding it together. If it was a ship, you really wouldn't have wanted it to sail too far out of sight from the harbor—you simply couldn't trust it to not sink. The walls leaked when it rained; speakers routinely fell off the theater walls mid-movie, scaring the shit out of patrons; the screens were all speckled with soda and whatever else the cleaning crew got on them when they played baseball with brooms and the leftover concessions. The carpeting wasn't carpeting anymore so much as stained pressings of reds, yellows, and blacks. Plaza 8 was ratty, threadbare, and I loved every second of being there.

I was going to live it up that summer with the misfits that called themselves Plaza 8 employees. Once I learned how to use the cash registers, negotiate the CO_2 machines, refill the oil butter, and know the exact millisecond to dump the popcorn popper without giving yourself a second-degree burn—it was pretty straightforward. The people there weren't normal. (They'd probably all be *Lower Basic* by Milan Elementary standards.) Oddly, I felt at home. I'd just graduated high school, was ready to go to "High School: The Sequel," and planned to keep the job. All around me were high-school dropouts, people with minor criminal records, drug dealers, couples barely holding it together, thieves. Even an exchange student from Australia inexplicably worked there. One dude was a deejay who performed at shady hotels and moonwalked while he served popcorn. Another guy in his fifties drove a car to work with a wooden bumper.

Most everyone had slept with one another, too. There weren't icy chills between anyone—everyone just laughed off the sex, like it was something to check off on a list somewhere.

Oh, yeah. I slept with Troy. No big deal. I brought Big Neal into the fold of Plaza 8, if only to witness the insanity for himself. All he had to do was endure the madness and see all the free movies he wanted. It was heaven on earth. Big Neal settled right into the job, donning the burgundy vest and black slacks, and juggled that job with his other job of working as a morning radio host. (At some point, Neal printed himself a nametag that said "Navin" from *The Jerk*. He went by Navin for three months without our manager ever noticing.) I'd sneak into the movies between shifts where I could that summer—*Die Hard 3, Congo, Friday*. And then someone asked me if I was going to one of the "late nights" that Wednesday. I had no idea what that meant, but since I now lived with my grandfather, I didn't have to worry about a curfew. It also sounded fucking awesome— like I'd been invited to a party, which had never happened to me before.

"Late nights" were when the theater was closed for the night, then the projectionist threaded up whatever new movie we had. People smoked; free pizzas were inhaled, thanks to the friends who worked at Domino's or Marco's or whatever rathole pizza place was closest; cases of beer were drunk; employees made out in the dark. More adventurous couples got busy in the neighboring, empty auditoriums. We invited friends and anyone else in arm's reach to sit with us in the dark, propping our feet up on the seats in front of us. Once, I remember Big Neal sitting with an enormous weather-balloon-sized trash bag of popcorn on his lap. I was so happy—I sometimes tilted my head back, gazing up at the ceiling like someone gazing up at the night sky in admiration of constellations or meteor showers. I'd watch the projector's beam over my head—streams of shifting colors and light, catching all the dust and smoke on fire.

It was the first time I had alcohol, in any kind of actual social setting. I'd even happily pitched in for the beer, giving them a whole twenty dollars, which was a lot of money at the time. I felt ownership, as much as I hoped they'd like me more. The Busch Lights were passed around like party favors, handed out with insistence and expectance. All through the movie, there'd be one beer cracking open after another. I loved the comfort of that sound, like wood crackling in a fireplace. And I distinctly remember being wordlessly handed those cans—tickets to another world. I felt accepted. More than that, I felt the beer bring me to a sort of cruising altitude that I never wanted to come down from.

I quickly became friends with the resident projectionist, Mark—a tall, quiet, lanky redhead who ran something of his own movie studio on the side called Blade Independent Studio. He'd recruited most of the theater staff to act in his productions, too. Titles like *Witchface. The Evil Eye. The Natives Are Restless. A Darker Light.* They had connections all over town: they filmed in court rooms and restaurants and places normally requiring permits. They secured police cars. They had fake shootouts in public places. The plots ranged from the weird to the absurd: Vampires who lived in daylight. A comic-book store owner who gets caught up in a plot involving genetically mutated eyeballs. A timid guy who raged out whenever he was called a "wimp."[8]

Most of the scripts weren't even written. They were simply free-associated. But Mark had such nice equipment, no one ever questioned any of it. He was the man with the expensive VHS

---

[8] There is an honest-to-God trilogy of movies out there called *Wimp.*

camera, and that gave him legitimacy. Once, after a bunch of us downed many beers in a cramped apartment, Mark started talking about needing a shower scene. This was just moments after shooting a few scenes without dialogue. In the course of five minutes, he convinced the only girl in the apartment to go topless. It went like this:

"So, I'm thinking, uh, of a shower scene."

"What kind of shower scene?" the girl, Michelle, scrunched a face. "Like, sexy?"

"Naw," the girl's boyfriend, a brooding musician named Shawn, shook his head of long, ragged curls. "Not like that. Right, Mark?"

Now, suddenly, Shawn was an auteur. A bunch of drunk twentysomethings in a shitbag apartment trying to figure out how to get Michelle out of her top on camera.

"No," Mark narrowed his eyes. "What if she's killed by one of the cult members?"

"Which cult?"

Shawn did his best impression of someone remembering details of a movie plot that hadn't even been invented yet.

"The vampires."

"The daylight vampires?"

"Yeah."

"But it's night," I offered my genius take on the situation. "They wouldn't be out."

Mark immediately shot me down—mainly because I wasn't following where his brain had already gone.

"Doesn't matter what time of day it is," he said. "I can make it look whenever. But she'll be taking a shower and they kill her."

"With what?" She poured herself another shot.

"I don't know, a knife."

"I've got a sweet machete in the back," Shawn nodded, getting into it.

"You serious?"

"Yeah, I'm fucking serious. You gotta see this."

Seconds later, we watched Shawn unroll a length of cloth to reveal a Smith & Wesson Bush Hog machete. Shawn handed me the machete and I gripped the rubberized handle, seeing the blade gleam in the scattered Christmas lights. I was terrified of it almost as much as the reality of maybe seeing a real, live, naked woman in a few minutes.

"So, she maybe gets fucking flayed with this thing, right?" Shawn took the machete back.

Mark was nodding, light years past the machete. He was already figuring out how to jam a lighting rig into the bathroom, not to mention the power strips and all the extension cords they'd need. But sure enough, seconds later, it was set up.

"I'm going to shoot this point-of-view style, I think," Mark said, taking the camera off the tripod. He slammed down another beer, forcing to keep it down as he scratched his red beard. "Like the killer, coming at her."

"Oh, that's fucking money." Shawn's eyes were alive.

"Quick jabs, you know?" Mark smiled.

Even Michelle seemed to distantly understand what was going on, though six or seven tequila shots only let so much information through. There was a brief second where she surveyed her apartment, looking at the bathroom that was now lit up like a crime scene with the utility lights and the running water. I could see it in her eyes: fight, flight or fuck-it.

She went for the latter.

She downed two more shots and off came her T-shirt.

"I don't care," she said. "Screw it."

Some part of me still thinks she *did* care at that moment—like she was crossing some imaginary threshold for things and compromises and substances and places in which you don't even want to find yourself. Your first narrow rail of cocaine in a restaurant walk-in; your first missed month's rent check because you decided to party in Windsor, Canada instead. This was no different.

She wasn't thin or athletic; she was just a naked woman. Almost as featureless as some of my parents' crash-test dummies. She slipped into the bathroom and I tried to follow—you know, as an assistant or something—but Mark made sure I knew that there wasn't going to be enough room with all the stabbing and the fake blood.

That's when the night's true genius came.

"Stop," Mark said, admiring Shawn from a different angle.

"Yeah?"

"Your hair," he said.

"What about my locks? You love them, Mark?" he teased.

"Yeah. Let's turn this into a *lesbian* vampire scene. We'll only show you from the back, kissing her. And the audience will think it's another chick."

"I'm not a lezzie, Mark," Michelle got serious.

"We know, Michelle."

Mark turned to me.

"You're going to have to go."

I was hurt. Shut out of the party. But I went outside. Since they were shooting on the first-floor bathroom, I desperately tried to see it all from outside. There was something of an ornate gate ringed with ivy where if you climbed *just* high enough on one of the designs, you'd either slip and twist your ankle, or have a clear shot into the bathroom where the alcohol-induced carnage was taking place.

I felt my buzz and the electricity of the moment fading—especially since, outside, I was much more of an actual creeper. I decided to wait until the next day, in muddy VHS quality, to see Michelle being attacked by a huge machete. Rivulets of red corn syrup over tiny little nipples. Unconvincing screams. A long shot of the shower curtain rings coming out, one by one by one. Lingering shot of blood pooling at the drain.

They'd shoot their movies and then rent out a room at a local hotel to host their premieres. Mark was never in the room where his movie was playing. He was at the bar, downing beer after beer. I found that fascinating. I'd join him in the hotel bar and he'd slide shots and beers my way, as if thanking me for keeping him company. Mark had an entire room in his apartment dedicated to film editing equipment: decks of VCRs and monitors and receivers and wires snaking in countless directions. He edited everything by hand. It's almost mind-boggling to think about now: how he assembled all the footage and spliced in the sound and made something out of nothing. No computer. That, more than anything, impressed me. Even then, I remember being so blown away by the tactile sense of *making something*. He even went balls-out and created gigantic movie-lobby standees with three dimensions.

Mark took a liking to me right away and suggested to Margie that maybe I wasn't like the other dunderheads downstairs who couldn't be bothered to do more than the bare minimum between their cigarette breaks. So, after about a month of vacuuming popcorn kernels out of the bins and wiping down countertops and bagging uneaten popcorn for the next day,[9] I was asked to work in the projection booth. Now, to me, this was like getting knighted. My first time upstairs was dark and disorienting, sort of like being on an alien spacecraft whose crew didn't know you'd invaded their ship. In the blackness of the booth, I could make out the shapes of hulking projection equipment: the massive lenses, the sound towers, the film *clacking* through the sprockets of the projector. Enormous silver spinning platters, feeding film to the projector with the proper amount of tension and then back to another platter. There were eight projectors in all (not all of them were guaranteed to work at the same time), and they noisily worked in the shadows, pumping images and sound out into dark auditoriums, their corrugated exhaust systems pumping hot air out to the roof.

I felt that first, primal instinct all alcoholics need: control.

I was in control up in that projection booth. After a few weeks with Mark, I'd gotten the hang of how to thread a projector (which is funny, since I don't have an iota of mechanical sense about me). I think some part of my brain unlocked long enough to learn how to thread a projector because I knew I'd be able to control eight movies simultaneously in a movie theater. In another generation, I'd maybe be able to harness this learning power for using machine guns in WWII.

That summer, I melted into movie theater life. I genuinely loved being there—I even visited the theater when I wasn't scheduled to be there. I came to look forward to that first blast of air conditioning and buttered popcorn like some junkies

---

[9] Yes. This is true.

look forward to their morning fix. It was a magical alchemy. I'd sit at the desk upstairs in the projection booth, all the projectors working their magic behind me. And the theater itself was something of its own mad city. Some of the employees had scams running between the front desk and the ticket booth, printing up passes and pocketing the difference in cash. Some of them were routinely high while they swept the theaters clean between shows. We even hired a ticket guy named Jay who supposedly had special needs, but I think he was secretly just an asshole. He used to mock people's movie choices when they handed over their tickets.

"Bridges of Madison County? Wow. Good luck with that one. Theater 4."

Someone died there that summer, too. An old lady shuddered in, put her sunglasses on her head, ordered two tickets—one for her daughter and herself—and fished around in her pocket for money. While she did, she collapsed and smacked her forehead on the box office. I knew right away she was gone. I locked the doors to the theater and waited for the police to show up, but I was so cowardly. I hid in the projection booth and let most everyone else deal with the dead body on the floor, blood pooling around her head. EMTs carted off her body and that night we all watched *Dangerous Minds* with Michelle Pfeiffer—the hobo version of *Dead Poets Society.* The one where she implausibly gets through to inner-city kids by means of poetry. We drank ourselves silly that night.

Can you fucking believe someone died?

Her eyes were open the whole time.

Can you believe Paul hid up in the booth and made me stay at the box office with the body?

I fought back embarrassed, ashamed tears. People were banging on the glass doors to get in, even though the body was right there. They really wanted to see *Pocahontas*. I downed four Icehouses in a row—enough to allow me to go along with the Michelle Pfeiffer movie where she's an inner-city high school teacher—and I could feel the beer tugging me away from the thought of that dead body—the slow tide pulling me away from that nameless woman in the movie theater lobby. It made it okay. It was just another thing that happened.

MY GRANDFATHER USED to visit the family farm in West Virginia a lot. He'd be gone for a week at a time—enough for me and Big Neal to tinker around in the liquor cabinet. Our experience with alcohol began and ended with shitty beer and the occasional shot of Chivas or Cuervo. We rooted around, not quite knowing what to do with the rainbow of bottled glass that stared back at us. There were dozens and dozens of bottles, carefully curated and savored by a real man who understood how to drink. We were teenagers, let loose in a sprawling house with too many rooms and too much time on our hands. Greens, reds, yellows. We'd pull out two or three bottles at a time, line them up on the kitchen counter, and pour small measures of each into a juice glass. The colors would bleed into one another—excellent single-malt Scotch whiskeys, brown amarettos, cherry-red grenadines. We watched as our glasses suddenly contained something that looked more like a quarter-glass of swamp water. We counted to three and slammed down the concoctions. After a while, I used to pretend I knew what

I was doing. There was something so romantic to me about being knowledgeable about drinking—the art and craft of putting something together. Big Neal didn't believe me, but he went along with it anyway. I pretended and poured. After a while, my only goal was reducing him to a wobbling mess as quickly as possible. I once told him that a drink was called "The Darth Vader" and he immediately threw it up in the sink, some of the black mixture coming out of his nose. (Success!)

My grandfather had crazy beers scattered around the house, too. Things no one ever heard of. Hamm's. Schaefer. Henry Weinhard's Private Reserve. We had a Great Lakes Edmund Fitzgerald Ale once, and remarked that it tasted exactly like the hull of its namesake sunken ship.

The empty-house routine also became crazy popular that summer. My friend Mackenzie, a tiny, artsy girl I'd known since elementary school, had somehow fallen into my orbit between semesters at a liberal arts college in California. She was a mainstay after a while. She had a home life that reminded me of a lonely pier leading out to a frozen lake. There just wasn't anything there for her. She seemed to change her hair color and style every other week and became a target of misdirected attraction from all the guys in high school—and beyond. In other words, she was one of the few girls I knew who talked to me. She was attractive, but she was also ethereal. She was like working with water—she was constantly slipping between my fingers.

Mackenzie was intelligent, funny, and liked interesting music: bands no one had ever heard of, their names scribbled in magic-marker on blank CDs. I think the school she attended gave dolphins and gold stars instead of letter grades, but she confused me. She had that sway all young women have over young men: they're aware they're attractive and yet they don't know quite how to harness it, like a Ghostbuster proton stream—it's all messy and electric. I had no idea why she hung out with me.

Once, enough confused hormones collected around my thoughts before her next visit to the house. I felt them swarm around my synapses, accenting every thought. I'd also downed two cans of whatever nameless utility beer Granddad had sitting around. So, we spent the afternoon as we normally did, observing nature and listening to music. She'd bring over a Kate Bush record and we'd maybe go outside and lie on the walkway, watching ant colonies do their thing. Then we came back in and listened to more of her CDs. Even if they were horrible or if I didn't understand them, I pretended to dig them.

She could sense something was wrong.

"What are you thinking about?"

Given the nature of our conversations, the answer would likely be some bullshit I'd just half-learned about Ayn Rand or whatever author Mackenzie was into. Instead, I turned, feeling the beer driving my thoughts.

"I think I want to kiss you."

The look of instant horror that seized her face is something I'll never forget. Years of friendship toppled like a Jenga tower. She literally folded up on the couch, protecting herself as I approached. I had one arm outstretched already. This was how I'd made out with my pillow, after all.

"No. Please, no, just don't."

I didn't understand. I thought that it was what was supposed to happen next. My brain told me to be bold, but looking back,

I'm convinced it was the explosion of beers in my brain. The liquid courage. Regardless, you couldn't pay Mackenzie to want to kiss me. I'd betrayed something—some fundamental understanding between us that I didn't quite get.

We sat there for a real ten minutes in silence.

Later, one night at the house, Big Neal, Mackenzie, and I got completely blotto. Tori Amos was shrieking on the stereo. Neal was passed out hard on a couch. After three or four rounds of shitty mixology, Mackenzie and I ended up naked in a soapy bathtub.

This was the greatest moment of my life.

Everything was messily colored in, but the world kept telescoping away from me. Everything was now on a gimbal, constantly trying to put me at a thirty-degree angle when I didn't want to be. My familiar bathroom, now with a naked girl in it, wasn't at all what I expected. I couldn't enjoy one second of it. But there she was in the world's largest bubble bath, water trickling out the sides. I put towels down along the edge because my drunken brain told me that this would cause water damage. Especially if we started having sex or something—which I was *definitely* not prepared for. In fact, there's a weird sort of inertia that hits you when you're an overweight teenage boy who has a crush on Gillian Anderson.

If and when reality ever hits, you're paralyzed. I'd somehow gotten from Point A to Hell Yes, but had no idea what was going to happen next. My brain conspired against me. I lay against the ceramic tile, far away from the naked teenager with large breasts—the ones most every guy in school wanted to see. And now they were loose and hanging free in my grandfather's bathtub. Her brain was clearly at half-mast, too. She thought everything was goddamn hilarious. She began speaking in singsong, referring to me as "Phillip" and her as "Minnow" in a thick British brogue. I was so blown away by the presence of an actual lithe teenager who was jockeying for space in the tub, her legs snaking around mine in the water. We were touching, my brain was going off, but I was also trying to keep pace with the Phillip-Minnow one-act play she was spontaneously writing. I didn't know if I had the mental energy for that, or if I could keep up with it.

"Phillip?"

I liked how she barked at me, though tenderly. We'd only agreed on our character names—we had no reference point for what their actual jobs or lives entailed yet. She was much more skilled at Naked Bathtub Drunken Improv. Right now, I was just a friend in whatever Brigadoon she'd invented there, her back to the showerhead.

"Yes, Minnow?"

"Phillip! I am displeased."

"Oh dear," I said in my best servile English, swallowing back the black slick of Jagermeister creeping up my trachea. "What now?"

"I have found myself in a state of cleansing. I require cleansing. I am most displeased."

"Cleansing."

"Yes. Please cleanse me."

"Cleanse you."

Her eyes, narrow slits as she channeled her Englishwoman, went wide. She broke character, just for a second.

"Yes. Clean me."

I couldn't control what happened next, but I was going to

clean her.

"Where?" I trembled.

"Why, Phillip! Everywhere!"

"Even…?"

She let out a dramatic sigh—the sigh of several years' worth of defenses coming down.

"They're breasts," she grabbed my hand and guided it toward her chest. "See? Feel it. Breast. Boob. It's nothing."

It was something.

"And this," she saw me beginning to periscope through the suds, "this is just a dick." She grabbed it and yanked it in the way you played *Pole Position* on an Atari 2600 joystick.

None of it excited me. I became very scared.

This wasn't us as Philip and Minnow, and this wasn't us as Paul or Mackenzie. This wasn't the sort of thing that happens to two lifelong friends if they're stone-cold sober. The neon-bulb fire in my veins dulled a little, and I felt the alcohol washing over my thoughts. For a little while longer, we stayed in the tub and turned the shower on, pretending that we were in a submarine that had gotten torpedoed. Broad strike—not a deadly one. I was barking orders and she kept coming back from the engine room with a Scottish accent telling me, "I'm giving her all she's got!" She was mixing ideas, but I didn't care.

Finally, we decided the hull was breached by water, just like the bulkheads in our brains had been compromised by one too many waves of alcohol. It was time to board the life rafts. Mackenzie perched herself over the edge of the tub for about a real sixty seconds. She looked as if she was actually seeing our shared illusion coming to life. I'm not going to lie: I stared for the entire time she was there, much like a sketch artist would—

only I was a creepy teenager. She appeared wistful, globs of soap sliding off her arched naked back, as she prepared to clamber out. I considered that she was imagining a world far below: churning waters, enemy ships, torpedoes, engine-room fires. She was really selling the illusion.

And then she vomited all over the carpet.

It came out in violent gags—the kind you see in sci-fi movies where someone's infected with an alien virus. I expected her to retch up the telltale black-green goo that means she's a carrier or a clone or something. No—it was just my stab at making a Long Island Iced Tea. She colored the carpet with wild curlicues and Mayan symbols. For a second, it looked like a crop circle. Then she collapsed onto the floor, drowsing off, mumbling something about a guy she'd met in college named "Kenseth." I immediately hated him. It sounded like such a made-up name—a Pacific Northwest warrior who wore samurai gear and slashed esoteric phrases with a saber. Lazy on Sundays, devilishly intelligent, charming stubble. He was the philosopher king of their liberal arts college and was poisoning my drunken mind even more. I could feel actual vitriol for someone I didn't know boiling inside me. Jealousy with me is never green or clear-cut: it comes from deep within the earth, it's harvested, it comes in giant black globs, bubbling up. Who the hell was Kenseth to ruin a drunken night? Alcohol had opened up a Neil deGrasse Tyson shortcut and now none of it mattered. Anyway, I tended to the most important thing at hand: the carpeting.

I staggered around the bathroom and cleaning closets, naked and trailing soap everywhere, and got towels and Scrubbing Sponges. I stared at the bleach for a bit, wondering drunkenly if *now* is when you used bleach or if it was for later. I couldn't remember if it was like primer paint or something. Used first, ahead of soap. I decided not to use it. I got on my hands and knees, alongside Mackenzie's stretched-out naked body on the floor. I stopped staring. It didn't feel right. It felt sort of like seeing Donna, our next-door neighbor, who used to leave the windows open. She didn't necessarily care, but she wasn't inviting me, either. This wasn't part of the plan. She was already asleep, making cute little muffled snores as I worked. I scrubbed and she didn't move.

One rule of living in that house was that I couldn't leave any trace behind, no trace of fun. Certainly no trace of Mackenzie yakking all over the bathroom floor. I scrubbed for at least ten minutes until it was palatable—I was watching my work with one eye open. Finally, I helped Mackenzie to her feet; I slung my arm around her after hoisting her up. She felt warm against the right side of my body; I flashed again, alive with car-battery voltage, just by touching her. It felt good and foreign to be that close to a naked woman. I saw her in the shadows as I helped her to bed.

I knew this wasn't our time—and more than that, it would *never* be our time. This wasn't meant to be. Nothing would ever come of this. I knew that she would soon be returning to her school. This was a minor interlude in her life. For me, it'd be the highlight of the year. I wanted more of it. I had to get better at mixing drinks—that much was for goddamn certain. I had to make sure I mixed and measured and served the right amounts so that interesting people didn't suddenly pull the emergency chute midway through a conversation, get naked in a tub, and puke everywhere.

I began passing out near her, also naked, for the sheer and conscious reason that I wanted to be able to say that I slept naked with Mackenzie. (Life is short, man.) Anyway, I watched the digital alarm clock in the dark—its red digits imperceptibly moving upward into the air over Mackenzie's chest in the dark. Just rising, always rising, into the dark.

I kept trying to follow its arc with my eyes, fighting back the waves of nausea, but couldn't.

I fell asleep. Sort of.

5

WHEN YOUR DRINKING PROBLEM is first starting to take shape, it's not unlike attending a glorified community college for three semesters: you're adrift, not quite sure why you're there, going through the motions, and haunted by a nagging sense of emptiness. You're well aware you could be doing so much more with your life, but you're not—and you're strangely okay with it, bleeding out opportunities and chances and hope. You're just there.

Like I said, Firelands College was where my parents met, and perhaps it seemed like a larger place to them back in the Seventies. It's not like I could complain—it was paid for. To me, it was just like high school, though: gymnasium, auditorium, modest library stacks, a self-serve "vendeteria." Hell, lots of familiar faces from high school sat in the same classes as me. During that first semester, I took classes that were far easier than anything I'd ever taken in high school. Best of all, there were giant gaps in between the classes where I could do nothing at all. I was taking classes from instructors my own parents had taken classes from. They were professors so old and out-of-touch that they likely would have found their names in their own research materials, had they been relevant and produced research materials.

It was just an idle place to be. Low-wake learning.

I ping-ponged between Firelands and the movie theater, which is sort of like commuting between a trailer park and an abandoned arcade. Eventually, my parents decided that I should probably transfer to main campus in fear of me becoming a full-time projectionist, afraid of daylight.

IT'S A GOOD THING I went to Firelands first. I wasn't built for main campus. Bowling Green State University sits amidst miles and miles of farm country—an area "flatter than a pool table," Granddad used to say—and touted itself as "Home of the National Tractor Pulling Championships." Campus itself was a mess of unflattering faded-brick buildings with small lecture halls.

Since I'd washed up in the rocky shoals of an English degree program (I wasn't testing myself whatsoever), most of my classes were in the same two buildings. They were all musty with mold-speckled ceilings. The instructors weren't much better. Many of my classes were tucked into basements where, upon first visits, I almost got lost, thinking: *There's no way it can be past here.* One class was so deep into a building's basement that I felt like Mitch from *Real Genius* when he goes chasing Lazlo into the basement lair. It just kept going and going, with two or three taped-on arrow signs saying: "Keep going" and "Class this way."

I enrolled in classes like Victorian Literature, Contemporary Fiction, and Shakespearean Sonnets. I had classes that required little more than reading and then writing papers confirming that you'd read the books and articles you were assigned. The program wasn't exactly a challenge by any stretch of the mind. I even artfully dodged taking biology, chemistry, and physics by cobbling together enough astronomy and meteorology courses to satisfy the science requirement. (I shit you not: my declared minor was the self-designed "Sociological Meteorology." Somewhere in some BGSU archives, confirmation of this exists.)

Since the actual course load wasn't exactly taxing, I immediately took to life outside the classroom. I landed in the brand-new dormitory on campus—Founders Hall—which was just mind-boggling to me: sleek steel-and-glass, sailing walkways, giant common areas. My room was part of a suite of rooms. I moved in with a roommate nicknamed "140," which was his high-school wrestling weight. We didn't get along. I'm not sure what lazy campus intern paired us together, but 140 sure as hell wasn't the person I had in mind when I filled out my dorm questionnaire. He liked WWE; I liked Bond movies. He liked country music; I liked R.E.M. 140 did, however, play a critical role in my GPA by waking me up one morning to take a meteorology final after I passed out around four a.m. cramming for it. (So there's your credit, 140. I don't remember your name, but I remember that you saved me from an F.) Maybe he just saw through me or something. I'm sure most people did. I was scared, lonely, and afraid—and, worse, scared, lonely, and afraid because people saw through me. One time, I got the flu and called my mom, tears welling in my eyes, because I hadn't been sick away from home before. I remember looking up and seeing one of my other roommates' girlfriends standing there, having heard the whole exchange. She tried to not acknowledge me, like I was a homeless person with a sign asking for change. She didn't want to contract whatever it was that I had. (Not the flu—the lack of being able to function alone at nineteen years old.)

My other roommates were more tolerant. Life sprouted out from the common room where we all lived. They weren't the most engaged dudes. One guy, Kyle, was in his mid-twenties, so he was our source for alcohol on the weekends. We'd pile into our car with Kyle, go to the liquor store, he'd buy an enormous amount of beer, and then we'd lug it all in two or three duffel bags. Every weekend, we looked like we were moving in.

At first, I wasn't comfortable being there. It was too much like being tapped directly into an electrical source—I couldn't take it. I wanted to blend my worlds, so I started inviting my movie theater friends to college parties. It was an awkward fit. I also had a weird affectation where I took photographs of everyone with a disposable camera. I needed to document everything. I started videotaping them at parties. I was the guy with a VHS camera on his shoulder at most every turn. It also helped me distance myself from everything—helped me feel at home.

But what made me feel most at home was alcohol.

I used to ask Kyle to buy me beer on, say, a Tuesday and I'd take it back to my room. To practice.

This wasn't a good sign, and both of us knew it.

THE ONE GUY WHO completely got me was Erik Bell, who they'd already nicknamed "Crow." He was tall, impossibly thin, and quick with a laugh. The Halloween before, Erik had dressed up as Brandon Lee's Crow character, complete with the greasy, scraggled-black hair and crazed-kabuki makeup. Even had the leather jacket. It was eerie how close it was. But Crow and I immediately hit it off. He tolerated me and just how "not from this world" I was. He asked me questions, liked my friends, always gave big hugs. The ladies loved him. He skated between classes on roller blades.

Crow used to hide in trees. He was the type of person who'd hide in the bathroom in the dark for a full twenty minutes, perched on the toilet like a gargoyle, to scare the shit out of you when you'd flip the light on. Crow and his outdoors-equipment-obsessed friend "Koz" invited me everywhere even though I didn't belong there. I'm fairly convinced that if Koz died, he'd come back as a charming piece of climbing gear, like a carabiner. He spent about six years getting a degree in Outdoor Recreation, but I loved him. He had dimpled cheeks, and everyone seemed to gravitate toward him. I piecemealed outfits together from my big-size JCPenney purchases and tagged along to parties where women were oblivious to me.

I was fat and getting fatter. The slow rise of discomfort and tightness has always been the barometer of how I'm doing in life: if I'm excelling at school or business, my waist size is climbing. My life has always been that piece of transparent tape against a wall where there's a little air bubble at its center—no matter which way you nudge it, the bubble's going to be there.

Alcohol didn't ignore me, though.

My flirtation with alcohol wasn't so much a flirtation as it was an awakening of the senses. Drinking was excused, expected. I needed to harness the way it made me feel. It loosened up something inside me, thawed out all the frozen parts of my better judgment. I gravitated toward the kegs in kitchens and stayed there, drinking more than I should, feeling myself understanding life—like it was unlocking all the mysteries of my past.

WE WENT TO COSTCO to buy a Rubbermaid container and industrial jugs of Hawaiian Punch, orange juice, and cranberry cocktail. We did math in the aisle on a crumpled piece of paper, trying to figure out just how much fruit juice we'd need to fill the Rubbermaid container. We wanted to be precise about it, like we were calculating how to get the Apollo 13 astronauts safely back to Earth. We did the math three or four times— none of us were good at it—as we tried figuring out the right ratio. We drove straight to Kroger and bought about $50 worth of pineapple, blueberries, and cherries. Then, by the time we got back to the apartment, one of our older neighbors had come through for us: our kitchen table was topped with bottle after bottle of well booze: vodka, rum, gin, tequila. I remember very clearly that it was a Tuesday night. Our party was to be on Friday.

Crow, Koz, and I laid everything out carefully. We got cutting boards out. Both of them worked in kitchens—Crow in a pizza shop, Koz in the Founders cafeteria—and set about chopping and peeling and mincing and dicing. They worked steadily, as if they were in a high-end kitchen line. I remember being so impressed with their careful knife work, their skill in cutting the pineapple rinds without losing much of the meat. My job was to load the Rubbermaid container with the fruit juices. I twisted off caps and poured. But not the booze—that was for the three of us to do. Before I knew it, about half of the container looked like where you kept all the fake blood on a movie set. It was so red that it was almost black.

"Dude, this is going to be epic," Koz shook his head, staring at it.

We then dumped all the diced fruit into the container, watching everything bob to the surface. Then, with glee, we unscrewed all the tops off the booze and each poured a bottle into the container. About seven bottles later, the Rubbermaid bin was full to the brim. Koz took a wooden spoon and began swirling it around, mixing it like the witches' brew from

Macbeth. I remember staring at the fruit as it circled around and around the purple hurricane eye. After a good two minutes, Koz was satisfied and slurped some off the spoon.

"Hoogah!"

"Let me get in there," Crow giggled and took his own spoon to it.

I took a ladle and scooped some up, too. The smell hit me almost immediately: a bright gasoline reek underneath all the fruit. The fruit was like a too-small tarp covering a giant anvil. It was as sickening as it was amazing. I remember thinking I could drink cups of it and not taste the booze straight off. Which, of course, was the whole idea. It'd rot your teeth as quickly as it'd rot your belly.

"We've got ourselves a Hairy Buffalo, boys," Koz nodded.

I was beyond excited.

Convinced we'd not only achieved some plateau of teamwork but culinary wizardry, Crow saran-wrapped the bin and the three of us carefully hoisted it up like it was a thermonuclear device and moved it into the fridge. We'd planned ahead that week and gone light on groceries so there'd be room.

"Now," Crow instructed us, "don't touch it. We let this shit settle until Friday. By then, the fruit will be just as potent."

We agreed and, believe it or not, I didn't peel back the saran wrap to test it. Not even once. I wanted it to work its dark magic, believing that over the next few days, there would be a sort of beautiful alchemy going on in the refrigerator.

I was curious if it'd even hit me.

🍾

I'D JUST SCREAMED "I'm Spider-Man!" and thrown myself against our apartment wall, hard. I was upside down, legs akimbo, lying against the tie-dyed tapestry in our kitchen area. Warm keg beer and Hairy Buffalo throbbed inside me. I'd gotten a good running start from the hallway and hurtled myself at full speed. We were having a "White Trash Bash" where everyone was wearing white wife-beater T-shirts, cut-offs, trucker shirts, and carrying around giant plastic mugs. It was one of our first apartment parties, and I'd spent days ahead of time making mix CDs for the event. Pretty sure Kid Rock and Lynyrd Skynyrd were all over that party. We were known for our theme parties. I'd spent so much time planning out the music playlist and so little time considering the snap-second decision to race through several dozen partygoers to throw myself against the wall.

It got the result I'd hoped for: gasps and laughs. I felt like a goddamn cartoon character. It felt good.

I'd flirted with drunkenness before. Now I was in it to win it. The first time I got drunk at college, all bets were off. It's like when you dip your paintbrush into watercolors in elementary school art class, then flick the tip of the brush with your fingers. You know what's going to happen, but you do it anyway. Paint speckles everywhere. Splatter marks and splotches—that's what I was when I was drunk. I was messy. You couldn't trust me from one second to the next.

I'd tell anyone anything they wanted to hear; I got mean; I got sad; I isolated; I pouted.

Some examples:

° This girl lived down the hall from us in the dorm, and she was into my movie collection. More than that, she was into my roommate. Still, I spent an inordinate amount of time trying to impress her. I told her I'd worked on a rare independent movie she liked. I suddenly had to make that lie true.[10] I created a fake version of the DVD art, carefully layering my name into the credits, then printed it. I spent actual time cutting out the artwork, slipping it into the DVD, and then nonchalantly leaving it in my collection for her to find. She never did.

   ° I got drunk and played acoustic guitar in my room with the door closed for a few hours at a party. Alone. No one was interested enough to come back and find out what was driving me to play the same three songs over and over again.

   ° I once replaced all the water in our ice-cube trays with Icehouse. I was convinced it'd build up my tolerance like I was an imperialist fortifying myself against arsenic poisoning by having a little of it every day.

   ° My friend Paula drunkenly kissed me in a stairwell, telling me she wished I was more athletic. I told her I lost weight fast. (Not true.) She'd already lost interest in the second she walked back into the party.

   ° I racked up a massive bar tab with some friends at a pool hall and didn't return until after senior year. Somehow, the owner recognized me and untacked a wrinkled $180.55 bill off the wall. Before he could even confront me with it, I was gone. I still stay away from that place to this day, praying for its closure.

   ° See if you can follow this one: One of my roommates made out with some random girl from another dorm room. That girl got drunk and made the mistake of telling me. I thought it was a good, solid, righteous thing to do to tell my roommate's girlfriend. It was like throwing a bomb over a wall.

---

[10] Three-quarters of my alcoholic life was doing this: making ridiculous lies true.

I listened to them argue and fight and scream at each other through my wall, him screaming *"Who told you?"* and every muscle in my body seizing up at the very real possibility that I'd get my ass kicked. I used the truth as a weapon—I liked to hurt people with it because I was so miserable myself. But I was pinned to my bed, worried that at any second, he'd lumber through my door and throw me through my mini-fridge.

   °   There was a guy who'd come to our apartment over and over again who I didn't like, so I set about letting all the air out of his car's tires whenever he did. I spent more time hiding out in the parking lot doing that than enjoying the party.

   °   I videotaped every single goddamn second of almost every party. Looking back on it, it had to be pretty weird seeing a guy with a video camera everywhere you went. My idea was to document the goings-on and get confessionals, like on *The Real World*.

WHILE MY DRINKING PROBLEM was still finding its shape and direction, I was also trying to figure out which shape and direction my Halloween costume would go. Every year, I gave it real time and thought. All my friends did the same thing, taking it super-seriously. When we'd hear a scream from the bathroom, we knew Crow had just claimed another victim when they flipped on the light switch. Halloween was his time to shine. In our senior year, he'd abandoned the Crow costume for something of a hipster vampire—Oakley sunglasses, bleached-blonde hair, fangs that barely hung in there. We'd find him, drunk as hell in a tree, just staring down at everyone without saying a word.

Knowing that our costumes had that sort of importance, I doubled down and went for Austin Powers. This was before the sequel and all the merchandising, so I had to piece that whole costume together myself. I went to thrift shops for the crushed-velvet jacket and the frilly white shirt, then hit novelty shops for the bad teeth and wig. With enough beer in me, I committed to my costume as much as Crow did his. Liquid courage kept me out there, too, loudly proclaiming (and half-pretending) to want to "shag" all our female friends. As the keg beer flowed, so too did the parade of people floating through our college apartment door: friends dressed as dinner table settings, cows with working udders, a deck of cards, and insane court jesters. A gaggle of girls came in dressed as Hooters waitresses. My friend Big Neal lumbered in as The Incredible Hulk, bare arms coming out of a shredded shirt, having only smeared green face-paint on. He looked more like a Hulk who had a really shitty cold. Still, it was all as dizzily creative as it was a bizarrely magical time.

But then it sort of tapered off from there. The time I invested in my Halloween costumes couldn't compete with the amount of time I was starting to invest in my growing alcoholism. In successive years, I went as Obi-Wan Kenobi and then Zombie Indiana Jones. There may have been a stab-wound victim in there somewhere, too—I don't remember. All I know is that none of them were particularly inventive. Much later, one of my first bottoms in grad school, I drank my face off and ate a shit-ton of mushrooms and staggered costumeless down Mill Avenue at Arizona State through a wall of dressed-up college students. I almost had a panic attack. I'm getting way ahead of myself, but it says a lot about where I was with the arc of my alcoholism: I was already out at the bars earlier in the evening, having forgotten it was even Halloween in the first place. It hadn't registered on my radar. The main event for me had become the alcohol—not the camaraderie of costumed friends.

DRINKING IN COLLEGE was acceptable on three days and three days only. Thursday, Friday, and Saturday. Sundays were for recovering, TV, and reading up for class on Monday. Relatively early bedtime. That's when I first felt the tectonic plates underneath me slipping—the sliding and grinding of earth. I remember it distinctly. I was in the kitchen of our apartment, making a sandwich or something, when I noticed there were some leftover beers from the weekend. This wasn't uncommon. There was always a surplus from the weekend—a scattered mix of orphaned brews from whomever came by. This time, there were three cans of Miller Lite, all lined up in a row, perfectly on display. They seemed to glow. I plucked one from the shelf and held it in my hands. Had I been alone when I saw them, I'd have drunk them by myself. But Crow and Koz were in the living room, textbooks splayed out on our table. (It has to be mentioned that our living room table was cinder blocks propping up a stolen yellow traffic arrow sign.) They'd say something, I figured. Crow certainly would mention it. He came untethered with the best of them when he was drinking, letting himself go far into deep space. But when it was time to come back to the shuttle, he did.

I cracked the beer in the kitchen and immediately pulled out a Diet Coke can.

At this moment, I felt it shift inside me: the dark machinery of my alcoholism starting to creak into motion. Casual deceit. It was coming fast and easy. I downed the beer quickly—not because I was full-blown already or anything. Not because I hated myself. Because I didn't want them noticing. I chugged it so fast and hard that my throat and chest were on fire. I crumpled it quickly and slipped it gingerly into the trash can, underneath all the other shit in there from the weekend's adventures. No one would be the wiser.

Then my brain started reasoning with me.

There are two beers left. Surely someone is going to notice you drank one of the beers. You should probably drink the other two. They won't notice all the beers are gone. It's less conspicuous that way. They'll forget the beer was even there in the first place.

I peered around the corner. Koz and Crow were watching *That '70s Show* when I plucked the second beer off the shelf. I opened it slowly and quietly, then made a real show of searching the cupboards for ingredients I didn't need so it sounded like I was in there at work. The can let out a soft, thankful hiss of carbonation. I chugged that one, too.

The third beer, I'd have to deal with on my own.

I slipped it into my pocket, bulge and all, and hurried into my bedroom where I'd finish that one by myself.

"Where you goin', Magnum?" Crow called.

(I have lots of chest hair, so my nickname was "Magnum," after Tom Selleck.)

I murmured something untrue. The beer was sliding down

the inside of my pants. I barely made it into my room before the can fell out of the pants leg. I closed my door, staring at the enormous vinyl *Star Wars: Episode I—The Phantom Menace* banner that I'd stolen from the movie theater that adorned my wall.[11] I cracked open the third Miller Lite and downed it fast. This was more beer than I consumed on a regular night out. But I'd awakened something inside me, something deeply cellular and generations-old.

ONE WEEKEND, Koz slept with a close friend of mine from French class. It wasn't the first time he'd moved in on my female friends, either. It cracked something inside me and let loose a geyser of envy. She told me, casually and almost matter-of-factly, over pancakes at an IHOP the next morning, explaining it in more detail than I needed. She didn't know how it happened. Just that it had. *Fuckin' wine,* she shook her head. That was the only explanation. It dawned on me through breakfast that she really just wanted to recreate the evening like it was the worst *CSI* episode ever. She also didn't have any clue that this not only destroyed me, but it turned Koz into something of an Andromeda Strain who needed to be destroyed. I felt like he was like a swift disease that was ravaging my female friends.

After paying the breakfast bill—the most bitter bill I've ever paid, tacking on 20% for the server—I went straight to the grocery store and bought a 12-pack of Miller Lite, took it back to my room, and shut the door.

I had some planning to do.

---

[11] This was before I'd seen it and realized it was an unwatchable piece of shit.

I had to become a good male specimen.

But not yet.

WHEN I TURNED twenty-one, it was Game On. For some reason, I waited for the real debauchery to start. Everything before had been a precursor to the main event. I'd been sneaking into bars with my friend Mark for ages, dodging every bouncer in northern Ohio. I wasn't always successful. I just played it off like I'd forgotten my ID and Mark tried vouching for me. Sometimes it worked; mostly it didn't. Most of the dives we went to didn't care, though. Still, I kept the drinking low-key. I was well aware that one false step meant that I'd be thrown out, or worse. I needed to be seen, blend in. I conspicuously stood near the door guy *after* I'd gotten in, trying to psychologically link him to the fact that I was allowed to drink. That way, next time, I'd be greeted with a head nod and a "You're good" sweep of the hand.

In undergrad, we had to drink *before* we hit the clubs. We'd stumble toward the bars where we couldn't drink. It was impossibly backward. But that's how our brains worked. It made some fucked-up sense to us, like getting a drink when we weren't allowed to was some sort of a puzzle we'd have to drunkenly unlock once we got there. It was a challenge.

I came to love bars, though. Absolutely love them. I discovered that to slip into the corner of a bar was to slip into a pocket hidden from the rest of the world. Walls seemed to open up like in a Harry Potter novel when I walked toward one.

My first bar experience, in fact, was when I was nine or ten. It couldn't have been super-late at night, but I remember going to my hometown's bar (The Wonder Bar) with my grandfather. He insisted we eat there, claiming that "bar food is some of the best food there is." I remember food coming out in baskets lined with crinkled, checkered wax paper. Things I'd never even heard of appeared in front of us: sauerkraut balls, fried mushrooms and peppers, burger bites. It was all percolating just under the surface, showing itself only at night. People could be loud: they could laugh, they could swear, they could be full of life. That stuck with me.

College bars, dive bars, it didn't matter. I genuinely loved everything about them. They were like private societies—places where the space-time continuum warped a little. Walking into a bar, there was always promise. Adventures lay in wait there on the barstools. It felt dangerous—romantic, even. To me, there is no more glorious a sight than that of a bar in wintertime: the glass all fogged from the inside, smeared colors, hints of animated fun going on. I wanted to hide inside them, collapse into their warmth and let the drinking dissolve me, maybe. I wanted bars to swallow me whole. I could get lost in them, get disconnected, come undone. I felt truly alive when I opened a barroom door—especially at eleven o'clock at night, catching that first blast of smoky air and jukebox music screaming from shitty speakers over a throng of people not paying attention to you. Back in those days, too, there'd be a fogbank of cigarette smoke hanging at the ceiling. You could smell the sticky floors and the bad decisions happening all around you.

Truths were slippery, secrets unsafe. Things were whispered; things concealed became shared. Loud declarations of love, an arm hung over another person, apologies.

It was true magic.

When I finally turned twenty-one, legal age, I already fancied myself something of an expert on alcohol. I had graduated from Icehouse and Schlitz[12] to Killian's. I felt refined, thinking it was a sumptuous, round brew—as sweet as it was bold. I couldn't imagine drinking anything else. I proudly waved my driver's license around, pissing off more than one bartender who'd been serving me for a year prior to that.

The night I turned the golden age of 21, we all went out. My friend Paula presented me a gift-wrapped bag of Goldschläger. It felt so adult to me, like a bottle of fine single-malt scotch—if only I could've appreciated scotch or understood what it was like to truly savor good alcohol at the time. That's not how alcohol functioned for me. It was just fuel for me to hurtle myself forward without thinking. I remember turning that bottle over and over in my hands, watching the gold flecks tumble from the bottom to the top like thin ocean surf at sunset, sparkling as it was dragged back out with the undertow.

We hit a few bars that night, and I went through the crazed motions of a twenty-first birthday.

"Don't you think you should probably eat something?" Big Neal cautioned me early on.

"No, I'm good."

"You sure?"

"Promise. I'm not hungry."

"Man," I remember him shaking his head, "I don't know."

"Know about what?"

---

[12] Actual Schlitz marketing slogan: "When you're out of Schlitz, you're out of beer."

"The drinking-on-an-empty-stomach thing."

"Dude, I'm fine."

Big Neal stared at me in his hang-dog way, alternately concerned and impressed. The latter part was important to me. I had to be strong for my friend.

"I'm four hundred pounds, man," he shook his head. "If I was drinking like you, I'd be out of it."

"You're *going* to be drinking like me."

"But I had two Whoppers on the way over here."

Big Neal, as he is about most things, was correct.

I remember the shots coming fast and furious and the hammer of drinking coming down on my head, hard. At some point, I collapsed outside a Buffalo Wild Wings in Bowling Green, with Crow trying to convince a police officer that I was fine. I was inside someone's car forever, too, until Big Neal persuaded me to get out by saying there was more booze in the apartment. I remember worrying that Koz was going to make out with Mackenzie—that she was going to somehow end up in his double bunk. For some reason, Crow and Koz shared bunk beds in college. Koz in the lower bunk where the girls with easy smiles ended up, like shells in shallow tide pools after the sea's gone out. And Crow in his "Crow's Nest," which was only a few inches from the ceiling, which made sleeping up there like lying in a coffin.

The Goldschläger hit me first, then the Jäger. They chased one another around in my bloodstream. I imagined them swirling, glittering gold and goblin-green, around in my body.

I remember gagging the alcohol out in heaves. I remember the porcelain and shitty tile of our apartment bathroom. The black crud around the toilet base where we never cleaned. Eons of pubic hair and speckles of Lord-knows-what.

I remember thinking that I'd never drink again. I promised whatever and whomever that I never would. I pleaded as the floor grew soupy under my hands and I wretched into the toilet again. It was just spitting now—nothing really coming up. My entire body seized against itself, and I was the shape of a cartoon lightning bolt.

A ragged sort of sleep finally took me.

LOOKING BACK ON THEM, my first true hangovers were quaint. Cute, even. No matter how much punishment I put myself through—foggy brain, cotton mouth, broken sleep—I could still get through the next morning just fine. My memory would snap back into view, locking into place relatively quickly. I'd get photos developed from the previous night at the one-hour photo at the Wal-Mart, and we'd flip through the previous night with a sense of distance and nostalgia for something that wasn't even a day old.

"Remember…"

I'd wake up Sunday morning, see Crow and Koz passed out on their beds with circular fans blasting white noise, and I'd have mental permission to sleep for another few hours until they eventually got up. The apartment reached a sort of quiet stasis like that. Once in a great while, the house phone would ring and cut the quiet but I had time to recuperate. Hell, after my twenty-first birthday, I'd managed to get moving and report back on the previous night's adventures after a few hours.

Email was pretty new back in my undergrad years, but

it quickly became a pretty effective tool for avoiding class. I remember logging into the Bowling Green email system—this green-on-black interface that looked like the JOSHUA system Matthew Broderick was trying to stop in *WarGames:*

WOULD YOU LIKE TO PLAY A NICE GAME OF CHESS?

Blinking cursor.

Sometime around seven-thirty in the morning, I'd groggily wake up, seeing dirty light leak through my blinds. My brain went through the classes I had that morning. Fridays, I had a Contemporary Fiction course with a young-ish professor named Dr. Whitworth who was gaunt with sallow cheekbones. His hair was a shock of gray, betraying his age. He liked to pepper his sentences with "fuck," and he adored anyone who adored him. He also liked to cancel class out of the blue. You'd drag your ass to class across a bracing, cutting February wind only to find a note on his classroom door saying *Class Cancelled.* You couldn't help but like the guy, even if he told some of the wildest lies imaginable. One time, he told us a story about loving a puppy so much that, when he was a little boy, he accidentally pulled its ears right off its head. There were whispers about how his health was secretly in swift decline; how he'd not only endured slurs by others, but slurs that were endorsed by the faculty; sordid stories whispered about him and other students. But mostly, it was the puppy story that told me he was completely full of shit. I knew he was full of shit because *I* was full of shit. And he gave me some sort of weird license to be that way.

So when the hangovers hit, I fired off emails off to my profs, saying I was sick. If some provost was collecting all the emails I sent to professors about being ill and added them up, someone would've alerted Campus Medical that I was dying. Seriously. I bet I missed a real three weeks' worth, combined, of classes. But I'd stumbled upon an alternate universe—a world where I was welcomed and I was funny and accepted.

But I was also about fifty pounds overweight. My clothes constantly argued with me. I wasn't fit like Crow nor did I own Koz's endless wardrobe of tie-dyed Peace Frog shirts. All of the other people I orbited around that junior year were in shape, too. They all seemed to consume the same amount of alcohol as me, too, yet with zero body consequences. Joe was in the National Guard—a tanned, lantern-jawed National Guardsman with a crewcut and the musculature of, well, a National Guardsman. He was always three beers away from putting someone in a headlock for no reason. Marsh was tall and reedy, like a quick-witted blade of grass. Kent was trim yet barrel-chested—the kind of guy who you could see kicking down a door with a shotgun and you'd follow him in, no questions asked.

And women all seemed to swarm in their wake.

I was the guy with the sullen lip of fat over his jeans. I wore oversized flannel shirts and size-40-something jeans. At the end of the night, no woman was talking with me. Doors were shut and I'd lie there in bed, hearing giggling and, often, creaking from other rooms—the punishing taunts that only an overweight kid feels in college. That hangs there in your room, by the way. You can feel its pressure bearing down on you. I was frozen out of that world. I'd only made it so far in the door. I was in the lobby, but I hadn't made it past the front desk. Alcohol made me feel like I could get there—that I could slip past the security desk and make it into the elevators without anyone noticing.

It would take real action on my part, I knew. For the first time ever, I wouldn't be able to fake it.

I WAS SUDDENLY resentful of everyone. I felt like my sex life suddenly had an expiration date, that it was a James Bond countdown timer ticking down to zero in giant red digits. I had one year left in my college career and I'd wasted the previous three on learning how to splice 35mm film, hammer out essays at three in the morning about books I hadn't read,[13] and scroll through the vast orange wasteland that was Ain't It Cool News. The minute my junior year was over, I hated everyone. Everyone was having more sex than me—at least, in my head. I craved attention like a potted plant set a little too close to the house, starved for sunlight. It struggled in the long shade, dying in the shadow, thanks to a careless owner.

I hated Crow and his breezy way with women. When he wasn't looking like the poor man's Keanu Reeves, he was carefully massaging the relationships around him like he did pizza crusts at work. Once, I saw him throwing pizza dough in the air, flinging it high and catching it with his fingers, casually playing with centrifugal motion while he laughed. The dough spun and formed a perfect circle, dancing across his fingertips. It was beautiful—and yet, he seemed disconnected from it. Some part of his brain had detached from what he was doing and he was carrying on conversations, laughing. That's exactly how he was with women. He didn't understand how his presence spun others into motion. And that was part of his

---

[13] Tell me *that's* not talent.

charm. And I hated him for it.

I wanted that.

But part of me knew that I'd be an impostor. No matter what I did, no matter how much weight I lost, they'd know. Someone would sense it, like a disturbance in The Force. So I drank over it.

But I also started going to the gym.

That summer, I threw myself into a self-made workout regimen that was little more than doing enough exercises in a row that didn't tire me out too much. I'd do just enough and then slow down. Then try some more. I had no idea what I was doing with the weight machines. I was too lazy to pay attention to other people when they sat down and worked their "delts" and "quads." I'd walk up to each machine and pretend to understand it. I tried following the graphic instructions on their sides and studied them like I was taking a vested interest in maybe purchasing one of them.

I hit the treadmill. I built up my time, slowly. At first, I ran until the buzzing in my brain started—the bee swarm of synapses telling me to stop, that I didn't need to do this to myself. It was all I could do to last ten minutes. Then I'd immediately jump onto the scale, as if the weight would have magically fallen off, but it didn't, like a child dressed as Superman running and expecting to take flight. But I had enough sense about me to know that I had to keep at it. I set about building a routine that involved an hour or so of working out.

And what got me through that torture? The thought of drinking later.

I'm not even joking.

I'd be doing leg lifts or chest pulls and all I could think of was a tall, slender pilsner glass filled with amber, beaded with sweat. I imagined it framed against the shitty bars we went to—and it didn't matter. I didn't need anything glorious. Some people, I hear, have mental places they go when they exercise. Some people summon spirit animals, some imagine calm forces and gentle winds. Desert flowers, butterflies pulsing their wings, penguins, raindrops.

Not me.

I pictured beer. Sweaty beads on glasses of amber.

I imagined that was my reward to get through something that would, in turn, lead me to a greater reward: women.

And still, here's the thing about me: I cut corners. I'm amazing at hemming my way around life, skirting edges and doing just enough to get by. My father, of course, was something of a terrific athlete in his day. Football player and wrestler. Bench-pressed with his buddy Doug in their garage. Really set his mind to it. It was part of his lifestyle. Dad was the guy, by many accounts, who people yelled for when a fight broke out at a pool hall. Dad would step outside and the fight would kind of just fall apart. Oh, and just to make me feel even more inferior: he got his pilot's license before his driver's license.

Growing up in that shadow meant I'd never live up to it, so what's the point? It's like: Well, if my dad understands all this real-world information, what the fuck does someone need me for? He knows how to fix radiators with JB Weld; he can fix a muffler to a frame with coat-hanger wire and duct tape; he built me a flip-face *Voyagers* communicator[14] out of sheet metal and blinking lights. He understood how a record needle produced sound, what all the solar system constellations were,

---

[14] If you remember this TV show, I love you.

how magnetism worked, how to draw a perfect circle, how to build things out of wood, what all the levels of the atmosphere are—not to mention every single sedimentary rock layer below. Name it—he knows it. It made me not care. I didn't need to. I just threw myself into all the things I figured Dad didn't know about. He had so many bases covered—athletics, included—that I delved into all the shit he didn't. (Oxford commas, here I come!)

He was the man I'd never be.

In the meantime, working out *sort of* gave me a glimpse into a world of manhood, of knowledge. Alcohol nudged me the rest of the way across the finish line. Whatever confidence I couldn't get out of exercise, booze provided. The going-out-at-night thing got me through the chin-ups, bench presses, and treadmill time. As my muscles burned and I gritted my teeth, I'd zero in on the mental image of tiny bubbles flitting up in a tall stein of beer. I kept my eyes closed, watching them rise and rise.

6

IMMEDIATELY AFTER COLLEGE, I was lost. I had a new body but I was the same idiot. I'd lost forty pounds in three months. I hadn't really started thinking about my future until February of my senior year which, of course, is when most everyone else had already accepted internships or was getting ready to move to real-world jobs that made the past four years' worth it. (See? I wasn't joking when I said that I really never thought too far ahead.) My last few weeks of school were dedicated to my buddy Rich Good and I, playing pool every single night,

Monday through Friday. My college career was also checkered with late nights spent at the movie theater projection booth, cramming for exams I should've been studying for on the weekends when I was partying it up and finishing up essays as the sun crept up over the computer lab. (That's all majoring in English is, by the way: writing papers. There are no tests.)

I met Carrie through friends of friends—which is to say: I have no clue where she came from. When Carrie and I started dating, I knew two things: I wanted to move out west and I wanted to go to grad school, if only to keep the real world at bay just a little bit longer. But she complicated things in all the greatest ways possible. She liked *me.* She didn't seem to like the work I'd put into getting myself into shape that summer. She liked what I had to say; she had interesting things to say herself. She was a nursing student, which meant she wasn't afraid of blood.

She was the quiet, black-haired one on the couch. Of our friends, we were the only two who didn't smoke. To this day, I'm not quite sure how we ended up the odd ones out of this group we found ourselves in. She was about my height with close-cropped black hair, cute angle of a nose, and opalescent eyes. She looked like a young Sandra Bullock. We traded emails back and forth on our dinosaurs of PCs—green screens that gave me a jolt of excitement whenever I'd see something like, "Good to hear from you too!" She was a strict vegetarian, track star, and someone who would meet us out on dance nights at the bar at eleven, even when she had to go to class at the hospital in just a few hours.

I want to go back in time to that moment and usher Carrie away from that version of me. That Paul didn't know what he was doing; he was operating under a different set of rules and instincts, I'd tell her. He was only destined to undo everything she'd worked so hard to set in motion for herself. After all, I wasn't ready for a girlfriend and yet, it was locking into place faster than I anticipated. She had it all figured out: she had a degree program she loved, a great family who loved her back, a car she bought with cash, a hefty savings account from working her ass off.

I had none of it. I free-associated conversations; I spouted off bullshit. I had no money because I didn't have to worry about it, thanks to my parents. But, as an alcoholic barely aware of his powers, I could warm my hands on her responsible fire and not feel too bad about it.

Soon enough, I wasn't able to sleep because of it. I drank more.

I declined the kindness. I disengaged. Hid in other rooms. Didn't want to make it real.

You have to understand that when Carrie appeared, my life resembled the first bloom of the mushroom cloud: almost beautiful in its epic rise against a desert landscape, like Chiluly glass tendrilling miles and miles in the air. You couldn't tell that my human blast-radius was toxic. The detritus of acquaintances and drinking buddies and people I barely knew from the movie theater. I surrounded myself with so many drinkers and n'er-do-wells that I'm shocked I didn't have an honest-to-God pirate in the mix, some night-student with a peg leg teaching us all how to successfully drink whiskey.

In my senior year, I wasn't exactly looking for a girlfriend, even though I'd spent the summer trying to look the part of College Student Capable of Having a Girlfriend. For the previous three years, plus the entirety of high school, I was the guy most likely to know the name of the episode where Data's brother commandeers a crystalline entity to destroy an entire planet.[15]

I had constellations of acquaintances constantly swirling around me, always ready for a good time. Somebody was always tapped into something cool or interesting: a vintage movie showing at the Eva Marie Saint Theater, someone reading poetry at a coffee shop, cover bands screaming No Doubt and Talking Heads. I couldn't get enough of Not Missing Out. I wasn't ready to have a girlfriend. I needed an escape route, fast, because she threatened all the good times I was having.

I kept telling myself something would happen and that this caring, loving, nurturing person would just vanish and let me be alone. I ignored phone calls; I listened to her knock on the door to Crow's new house when I was in the other room, telling others to say I wasn't there even though my Jeep was clearly parked out front. I embraced easy good times—not difficult responsibility. I was just appreciating the fact that my college coursework was winding down, and most of my classes were English courses, which meant it was just a nonstop parade of essays. I could write in my sleep. At one point, I recall writing my own papers while helping others with theirs. One week, honest-to-God, I remember having seven Word docs open at the same time, working among them like a concert pianist showing off on the ivories.

Then came graduation. I don't remember it, but I remember having something like three going-away parties. Everyone asked me what I was going to do, to which I just shrugged. I

---

[15] It's called *Silicon Avatar*.

legitimately didn't know. I knew what I *wanted* to do. I'd long had the romantic ideal fixed in my brain: the idea of driving through the desert, top down on my Jeep. Maybe I'd visit some roadside taverns on my way.

Nothing more than that. That's as far as my imagination carried me.

My parents got me a job at their crash-test dummy company, Applied Safety Technologies. I'd never worked in an office before. They gave me a half-cubicle and a computer workstation. I felt so important. I spent the days cataloging dummy parts—all the metal, cordite, and vinyl had a number that needed to be loaded into a database. Literally every single nut, bolt, and screw that comprised a dummy. It was mind-numbing and yet, I bizarrely liked the work. I liked shutting my brain off and zeroing in on building a crash-test dummy—all the thousands of little pieces and parts, each one numbered and organized and sub-organized and compartmentalized. It made sense to me. I went above and beyond and created separate folders and mapped out different organizational patterns. I built separate catalogs for the different styles of dummies, cross-referencing numbers.

I also had a weird thrill from working in an office space. The front of the building was organized into a small cubicle area, with some outlying offices and a main windowed conference room. There were a few testing areas where engineers stood around in lab coats and released giant metal battering rams from pendulums that swung dramatically from the ceiling, landing square into crash-test dummy chests. They furrowed their brows and measured the impact results on computer monitors—spiked wavelengths—then pulled the pendulum back to the ceiling where they'd do it all over.

There was a quiet, austere room where my friend Mark from the movie theater had gotten a job as a quality-assurance tester. It made some sort of sense seeing him there, measuring and testing each and every part against printed-out specifications, since he used to spend Saturday mornings in the movie theater, methodically cleaning out the projector sprockets and gears and dampers. There was also a modest machine shop, with computer-automated machines that looked like *Galileo* shuttlecrafts. A room dedicated entirely to vats of bubbling pink vinyl.

I'd spent so much time in musty college libraries, thumbing through silverfished hardcovers and bibliographies and cracking the spines of books that hadn't been opened in decades researching God-knows-what, that it was incredibly fulfilling to be around other people. Still, I was well aware that I was "The Boss's Son." I was twenty-one, just out of college, and everyone was super-nice to me. Literally everyone I met was Next-Level Awesome. I took their kindness sincerely. It took me years to realize none of these people really wanted me to be their friend. It only benefited them to have me in their pocket. It kept their world a little calmer. Everyone was secretly on high-level alert.

If I didn't like them, if I noticed they were chit-chatting beside the lathe or in the stitching area, I could screw them over. I was an unknown quantity. Until, of course, Charlie Steinmeyer cracked it. He figured it all out. Charlie was in his mid-thirties, vibrant and black-haired with a prominent bald spot. When he laughed, it was big and almost like a dog baring its teeth in anger. He fascinated me. He looked more like a fire hydrant than a man. Word had it that Charlie had literally run away with the circus in his youth, which came out at the company Christmas party when he'd do backflips on the dance floor.

Everyone loved Charlie. You couldn't not.

For me, Charlie also had an extra gravity about him. He was sometimes rough around the edges in the morning, bleary-eyed but still smiling. Proud up there in his office, surveying the plant floor with a cup of coffee. "Man, I got pretty brown last night," he'd say as sparks arced off a band saw. "What'd you get into?"

My brain raced back to the night before: me living at home watching *The Abyss* on my computer or screwing around with Napster.

What'd you get into?

The question seemed so natural and easy, like I should be entertaining any number of amazing opportunities while living at home with my parents. Just a few months before, I was entertaining the possibility of using my Bachelor's in English at the mall Waldenbooks. There weren't a whole hell of a lot of recruiters calling me, wondering when I'd come work for them. Getting a degree in English pretty much guarantees that. You're quietly radioactive. Unless you have "Dartmouth" or "Yale" attached to "B.A., English" on your resume, a lot of people assume you've given up on life.

Charlie, however, intrigued me. He seemed like he was attuned to some darker frequency—receiving something different than the rest of the people around me, like those creepy Cold War numbers stations where spies emotionlessly read off strings of numbers. Turns out, he was also a part-time bartender at The Old Dutch, a local dive bar. He also introduced me to the golden phrase: "Happy hour."

I like to think he could see the alcoholism in me even at that age, curlicuing through my personality. Another like-minded drinker. *Welcome to the club.* So, I started getting invited to happy hours after work. The beers came fast and furious. And free. People knew Charlie—and that had its own magical caché. Before I knew it, I'd been introduced to all his cronies—but clearly as his boss's son. So I got extra-special treatment. I was a curiosity. I got extra shots, free beers, no questions asked. I was in. I was accepted.

Now, some facts about The Old Dutch: it's Ground Zero for my alcoholism. There are no two ways about it. In that modest square, vinyl-sided box in the middle of nowhere, surrounded by a perennially potholed parking lot, it's where drinking swallowed me whole. I fell in love with the décor: the twin pool tables under shitty lamps; the strips of Formica peeling away from the bar; the men's bathroom with generations of phone numbers and insults peering back from hasty paint jobs. The Old Dutch is actually "Gerold's Old Dutch," too. It's where I came to pass a lot of alcoholic time—immersing myself in its bloodstream for a few hours at a time. Some nights, they had dartboard championships and volleyball, so not everyone felt like a massive alcoholic.

Either way, I fell in love with it all. Even years later, when someone hurled a brick through my Jeep windshield there, I still loved it.

WHEN I ANNOUNCED to my parents that I'd joined a band, I could see it in their eyes that their son was lost. Completely fucking lost. I may as well have been Charlie Steinmetz running off with the circus. I'd already tortured them enough with the English-major thing. Now, I'd decided to form a band with Shawn Daley—a mohawk-sporting friend of mine from elementary school who'd survived not only the Marines, but cancer. Shawn was the only person I knew who came out of the military as the same lovable doofus he was going in. Our drummer was a melon-headed computer nerd named Steve Lener who was always pushing glasses up the bridge of his nose, laughing at his own jokes, and launching into songs three seconds too early. I loved both of them but, as a band, we were pretty atrocious.

Also, I had no business being in a band. I'd taught myself how to passably play a few songs on the guitar the year before. I was better at coming up with band names than I was actually playing an instrument.[16] Shawn's dad had been a touring musician back in the day, having met Three Dog Night and played all over the country in his younger years.

That experience hadn't given way to the same deadness in his eyes, festering, that most middle-aged men have when they realize they'd given up on their dreams to become parents. It's kind of like looking at a half-blown-out lightbulb. You can still see the wiring and the frosted filament. After a while, it just becomes a resentment.

Not with Shawn's dad. He'd carved out "studio space" in his basement for keyboards and drum kits and guitars. That's what Shawn's dad had down there: work. In my younger years, I

---

[16] We were almost Right Star Mourning, Full Tilt Spock, F.O.C. (Friends of Charlie), Ten Forward, and Dan Rather Not. We settled on Short Bus.

remember it being a labyrinth—a musty, low-ceilinged network of discovery. I sat in folding chairs and listened to the man jam for an hour or two, letting Shawn in on the bass. Eventually, our "band" Short Bus played in that same space—mildewed tapestries hanging all around us.

I loved every goddamn second of it.

We never quite gelled because, well, I'm terrible. But we did achieve four or five of those moments I suspect any musician chases the rest of their life, much like an addict who spends the next few decades chasing their first high. Every once in a while, Steve would drum a consistent beat, Shawn would lock into a rhythm with his bass, and I'd nail a vocal and it'd come together. We couldn't possibly replicate it again, but it was enough for us to keep going back to that basement, trying all the same. Occasionally, my sister and one of her friends would come by and listen, then politely leave.

We got a few gigs right off the bat. Mainly due to Charlie. We showed up at the Old Dutch to discover they'd cleared their old piano to make room for us in the back corner by the men's restroom where it reeked of piss and regret. Still, it was a huge deal to us. We blazed through our sets. We didn't know how to take requests. I remember driving to one gig at the Dutch not knowing any of the words to one of the songs we were going to play, but I figured, just like everything in my life, I'd just wing it. The lyrics would come to me. Hopefully, while I was singing, they'd just emerge. That's how I lived my life. I'd heard the song enough on the radio, so I didn't need to worry about that detail. I counted on it so much, in fact, that I didn't even bother to write down the lyrics. (Old-Timey Alert: In those days, the Internet wasn't readily available with that stuff—you had to transcribe what you heard straight from the radio.)

I'll skip the part where we performed a St. Patty's Day night for zero money and free beer, lots of it, and flat-out tortured a guy, slumped in his chair, with a mangled version of "White Room" by Cream. He looked genuinely disgusted but I couldn't tell if it was from us destroying the song or his state of mind. I routinely forgot lyrics and just gave up midway through the songs, shrugging. Not the best way to build a following, I guess, but I was there for the beer.

We crammed all our gear into the back of my Jeep, where I'd torn out the back seats. Steve was fixed between guitar cases and a drum kit. He looked like he was E.T. trying to hide from the mom, staring straight and not moving a muscle. Without warning, two minutes after pulling away, the cops were on us. Adrenaline shot through me. *This is it,* I thought. *This is real life.* I just kept thinking about how furious/embarrassed my parents were going to be to have to bail me out of jail and, more than that, how angry that I'd put myself in this position. I wasn't there for the music, remember—that was just an excuse to play bars and get free booze and some college-age girls on vacation to sort-of pay attention.

Now, police lights were whirling in my rearview like I was in *Blade Runner.* That's also when we heard it: Steve. Shawn and I both turned to the back, where he was ridiculously hidden amidst all our gear. When I flicked on the interior light, searching for my insurance and registration, I could see the tears streaming down his face. He'd had a lot of Irish whiskey that night and now the tears were leaking out of him with no signs of stopping. Same old Steve from fourth grade.

"We're all going to jail," he was straight-up sobbing.

His entire body shuddered, so much so that the high hats clacked.

"Shut up, Lener," Shawn hissed.

The cop showed up to my Wrangler window, which I unzipped. I put myself into Overly Polite Mode. We ran through all the facts pretty quickly, and she asked how much I'd had to drink.

"Oh, not much," I heard myself say.

Cut back to the past four hours where I was drinking Labatt Blues like they were water and enjoying the occasional shot sent over by a table listening to us (I wonder now if they were sending over shots to stop us from playing "White Room").

After some small talk, I heard: "We're going to have to do a breathalyzer."

Everything inside me went ice-cold.

Steve started crying louder.

Mind you, we're in our mid-twenties and this was how we reacted.

"Sure," I faked confidence. "Okay."

She unwrapped the device, showed it to me, and instructed me to blow into it. I did.

And I kept blowing.

And blowing.

When she saw the results, she flinched. I could see it. She radioed for her partner to get out of the car and come see what she was seeing.

0.002.

Like, a toddler's accidental sip of alcohol.

I knew the device was broken. They knew the device was broken. I also knew that they knew that I knew the device was broken. But there wasn't much they could do beyond ask me where I was headed. Inside, I felt a billion hallelujahs and party streamers raining down from the heavens.

"Where are you guys heading to?"

"Oh, just a house over there," I pointed toward a building that was in no way, shape or form related to me. Sandusky is designed like a Masonic symbol, so all the roads came at you from odd angles. I was probably pointing at a one-way street. We actually still had twenty miles to go.

"Just be safe," she said, shaking her head.

A normal person would've taken this as a warning shot. I took it as a call to action.

I didn't feel lucky.

No.

I felt invincible.

TWO

*There's an empty space inside my heart
where the weeds take root.*

—Radiohead

7

WINTER SEIZED SANDUSKY, OHIO. There is nothing more depressing than the long, bleak sadness that comes with seeing a summer-vacation town hollowed out by a season. The sky turns gunmetal gray and the winds grow insult-sharp. Those spare cornfields will stare back at you forever. It's nothing more than space. You forget how empty it all is. You can feel the missing parts—as if three-quarters of a city suddenly got Raptured out. The gauntlet of shopping malls and strip malls and chain restaurants and all-you-can-eat buffets remained, curling north like a snow-swept scar, not quite healed. Sandusky didn't quite go into hiding or underground, like some coastal cities do when a hurricane blows through. And that's half its problem: most everything stays open, enduring the pain—the city was a dry socket or an exposed nerve.

That's kind of how I felt living there.

I'd had enough. Carrie was putting up with my weekends in Short Bus, coming to ~~see us perform~~ cringe whenever she had time off from the hospital. But she was working nights, which meant our schedules sort-of overlapped, but mostly didn't. She was usually sleeping when I worked and when I was finally passing out for the night, she was downing her second coffee. She was part of the equation, but since I'm amazingly self-centered, all I cared about was what was next for me.

I wasn't really living my life so much as coming awake in the middle of it from time to time. Every so often, I'd stop and look around and go: *Holy shit. I'm really doing this. I'm playing a guitar in front of people.* And then I'd remember Tuesday was the night I played pool at Buffalo Wild Wings, and everything would be okay again. But I decided that a life cataloging part numbers wasn't going to get me far, nor did I really have any business sense to keep my parents' company afloat.

I'd gotten accepted by Arizona State's graduate literature program, which is a lot like being handed a three-year vacation. I applied for three grad programs: Carnegie Mellon, Arizona State, UC Berkeley. They could not be more different programs, and I couldn't have tried any harder to impress any of them less. I wrote all the entrance essays and took the exams. The first time, I bombed the GRE so badly that I went back and hate-fucked it a second time. The test proctor seemed shell-shocked when I walked out after ninety minutes. After the verbal test, I guessed the answers on everything else.

When I told Carrie I'd got accepted to Arizona State, I really didn't consider all the earth she'd have to move to come with me. She'd have to quit a job she enjoyed, break a lease, and leave her family—all things that I assumed were super-easy to accomplish. And if they weren't, I genuinely didn't care. That's how much of an asshole I was.

There's a photograph of me, taken the morning I was leaving for Arizona: wide-eyed, full of happiness and adventure. Beside me is Carrie: scared, sad, forcing a smile. Over the years, thanks to me, she'd get used to that expression. We said our goodbyes and she said she'd figure out how to make it work. Deep down, I wasn't sure if it'd work out. My parents helped me move cross-country, and I was suddenly living a second childhood, studying Real-World Avoidance, Selfishness, and Debt.

Before I knew it, I had an apartment, a roommate, a part-time job at a shady nonprofit org up in Scottsdale, a few bills, and a cat named Captain. Life was beautiful. No one was looking over my shoulder, so I drank every night. In your twenties, your life has a lot of white space with lots of room to scribble in the margins. So I filled that white space with drinking and writing. I truly assumed that life would really take off when I'd sell one of my screenplays or novels that I hadn't written. That was a given. I just expected it to happen. I'm not even kidding when I say that I assumed this happened to everyone.

ARIZONA WASN'T SO much a landscape as it was the backdrop for horrible behavior. I was enamored with rustling palm fronds and the way lightning spidered through clouds during monsoon season. Beyond that, I was living a life teetering on becoming unmanageable. I'd oversleep and come up with some giant excuse why I wasn't where I said I'd be. I triple-booked myself on weekends, selecting who I'd show up for at the very last second. I scheduled early-morning racquetball games with friends and simply didn't show up. Credit card bills would arrive and I'd throw them away without even opening them, knowing full well that they were more or less transcriptions of my alcoholism: bar after brewery after nightclub, with some 2 a.m. Whataburger drive-thru action thrown in there.

I'd fought against normalcy for most of my adult life. I never wanted to feel tied down or beholden to anything or anyone. I feared appointments—and I'm not even talking about a trip to the dentist. Simply knowing that three hours of my day were spoken can cause anxiety to pool around in my brain. My days leading up to, say, the opening nights of friends' plays, birthday parties, or anniversary dinners were ruined. Obligations hung in the air and carried actual weight. So I chose what I wanted to do and threw out the rest. Drinking excused it.

I loved that part of life. I really, truly, honestly did. I loved the recklessness of it all—that quiet pivot around 10:45 on a good night out drinking, when someone orders another round of drinks for everyone. Things spun further out of control, and my chances of showing up to work the next day evaporated. I didn't care. It's not like I was living a real life. Nothing mattered. Over a decade was spent feeling as if I just had to keep everything on an even keel. Tell people what they wanted to hear, make sure those around me were pleased and happy, coast through the day and start drinking again. When I didn't show up or follow through or deliver or execute—which was quite often—I didn't care. Or that's what I told myself, anyway. There's always going to be a very thin-skinned alcoholic inside me who's very concerned about what people think.

I WAS AT the Backstage Bistro, an upscale restaurant I couldn't afford. Exposed rafters, linens, heavy flatware. In my 20s, armed with a credit card, I often pretended to be a grown-up with my new friends. I'd been drinking most of the day already, and my tongue felt like I'd been holding it to the end of a 9-volt battery. I couldn't taste any of the expensive food I was supposed to be savoring. I remember the server making a real show out of their seared opah dish, which I ordered and ignored in favor of a pinot grigio.

I was caught in the tidal patterns of brand-new friends. One of them was a fellow grad student, Matt—a kind, Beatles-loving, voracious reader who made extra money waiting tables at nice restaurants. We hit it off immediately. I remember looking through the stacks of books sitting around on the floor of his apartment, flipping through them and shaking my head at all the live-wire intelligence he'd drilled into the margins of the pages. He dared the words he was reading, challenging them with scribbled questions and comments and exclamations. He cared. I realized right then and there, sick to my stomach, that I didn't care about books the way he did.

I was pretending.

He'd been working in grad school at the Bistro, which was tucked into a shopping center in upscale Scottsdale. It was one of those multi-leveled jobs that kind of collapsed in on itself like a piece of origami that gave up halfway. Finding the Bistro was a job unto itself, tracing its entrance along narrow walkways past the offices of high-priced lawyers and tiny insurance companies that seemed to have spent more time working on their logos than culling business.

I was immediately taken with Leslie, the manager of the Bistro. She was slightly shorter than me, athletic, with a shock of blonde hair. Leslie always had the ghost of dark circles under her eyes, but a brightness about her that seemed to tilt that darkness in the other direction. She knew interesting things: all the dark machinations of restaurant life, how to lead people, the crazy choreography of an industrial hotel kitchen on a Saturday night. She could also quote all my favorite movies with alarming ease. When she said she thought *The Living Daylights* was the best Bond movie, I fell apart (in a good way). Watching her slip behind the bar, calm and collected, was intoxicating to me. I studied her as she calmly collected patrons' bar tabs with grace, swiping their cards quickly. I'd watch as she worked the POS station while others reported into her. She remained calm through it all.

The dude at Table 9 is totally jacked on coke and hitting on Tabitha.

They don't like the lavash at Table 3.

I think I shorted Table 5 an appetizer.

Her eyes told the story. She was a commander who surveyed things with an impassive look on her face, her lips pursed together. She never gave an inch.

Her job became unwinding other people's problems.

I'd typically take a seat at the bar all the way at the end and parked myself there for hours at a time. It wasn't convenient to get there from my Tempe apartment, but it was worth it to see Matt do his thing as a server, becoming another person who offered people specials and suggested good wines and delivered plates of food with pride.

Turns out, the executive chef was something of a blowhard with just enough money to lose it all in the restaurant world. He was a big, fiery Greek—a hulking mass of a man whose personality was pretty much isolated to the kitchen. He went through chefs and sauciers and kitchen staff so quickly, in fact, that he soon had his own children, nieces, and nephews scrubbing down plates and serving food. I'm not joking. I'm pretty sure those were strict health-code and labor-law violations, but the food still came out good and no one really seemed to give a shit that they were eating expensive meals prepped by sixth-graders.

Leslie and I connected right away, and I knew I was doomed. We discovered something of a shorthand with our knowledge of common 1980s movies: *Real Genius, Flight of the Navigator, InnerSpace*. These were academic choices, mind you. We weren't fucking around with *The Goonies* or *Back to the Future*. No way. Those references were child's play. Our waters ran deeper. Our conversations ran well into night, hours after the place closed. Booze flowed—it was free there—and we kept at it until daylight purpled the sky.

Throughout the night, I'd look down at my phone and see Carrie calling me. I ignored it and kept at it with Leslie.

"And what about *Remo Williams*?"

She'd laugh. "What about it? Isn't that the one where Joel Grey played the little old Asian guy?"

"Yeah, the kung-fu master. He won an Oscar."

She laughed. "For *Remo Williams?*"

I laughed. "No. For *Cabaret.*"

"He's spooky as shit in that movie."

"Yeah. The way he stares."

"And does that half-smile. He knows things."

"Tell me about it," I slammed back my drink.

And so on.

If I have one skill in life, it's being able to zero in on people just like me. I once remember someone pouring themselves another way-too-full glass of red wine and laughing, "I don't even want to think about how much money I spend on this a year."

This.

It was such a half-considered, ambiguous word, but it's always stuck with me. By then, "this" had already gotten me into some trouble, but the worst hadn't even arrived yet. The DUI, the broken engagement, and all the lost jobs were still around the corner. It'd be impossible for me to tally up the total cost of alcoholism in my life—financially and otherwise. I could never tell you how much I've actually spent on alcohol in the hopes of feeling confident, finding acceptance, being taken seriously, getting women to take interest in me, smoothing over problems, and drowning out the noise of reality.

That'd be the emptiest math problem ever.

8

A YEAR INTO Arizona State, I moved into a neighborhood that was sketchy at best: a series of low-rent apartment complexes surrounded by abandoned lots. At one point not long after I'd moved in, a body was found in the backyard of the house next door. A real-deal corpse. The cops lit up that backyard like it was an airplane crash scene: twenty-foot xenon lamps setting everything on white-fire. Earlier in the day, a neighbor downstairs had somehow videotaped the body lying face-down in the dirt, police unrolling yellow tape and taking photographs and measurements. He kept that video on nonstop all afternoon, inviting people over to watch it like a morbid CNN broadcast. I remember thinking that this is simply what happened in big cities: bodies were discovered yards away from where you slept.

I sat on that guy's couch for a good fifteen minutes, drinking a beer and studying the body in the long-zoom of the shaky video. I lost interest after a while.

My Wrangler was routinely tossed. I'd come out in the morning and all my belongings would be emptied across my seats. I imagined all the horrible things I'd do to the person who did that. Once, I got really drunk on a Saturday afternoon and, from our second-story bathroom, watched a dumpster diver in the parking lot. Every time he'd poke his head up like a nervous gopher and consider approaching our cars, I'd set off my Jeep's lock alarm. He'd jump back down into the dumpster. It was insanely fun for me. I even once threw in a whole garbage bag full of used cat litter when he was in there.

The complex had been a fraternity house at one point, its history murky and mythical, and it surrounded a courtyard pool. No one had bothered to paint over the Greek letters at the bottom of the pool, either. I'd moved in with a fellow grad student named Luke, an intense playwright who'd shut his door and hammer out one-act plays until the early morning. I remember hearing the coffee pot brewing at two in the morning, his door opening, him stalking off to load up, and then shutting the door again. Luke resembled a clenched fist, ready to strike. We even drunkenly got into an argument one night and, like writerly roommates, each left apology notes taped to our doors the next morning.

When Luke wasn't angrily writing plays, he was in the gym or terrifying his freshmen by hurling textbooks across the classroom at walls, just to see if they were awake or to make a point. (I called this "Textbook Luke." Nobody ever laughed at this joke, so I'm adding it here, just in case someone finally laughs.) I loved him, but he was one of those first people in the real world who made me think that maybe, just maybe, my drinking wasn't normal.

THE BEST ABSOLUTE worst part about that apartment was just how high the ceilings were. They guaranteed as many gasps from visitors as they did $250-a-month bills from the electric company. The bills were comically high. It's like our apartment was designed to trap Arizona heat. Oh well. The characters who populated the complex made it sort of worthwhile. For a few months, we had a group of unemployable outlaws in their forties living next to us who threw old furniture out the windows and played loud psycho-rap at 4 a.m. I called the cops on them twice and both times, they'd just crank the music back up ten minutes later. Directly below them was a unit rented by a skeleton with transparent teeth named Steve.

Steve only came out at night, skittering around the parking lot and peering into cars and trash cans and empty postal boxes. His skin was translucent, his eyes milky white. He was otherworldly, always in motion. "I'm just trying to help everyone out, man," he'd creak in his weird, sideways voice.

I made a brave trip into his unit once (yes, drunk), and I had a flashback to the time at the Milan Melon Festival where I'd dumbly volunteered to help one of the carnies load something onto a bus. I was pinned in the center of the bus. They could've shut the back door and all the windows, and that would've been that. I'd have been a prisoner of the local-fair circuit in 1987. With Steve, it was the same thing. He didn't have electricity at the time, so there were electrical wires snaking all over the damp floor to the empty next-door apartment whose missing tenant *did* have electricity. Everywhere had the bright ammonia smell of cat piss while utility lamps hung all over the place. In the dark, there were boxes upon boxes leaning every which way. All filled with junk carefully stolen from the neighborhood. What blew me away, however, was that Steve had an amazing cataloging system. He knew where everything was. Lights? He had them in all sizes. Car stereos? Covered. Need a complete collection of hardcover encyclopedias from the Seventies? Done.

Hispanics used to bicycle by our place and ask us if our apartment was where they could get "glass." I had no idea what they were talking about, but I'm sure they'd be able to find it. It always smelled suspicious inside Steve's apartment, and I'd later discover that I'd spent ten minutes touring the insides of an actual, working meth lab. He had a young, dead-eyed wife and an infant daughter he'd kick out into the Phoenix heat for hours at a time while he cooked. Because I'm a pussy, instead of calling Child Protective Services, I wrote their office a letter—a *handwritten letter*—and told them about the wife and little girl. Suddenly, we never saw the wife and little girl again. Someone claimed they'd seen them on a shopping trip at the mall, but that came from a girl who seemed to live on whippits. One day, Matt was jogging by my place and noticed that it was on fire. He called me at work to tell me black smoke clouds were billowing out of my apartment complex. Yep. Steve had finally done it. He'd accidentally blown up his unit. True story.

"What happened?"

"Uh, your apartment is on fire."

"What's it look like?"

"It looks like it's on fire, Paul."

"Has it actually hit my apartment yet?"

"I can't tell. Do you want to get down here or anything?"

I was already projecting to a scene, days later, where I'd be sifting through the smoking, wet slop of charred *Maxims*, bookshelves, and what looked like my old computer. But Captain would be missing. He'd have jumped to whatever existential plane he was from. I was confident he could. He'd escape one way or the other. He wasn't from this world anyway. He was just visiting. That was one goddamn magical cat. Turns out, the fire was limited. Phoenix Fire did their thing: condemned his unit and the one above it.

Not mine.

Steve, though—he still lurked around the apartment complex.

His unit was now a bombed-out shell, complete with police tape, but the owner of the complex didn't do anything about it. He just kept it as-is. We used to find Steve sleeping under our stairs, curled up like Gollum inside a cardboard box. He eventually slithered back into his apartment somehow and we'd hear him tinkering around in there, knocking stuff around like a squirrel loose in a garage. One night, we got ridiculously drunk and thought about all the ways we could scare Steve off for good. So I took an entire length of raw bacon from our fridge and put it on his door handle, complete with a handwritten note *"We're watching you."* Not long after that, the police found Steve dead a half-mile away in a vacant lot.

The two events aren't related, but I still feel like they are.

SOMETIMES I'D WAKE up at eight in the morning, seeing perfect-blue peering through the closed blinds of my room—the blare of cicadas outside my window beckoning me—and I'd just lie there, watching the fabric play with the light. I wondered how I'd gotten there. Captain would be nosing around in his food dish in the kitchen. I'd get up and stretch. And sometimes, just sometimes, I'd forget that I actually had a job to do. I had a class to teach, maybe. Going to classes wasn't hard—I'd very often just show up, not having read any of the assigned work, and just bullshit my way through a quiz about psychic decomposition because, well, if you're in grad school for literature, it's all bullshit anyway. But the days I forgot that I was teaching—that was a real shot of adrenaline. I had to remember what nonsense I'd assigned them. I routinely assigned stuff that I'd never even read. I'd keep putting it off and off and off to the point of absurdity. I'd artfully dodge questions in class when a student would bring up a specific point to discuss. I'd feel pinned against the wall for a second until another student would refute that point.

"Maybe this just means nothing," he'd say, staring at me, my insides going cold.

Then another student: "Well, maybe it means everything."

I told myself I needed to prepare more; I needed to act the role of Teacher; I needed to be responsible and present. Instead, I simply winged it whenever I wasn't regularly sleeping through alarms to go to class or work. Those were suggestions. After all, I was Paul Fuhr. I was above the rules. And sleep, after

I'd call or email in, wasn't exactly blissful, carefree, vacation-like sleep. It was fitful and restless—tortured sleep.

But I never changed.

It was easier to pretend and just get by.

I CAN'T EXPLAIN the black relief that came from not turning work in on time, skipping appointments, or ignoring obligations and responsibilities. I handled regret far better than I handled success. I did the same thing with my master's thesis. While graduate school was an amazing place to avoid the real world, I somehow also managed to avoid working inside the fake one, too. While my colleagues were busy in ASU's Hayden Library, I spent hours at the local brewery, pretending to put important thoughts together down on legal pads. I was even hired to a part-time job wherein I had to teach Microsoft Access courses to fellow grad students. I hadn't done a day of Access database work in my life, but my alcoholic ego told me: *You can do anything. How hard can it possibly be?* Even with a three-month lead time, I decided to start teaching myself two days before I had to teach others.

It did not go well.

I'd studied something that the class, mostly my colleagues, already knew. Probably from reading the back of the software box.

People were starting to zero in on me.

I could feel the noose tightening.

I was not long for Arizona State.

ONE SUMMER, MATT was sleeping on my couch and we both had morning composition classes to teach. For some reason, on one of our off-days he insisted we stay up all night reading *Little Dorrit* by Charles Dickens—a 1,000-page slog about a debtor's prison—and then watch the sun rise over Phoenix. I drank wine all night while he furtively read, taking notes. I illegally downloaded hard-to-find music to distract me from feeling queasy from the thought that I should be sleeping.

When five o'clock rolled around, we drove out to Papago Park, a collection of rosy-red bluffs, and I started to feel like I was outside the bloodstream of reality. I watched the city awaken to the idea of itself, growing in blacks, deep reds, then yellows and greens. The entire valley emerged into view. I saw the glints of all the cars trailing on the 202 and the 101—the chain-link fence of commuter traffic clanking deep into Phoenix. We sat there on a rock, watching it all knife into view—bright, vague, shimmery. It was everything and nothing at the same time. A great green swath of smog haunted the cityscape.

It was now officially Tuesday morning.

I didn't have anything to do that day.

It was meant for studying up on my Wednesday class, which the back of my brain told me was unnecessary. That's the problem with a graduate degree program in literature: it's full of hours that you can't account for. Nor do you have to.

Matt went to the coffee shop to read.

I went to the first bar that opened at 11.

I was starting to feel like a tourist in my own town—daydrinking and enjoying all the things no one else could. Those poor schmucks with actual jobs and salaries. *This is how it's done,* I told myself. I acted every day like I was retired at twenty-two. You get crazy good at something—writing essay after essay after essay—and then the rest just follows. I did the bare minimum with showing up to class, but my 4.0 GPA spoke for itself. I did just enough to get by, which was still bizarrely better than most. This either says how lax the academic standards were at ASU or how hyper-intelligent I am. (I'm not.)

In fact, if you'll allow me, please be my guest here for a few moments. Let me take you on a tour of the sprawling, two-mile radius I called "academia" the day after Matt and I stayed up all night. In many ways, it's a pretty good summary of how I regularly spent my time.

Ready?

Good. Here we go.

MILL AVE. CUE CLUB (11:00—11:45 a.m.): I start here almost alone. Mainly because it's right across the street from the coffee shop where I've left Matt. I can see him through the windows here. Sure enough, he's studying. Look at him over there. He's got two books open. Furiously marking up a notepad. No one notices me standing here. It's because it's still that weird nether-time between 11 and noon when the opening bar staff doesn't really notice you or care. They're probably hungover themselves while they count their registers. They're probably just praying I'm not asking for an application. I'm in a nice, darkly lit pool hall with curtains separating the sections. It's nicer than it should be, but its nicety is betrayed by the bros in cut-off muscle shirts and backward baseball caps who don't have jobs, either. You pay by the hour here, and the service is actually pretty good when they notice you. They insist you put your drinks far away from the pool tables, which, of course, I do not. There are maybe three people in the entire place. At night, there will be a line. Right now, there isn't. I pay twenty dollars for an hour of no one playing against me. I practice angles and drink.

LONG WONG'S (11:45 a.m.—1:30 p.m.): I meet my friend Scott Welsh here, just down the street from the Cue Club. Scott's one of those guys who's successfully figured out how to be in his thirties in a grad program and not come off as sad or creepy. He's lived in Arizona all his life and Long Wong's is one of the few "legit" places he can swallow—especially this early on a Tuesday. This is a broken-down chicken wings spot with a little stage where several bands have gotten their start, including the Gin Blossoms. There are a few people here for lunch, but not many. As usual, I'm here for the drinks. Scott gets hungry, but not for wings. We stay for a few of his picks from the jukebox, and I hit the bathroom twice—a heavy corrugated metal door that belongs on a battleship. It looks like it could take a bullet.

THE CHUCKBOX (1:45 p.m.—2:20 p.m.): This is a thatch-roofed hole-in-the-wall with an open barbecue pit. Smoke billows out the top into the desert blue. The second you walk in, you're being yelled at for your order. It's the best cheeseburger I've ever had in my life, but it's also probably because I've been drinking and awake for over 24 hours at this point. You sit on thick, lacquered tree trunks in this place. My brain has locked into a sense of delirium. The thought of sleep actually terrifies me at this point—it's like I'm standing in a high-rise and my lizard brain does the math on just how unnatural it is to be this high off the ground. If I go to sleep now, I'll feel myself hurtling toward earth, and I can't bear that sort of panic. I down a Corona and Scott suggests we move on. "I need to catch up to you," Scott says, referring to my state of drunkenness. He's just trying to figure out how fast he needs to start running before he catches my train.

FOUR PEAKS BREWING COMPANY (2:30 p.m.—6:00 p.m.): This is where shit really goes sideways. All the daylight drinkers are out to play here. Outside this brewery, there are water-misters lined across the roof to give you a brief reprieve from the blistering heat. We have one too many high APV beers and some scattered nachos, and I can feel myself not even engaging with what Scott's saying. He's laughing at me, but not in a way that makes me feel like I'm good company or funny. I must be repeating a story for the third time. I'm probably telling him some bullshit story that's clearly bullshit. His girlfriend calls. Ever feel like you're crying when you're actually laughing and smiling? That's how I feel right now. I feel like I've opened up, told him something way-too-true, and I'm just seconds from sobbing. The muscles that work my face are exhausted.

BANDERSNATCH (6:15 p.m.—7:30 p.m.): By this point, the day is a smear. This is the low-slung bar with the too-large patio where all the English majors like to hang out. Probably because its name is from Lewis Carroll. I see quite a few people from my program here, but I can't make eye contact with any of them. I'm ashamed. I routinely miss classes with them, and we both know that I'm just an academic tourist—I'm not a person who's serious about studying. I'm not here for the long haul. Matt's here. He's clean, his hair washed and slicked-back, and he looks rested. Fucker probably even got a nap on my couch. He makes grad school look like cultured fun.

CASEY MOORE'S OYSTER HOUSE (7:45 p.m.—10:00 p.m.): By this point, I don't even know how I've arrived at this place— an Irish pub with dark walls and low ceilings. This is where you take your parents when they come visit or when you're feeling especially fancy with your friends. It's an actual house but I don't feel dexterous enough to wander its staircases. I'm annoyed by the server who keeps asking me if I want food. I knock over a pint of beer; I'm drunk enough to not apologize. Scott's left me and I'm all alone now, just like how I started the day. I keep drinking. It tastes empty, no matter how much I put in my body and how much I take out of my bank account.

It occurs to me that I've seen nothing of the actual desert southwest. Not in any real way, at least. I haven't hiked through arroyos or gone canyoneering with gear or watched buzzards as they caught the thermals. I'm surrounded by it every single day and yet, I hide from it at every turn. It's all wasted on me. All the reasons I wanted to move out into the desert, all the things that drew me out from rainy, gray Ohio—all the allure, all the spectacle—it doesn't matter. It's gone. It's all window dressing. In fact, if Arizona was a restaurant, I was caught in the hedges out front. I traveled thousands of miles to discover

I didn't know who I was, and if nothing else, I lost myself even more by the day.

My life is officially the thin tasteless swallow of foam at the bottom of a beer glass.

9

I WAS MASSIVELY HUNGOVER the morning of the 9/11 terrorist attacks.[17] Thoughts came slow; everything seemed underwater. I'd scheduled my Tuesday comp classes off that day, so they could work on their first papers of the semester. I hazily heard the house phone ringing over and over. Muffled, frantic messages from friends and family. I rolled over. Around 7 a.m., Luke eventually came hard-charging into my room and told me what was going on. He was already an intense, Henry

---

[17] It occurred to me very recently that some of you who are reading this book weren't actually alive for the September 11, 2001 attacks, so I have to impress upon you how surreal that morning was.

Rollins-ish kind of dude, so I figured he was embellishing most of the details for effect.

He wasn't.

"WTC hit! Pentagon hit! Missing plane somewhere over Ohio."

He counted them off on his fingers.

Minutes later, he and I watched the first tower fall on a tiny TV set that sat on a cinder block in the corner of our living room. We didn't have cable yet, so it was full of static and we had to ask each other, "Did that just happen?"

We weren't really sure.

I meandered to the kitchen. My heart leapt at the sight of two Strawberry Blonde ales. One of our new neighbors had left them behind the night before. I cracked one open without a thought, swallowing down the weird fruit brew in two gulps. Disaster, I believed, gave me license to drink.

Some time later that morning, Matt rang our doorbell, solemn and dazed, and came inside. He'd cancelled his classes for the day and told his students to get near a TV. We didn't say much to each other. I remember commenting on how FOX News had some sort of cartoonish *"Terror in America!"* subtitle at the bottom of the screen that was inappropriately jagged and cracked like an earthquake fault line. Once the second tower fell, they changed it. I wished I could've changed the channel, but it was the only one that came in.

I remember calling Carrie back home in Ohio, now my fiancée, to make sure she was okay. It was a perfunctory call. Sometimes I forgot I had another life waiting for me several thousand miles away. It's terrible to say, but Carrie was pretty much the only real thing I had in my life—even though she was very often out of sight and out of mind. I felt bad about it for an hour, then it'd evaporate like steam in the Phoenix air. My sister was still in college and she called me to say she and her friends thought they'd seen United 93 (it was just a 747 miles up at the time, no number) overhead. She may have.

Later that day, my office mate Lynn Houston and I decided to go on a random tour of the pubs around Tempe and try to make sense of what was happening. We talked about life and where we'd be in five, ten, fifteen years. We wondered if the rumors were true about terrorists attacking the nearby nuclear power plant. Where would we go? What could we possibly do?

We wondered if, since the FAA grounded all the planes, there were terrorists on the grounded planes who didn't get a chance to hit their targets. We talked about our families. I remember seeing everyone in the U.N. singing "America, the Beautiful." I remember feeling very close and disconnected from everything at the same time. I remember everyone being the heightened versions of themselves that day: extremely generous and nice and overly friendly to strangers, opening doors for people, smiling, infinitely patient.

I skipped classes and emailed my professors that it was because I couldn't handle the stress. It was just too much for me. Truth be told, I just couldn't handle the alcohol running through my veins. I'd been so proud of myself for not drinking for a full week before 9/11. Luke had been keeping something of a quiet watch on me, making sure I wasn't buying beer or wine. I loudly told anyone who'd listen that I wasn't drinking that week, and I wanted them to keep watch. Surely, I wasn't an alcoholic. I couldn't be. By not drinking, I was in control.

As our apartment complex was its own revolving door of

characters—seasons of TV shows with their own casts rolling in and out—I remember one girl, a new arrival named Holly, laughing at me.

"If you need someone to confirm that you haven't bought alcohol for a week, you're an alcoholic," Holly said.

"No way," I frowned.

She just laughed and walked off.

"You'll see," she said.

With 9/11, all bets were off.

WITH NO AIR TRAVEL or classes I cared to attend, I decided to drive. I jumped into my Wrangler, gassed it up on a credit card I wasn't sure would clear, and headed east into the Superstitions. The mountains cut a jawline several thousand feet into the air but without any real shape or outline. They're just there—a forbidding row of peaks with more stories in them than spectacle. Apaches famously believed that the route to hell is tucked away somewhere in there. I shifted the Jeep into fifth, noticing just how unnervingly blue the sky was above me with not one single contrail marking it. Normally, the sky was filled with sketchmarks.

As I drove, I shot past the touristy Old West town, with its saloon and fake gold mine, and drove until the road narrowed into a valley clustered with wildflowers. The farther out you drive, the faster you find yourself in some future movie producer's location setting for Venus. Everything ceases to look like Mars and starts to bleed yellow. Everywhere you look, the landscape gives way to boulders of yellow-lime lichen with iron oxide leeching out.

The asphalt road gave way to dirt, and I hit the first of three man-made lakes that I only peripherally knew were out there. I was too lazy to reach the last two. The first was surrounded by vacationers and people just chilling out. Nothing better to do on a Wednesday afternoon, I guess. There was a low road that led to Tortilla Flat—a forgotten little section of civilization barely hanging on as a tourist attraction: a claptrap strip mall with uneven floorboards and a dead 1960s Coca-Cola machine. A pickup truck filled with Latinos was parked there—four of them splayed out in the bed, getting sun. They had a cooler open at their feet where they were opening Sol after Sol.

I pulled up, fully expecting to get a bottle of water inside the shady convenience store after getting sand-blasted from driving a half-hour with the top down.

"Cerveza?" one of them called out.

I didn't even think twice.

"Sure."

I grabbed one of the icy cold Sols they offered me and twisted the cap off, nodding appreciatively. I couldn't think of a more perfect setting to enjoy a beer: standing in a tourist-trap parking lot with strange people, not knowing Spanish, drinking a Mexican beer. But it tasted good. Plus, no one knew me there. I downed it too quick and felt it go to my head. I even asked for a second one. Someone in the truck bed leaned over and threw another one my way. He didn't hand it over. I could feel the goodwill dying out, but I didn't care.

I still think of those beers, believe it or not—the thinness of the glass, the way the melted ice beaded over my knuckles, the romantic sense of being nowhere alone. I tried thanking them, but it was no use. I'd driven all that way and still managed to find alcohol. I didn't push my luck for a third beer, though it was already crossing my mind in my first swallows of the second.

I'd gotten lost, but I'd found myself. I was definitely, without question, an alcoholic.

SOMEONE KINDA/SORTA/MAYBE suggested that I was an "alcoholic"—or as close to one as they knew. That was a word reserved for people who lived under bridges—not me. I promptly disconnected from them on MySpace and didn't buy beer for another whole week. I was so proud of myself. Then I started hearing it from various corners:

I love Paul, but you can't believe anything he says.

Don't trust Paul.

You know how Paul is with the truth.

My stock wasn't exactly rising in grad school. I was hemming myself into a very narrow bandwidth of friends who could tolerate time with me. I'd get drunk and tell people all the things they didn't want to hear. No one believed a fucking word I was saying. In fact, the most expensive thing I ever bought in Arizona was my own bullshit. I believed everything I told people: I knew famous people; I was on my way to becoming a screenwriter; I'd sold a script, but was between agents. And if that wasn't enough, I was doing ridiculously awkward things like asking someone's dad in a crowded bar, a Vietnam vet, how many people he'd killed in combat. Someone would inevitably sling an arm around me and pull me away to a safer place.

I simply couldn't face being me. I thought alcohol gave me courage and confidence and authenticity.

It did the complete opposite.

I'm not cool; I never have been and never will be. In my active drinking, this fact absolutely haunted me. I tried Way Too Hard in my 20s to muster any shred of coolness. Fox Mulder Cool. But I always came up short. Always. Coolness eluded me like the details of a dream when you first wake up. I burned so many calories trying to say the right thing and dress the right way—all while looking like I didn't care. But being cool never looked good on me in all the same ways I never felt comfortable with it. No amount of J. Crew or Banana Republic could disguise the geekdom that was hardcoded into my DNA. People could smell it on me when I was drinking, too— figuratively and literally. I grew up on a steady diet of Starfleet Academy, AT-ATs, Super Mario Bros, and *Quantum Leap*. For years, I desperately tried to hide that fact. All it did was start the long, sad spiral of me getting lost in my own alcoholism. Not because I immersed myself in TV shows about aliens and government conspiracies, but because that was the last time I'd actually, honestly been me. Fox Mulder never found his sister in all the same ways I would've never found coolness, with even the brightest xenon *X-Files* flashlight on the planet. And I may be gloriously uncool in sobriety, but I'm authentic—and that brings me all the credibility, charisma, and confidence that I'd been searching for in the dark (and drink).

One spring break, Mark from the theater came out to visit. Under ordinary circumstances, I would've scribbled his visit on a calendar. My school schedule had become such a "suggestion" that I stopped paying attention to anything else, including when friends might be paying me a visit. It was Luke who noted that maybe I should be giving movie-theater Mark a ride from the airport.

Shit, I thought. I didn't have the electric-jolt excitement I should have from his visit; instead, it felt like someone from "home" checking in on me. His visit totally occurred during spring finals, no less. I had to be present during class, which really put a wrench in things. I'd probably even be observed by my English program's director, too. I didn't care, though. I honestly didn't. Mark was coming. I went to the grocery and liquor stores and bought more than two people could possibly need. When Mark arrived, he was ready for vacation as much as he was the same old Mark I'd described to all my new friends: lanky, bearded, athletic, red-headed Mark. He'd never been out West before, so it was my job to take him around and show him a good time in Arizona—not showing him the interiors of my classrooms where I should be holding tests about what my students had learned that semester. (I'm not sure I could've passed the same test.) I had Matt cover for me.

"So, what do you want to do first?"

"You tell me," he shrugged.

Mark wasn't much of a world traveler. Getting him outside the microchip of Sandusky was a tall feat.

"How about we hit this sushi place first," I started. "They have a really great happy hour. Killer sake. And then after that, we can walk across the street and meet a few people at Rula Bula, this Irish pub. They carried the pub over, brick by brick, from Ireland, I think. Can you believe that shit? We can have some Irish car bombs there. And then, hmmm, let me think…"

"Why don't you just show me where you live?" he said. "Go for some drives, some hikes. I brought my boots."

"Okay."

I frowned. This wasn't the Mark I remembered. I couldn't recall where I'd put my hiking books, even though they were an expensive pair of Vasques that I bought with a credit card I couldn't afford to use.

Within a day, it was clear that Mark had no idea who he was visiting. I was tapped into something different. I was having too much fun. There wasn't a lot of downtime for the two of us to just sit and talk. After Steve blew up his apartment and the one above it, those psycho-rap fans came by a while later and totally demolished their apartment: they came in with sledgehammers and crowbars and tore everything apart one night. They smashed the sliding glass doors, shattered the porcelain toilets, pissed into the oven. Weeks later, I found myself hanging out with the kids who moved in.

They couldn't have been more different than Mark.

The band members were barely into their twenties, smoking and growing weed in their shiny new apartment. We sat around their living room table. I pretended to be fine with all the joint rolling while Mark was counting seconds before the cops showed up. Their band was actually doing pretty damn well on the local indie station, and I went to almost every one of their shows, largely because I knew there'd be booze there. I hung out with them, designed a website for them, and stayed somewhat in their circle for a while. It made me feel welcome and out of place at the same time. Even then, I was too old to be hanging around with that crew of barely-twentysomethings. At a house party following one of their record releases, I remember thinking the floor to their apartment was certainly going to collapse after all the damage Steve's apartment had experienced. It was kind of how I felt about my drinking: the fires within had done damage, weakened walls, and charred things unseen.

Back to Mark: I could see it in this eyes that this wasn't the Paul he said goodbye to in Ohio. Something had happened to his friend.

The sun was going down outside and, so too, were the chances of our day hike through one of the nearby mountain ranges. We'd have to try again the next day, right after I faked my way through delivering a two-hour competency exam to my students. Later that night at Four Peaks, my favorite brewery, Mark wiped a sheen of sweat from his forehead.

"So, this is it?"

"This is what?"

"This is pretty much what you're doing out here?"

I beamed. "It's great, isn't it?"

He nodded, then took a pensive swallow of his beer. His flight was in a few days, and we never once got in a real-deal hike. It was a tour of air-conditioned pleasures, through and through.

I wouldn't see Mark again for another year.

I TAUGHT CLASSES like an afterthought. Most times, they'd appear on my schedule and I'd think: *Oh, that's right. Today, I have to teach.* I wore shorts and flip-flops to class. I rarely combed my hair. The only thing I took seriously when it came to my students was their writing. There was nothing my students and I would share that would be as intimate, insecure, and profound as the words they wrote me. I gave them lightweight writing prompts "Describe your best day" or "What was your happiest moment?" at first, full well knowing that they were eighteen. Then, I started getting into papers about their fears, their worries, their troubles.

I'd collect all their papers, bind them with a rubber band, and bring them home with a bottle of wine and light some candles. I put on music and marked them up. I used a pen to correct grammar, make suggestions, call out good examples, praise. It was my very favorite thing to do. I felt like this was what I was truly being paid to do: review and evaluate my students' writing. I was taken with their stories—so much so, that by the three-quarters mark of the wine bottle, I'd often be wiping away tears.

It took me a long time to realize that I probably wasn't having that deep of an emotional connection with some freshman's bulimic history. The cheap cabernet was probably responsible for most of that. Many of the papers I returned were splotched with purple.

AT THE TIME, I was also working at an educational policy office called the Internet Education Exchange (iEdx)—a suite of offices and a conference room that occupied the fourth floor of a forgotten Scottsdale industrial complex. Most of the floors were empty. I researched educational options for families living in specific states (school vouchers, grants, magnet schools). I'd been so hungover for the first interview, I'd simply no-called/ no-showed for it and rolled back over. A few weeks later, I got an email asking me if I was still interested in trying. I shrugged, went, and got the job that afternoon. Easiest interview of my life.

I worked part-time in a pretty big office obviously meant for the COO of a much larger corporation that didn't occupy the suite. I put framed photos of Captain and Carrie around my computer. I was a good employee when I wasn't calling off sick or stumbling to the bathroom to vomit up the previous night's adventures. Still, I'd managed to leave a pretty good impression: I did all our website's graphics, edited most of our content, and turned in stories way ahead of time. I might not be reliable, but I put enough work in the gas tank that you didn't really notice I was running low until the light came on.

One Christmas, my boss Christopher—a kind, athletic, quietly bizarre man with hair that curled around his shoulders— invited all of us over to his house. The office staff (all six of us) drove deep into north Scottsdale, where everything is pitched up at an angle or at the base of some mountain range or another. I remember pulling up to his place, a low-slung desert ranch house in the shadow of a mountain. There was a decorative javelina in the front yard with a Santa hat on its tusks. Luminaries lit the way to his doorstep. Christmas carols were sung. Gift cards were handed out for trivia questions. We had a white elephant gift exchange. I loved every second of it— but most of all, I loved his house. I loved the built-in cabinetry, the granite countertops, the immense library of things he'd read and planned to read. The vintage, first-edition Ian Fleming hardcovers. I remember thinking that it was exactly what I wanted when I grew up: the adobe floors, the archways, the open kitchen with turquoise etchings. He poured me a generous glass of single-malt scotch and put an arm around me, leading me up a winding stone staircase outside to the roof.

It was a perfect evening, maybe sixty degrees. The entire valley yawned around us. We said very little, but we both leaned against the stucco and studied the lights. For a second, I thought he might talk about my attendance problem. After all, I'd called off more days than humanly possible. But, no. He was a curiosity himself—hammering out epic-length emails at four in the morning and disappearing for days on end before returning to the office as if nothing was different.

Still, I liked him. I sipped the scotch and savored the surroundings.

"You can come here whenever you want, you know," he said. "All of you. You're like family."

It was sticky-sweet, but in the way that most buzzed people speak to one another before the pendulum swings in the other direction. Still, I believed him.

"I know how hard it is living by yourself. Being away from home like you are," he nodded in the dark. He was something of a surfer back in the day, a lover of Dead music who'd somehow gotten wrapped up in Arizona politics. I pictured him living in a VW van, going where the waves were, up and down the PCH. "You come here whenever you want."

"Thanks," I nodded back, meaning it.

I felt at home up on that roof, watching the valley lights shift and melt and bend. I could see all the red and green decorations shivering in the temp differences.

Suddenly, I felt it.

I was going to tell him everything.

I drew in a breath to admit that I had a problem I didn't have a solution for.

Right then and there, I was prepared to tell him about my drinking problem. I was just going to let it all leak out. About how I couldn't get anything done without drinking being in the foreground. About how I missed my parents so much it physically hurt my head sometimes. About how I was getting married because it was the one sure-footed, stable thing I could think to do. About how alcohol curled around every thought and impulse and desire.

It just didn't seem right burdening him with it, though, since I was holding a heavy tumbler of expensive scotch. Still, it seemed like he was teasing it out of me, waiting.

"I look forward to the new year," he said, finally.

"I do, too."

Unfortunately, not long after that, the Phoenix police department would, shockingly, find him dead—the victim of a gunshot wound to the head, in a bad neighborhood somewhere on the west side.

Drugs.

We all have demons, apparently—some hidden better than others.

I TOLD MYSELF that my Master's thesis was going to be mind-bending. All these other people in my program—well, they were just arguing over who could pull the most esoteric quotes from the air or weave together the most fanciful phrasing of literary terminology. Me? I was better than that, I told myself. I was going to write a *book*. This is also, by the way, the same exact, sad, *fuck-you* wall that goes up every single time I feel threatened and/or out of my element. I don't care about anything or anyone. My way is better. I'll outsmart you. Everyone else is just playing catch-up. So I decided, very early on, to write a book. I could do that. I hadn't decided what my thesis was going to be, but it was going to be more impressive to turn in a volume of thick pages. (In the end: my page count was just *one* page over the minimum required of 59 pages.)

But weeks went by, and not one page got written. No planning whatsoever went into my thesis. Like most things, I talked about it a lot with colleagues, but mostly I pretended it was coming together. Matt would take weekends where he'd vanish off to Flagstaff or sequester himself in his apartment and hammer out plans for his postmodernist deconstructions of Irish colonial novels. I was above that, I told myself. Matt needed the extra time. I could hammer something out quickly or the magic would just come to me in time. It'd be a lightning bolt. Hundreds of pages would just erupt out of me. And then as the semesters wore on, I quietly resigned myself to the fact that my thesis was going to be something I threw together over a couple of weekends instead of a couple of years. Never mind that this goddamn thing was to be bound and kept in a university library for posterity.

Instead of doubling down on studying, I fell into a darker routine of hanging out with Leslie, attracting a new debris cloud of acquaintances that orbited me and drinking night after night after night. And when you grow further away from something, you usually grow resentful of it. The English department wasn't my home anymore, not that it ever was. I grew resentful of my colleagues to the point where I actually hated them. I started having conferences with my students in taco bars in the afternoon instead of my office. (That didn't last long before the department chair formally frowned on that and insisted I hold meetings where beer and salsa weren't condiments.) I found everything they did to be pointless and stupid and futile. I quietly mocked them. I made lists of all the words and phrases that I knew couldn't be traded in the real world as currency.[18]

I went to grad school simply because I liked writing. End of story. But I didn't enjoy taking literature apart like my cousin Brian and his son Eric lovingly dismantled a vehicle in their garage before putting it back together again. That's not why I signed up for it. I didn't enjoy working in one of the shittiest, most underfunded buildings on campus. I just wanted to be around writing. Same goes for my alcoholism. I just enjoyed drinking. I didn't understand the distance I'd crossed with both—ignoring all the mileposts along the way, telling me that I was hurtling in the wrong direction.

SO, LET ME TELL YOU what happens when you spend three years *not* writing your thesis—and then you have to defend your thesis in order to graduate and collect a diploma. This

---

[18] By the way, here's a list of literary terms that probably aren't going to get you far in the real world: *acatalectic; acrostic; anastrophe; animism; astrophic; Bildungsroman; bibliomancy; caesura; calligram; catachresis; chiasmus; choriamb; circumlocution; dibrach; duodecimo; elision; ekphrastic; fourteener; Freytag's pyramid; gnomic verse; hypotactic; marginalia; pathetic fallacy; periphrasis; spoonerism; synthesezia; verisimilitude.* Drop one of these words in a casual conversation and tell me what happens.

is what it feels like when you haven't practiced or prepared or really even expected to get there: You walk into a tiny, low-lit room, you see serious people staring at you, and you realize you're probably going to pass right the fuck out. It's stage fright, cubed. First, you get light-headed. Then your fingers tingle. Sweat beads on your skin. When it *really* dawns on you, when the gravity really pulls down on you, there's a little tug on your belly that tells you that you're going to vomit. Your future hinges on this moment. The past three years of Four Peaks and Nita's Hideaway and too-nice-for-me Scottsdale clubs like Axis/ Radius were no substitute for this moment. I recall the room but not the people—I'd collected three defense chairpersons that I barely knew. I hadn't worked with them like I'd promised to, so they may as well have been stone-faced strangers.

This was my *thesis defense committee,* for Chrissakes, not another class I hadn't prepared for that I could wing my way through. My uncle Steve would be so disappointed in me. I sat there, suddenly envisioning his own black hardbound thesis back on my grandparents' shelf. It used to call to me, Uncle Steve's Ph.D. dissertation. It directed me from that shelf, telling me to follow in his footsteps as an academic. I used to thumb through the pages, not understanding any of its strings of heiroglyphic math. I'd be feeling its weight—not necessarily its heft, but its sheer intellect.

What the hell was I thinking?

I had no time to panic, though.

I had to dig deep.

In front of each of the thesis board members was a copy of my thesis—a shamefully slight tome that topped out at sixty pages in 12-point font. Maybe. Each one was fastened together with a series of twisted copper brads. Without boring you, here's what I eventually cobbled together as a topic: The way that Victorian authors like Charles Dickens wrote about dreams is the exact same way that, later, postmodern authors were now writing about cyberspace. They used all the same adjectives and descriptions. And therefore, in my argument, cyberspace is a psychological space—a complex, psychosexually dynamic sphere with the same light, airy, ethereal weight of dreams.[19]

Still with me?

So, there was my tiny little thesis, neatly printed in front of three individuals: a bearded, perpetually depressed English prof whose wife had left him at the same time his interest in ironing his clothes had left him, too; a thin Texan with a tight John Waters mustache and bolo tie whose sole pleasure was smoking cigarettes in his office and blowing the smoke out his tilted window; and a recently-divorced postmodernist who I was somewhat enchanted with—mainly because she pronounced "Chthulu" correctly.

And Matt. God bless Matt. He came, too.

There were five of us in there, and I was fighting to stay conscious as the blood drained from my face. I had nothing but a notepad. I didn't even think to bring a copy of my thesis, let alone a bottle of water.

"So, how does this start?"

"Why don't you explain the little germ of an idea you brought to my office years ago," the ruffled prof began, flipping my thesis in the air, "and what you think you've accomplished with it since? That sound okay for everyone?"

Nods.

---

[19] I just used Google to find my thesis title, by the way: "Simulated Dreams, Virtual Truths: The Narrative Equivalence of Dreamspace and Gibsonian Cyberspace." Good Lord.

The defense was scheduled for noon, which was deliberate. I was terrified of being too hungover for it. Still, I'd drank at least two beers at the shitty Mexican bar across the street. For nerves. It'd only just dawned on me that maybe they could smell it. Fuck it.

I went for it.

"This is about Gibsonian cyberspace…"

"Tell us about Gibsonian cyberspace. What does that even mean?" my bolo-tied chair said. "I know we discussed you clarifying this concept a few months ago, but I'm not seeing that work in these pages. At least not in this draft."

"Agreed. What makes William Gibson the gold standard for constructing what you call 'cyberspace' beyond him being lucky and coining it in his most mainstream, accessible work?"

I could always count on Prof #2 for rumpled clothes and piling onto an already-asked question.

"Right," the female prof leaned in. "What makes his view of cyberspace the actual baseline through which *all* literature analyses and critiques should be measured? What hallmarks are there?"

I threw half-answers everywhere I could. As quickly as they emerged, they were out of my dry mouth. And before I subject you to a whole transcript of my thesis defense, let me give you some of my committee's greatest hits:

○ *"And Part 2 really seems to be an extension of Part 3, except Part 3 just sort of trails off. We don't come back around to an actual point. You ask all these questions and then… nothing. Is that the point?"*

○ *"If the last half of your thesis is designed to act as a dream—in other words, if it's meant to lull the reader to sleep, it's a brilliant piece of writing, Paul. It really is."*

○ *"I'm not convinced you actually read two of the books you heavily rely on in your thesis here. And even if you did, they don't strike me as the two strongest books you could've used."*

○ *"You keep pronouncing 'illusory' wrong. I'd probably learn the proper way to do that."*

○ *"Choosing Dickens as an example of Victorian writing is something I know that we talked about over and over again, Paul. He's not going to get you published. Dickens is done. Over. No one writes about Dickens anymore... I sincerely hope he's just a placeholder. I really, honestly, didn't think you'd show up here with a straight face trying to apply a complex psychological framework, complete with Jacques Lacan, to* A Christmas Carol. *But here we are."*

○ *"You have a billion ideas in here—genuinely good ones— but none of them work together. I'd say you're almost too smart for your own good, but I actually think you've just spent very little time fleshing any of this out."*

For ninety minutes, it was awkward and it was terrible and it was queasy, but it qualified as a thesis defense. I fought their questions. I made shit up when I got backed into a corner. I had moments of brilliance. I recalled specific pages in my thesis. I quoted philosophers and thinkers who certainly didn't have a two-beer buzz going on. I countered them with second and third questions. I pushed back. I challenged their questions about why I didn't elaborate with my writing. I argued that, no, my thesis didn't need an extra six chapters. I occasionally stared blankly. I almost threw up. I wiped a tear away, unnoticed.

I came out of it with *Pass—No Changes*.

When I told Matt the grade, he froze.

"You didn't get a Fail?"

"No."

"You don't have to re-present?"

"No."

"You're too smart for your own good," Matt muttered in disbelief as we walked down the hall, echoing my thesis chair. "That's not a compliment. But, congratulations."

It's still not a compliment.

I want that time back. I want to do the thesis right—I don't want to get by because I had the right alchemy of booze and adrenaline in my system to get me through. I want to make my time spent in the program mean something. I didn't want to face a roomful of academic strangers, and go through the painful exercise of bringing the equivalent of wet tissue paper to their scrutiny. More than anything, I didn't want to work with words anymore.

Especially other people's.

WHEN MY NEIGHBORS bought a shuttle bus for their band Ember Coast, Carrie and I broke off our engagement. Simple as that. You could diagram it out—you could throw up the wireframe-workflow of our relationship on a chalkboard and have it annotated and arrowed: *I'm a not-grown-up-masquerading-as-an-adult* and *she's-an-adult-who-constantly-gets-her-shit-together* but the break really occurred when the band next door brought home an honest-to-God tour van.

Carrie had been patiently waiting for me to finish graduate school. She'd moved out to Arizona for me. She woke up on time, had a steady paycheck, a nice apartment, good friends and family members she went to church with. She was a study in how to live life, whereas I was steadily approaching thirty and finding new and inventive ways to avoid doing anything real or measurable with my life.

But when that old hotel shuttle bus came around my apartment complex, you could just see the color drain from her face.

"What's that down there?" she peered between the two fingers prying open the Venetian blinds.

"You're going to have to do a better job than that," I said, adding a sentence or two to an overdue paper.

"It's a bus, looks like. Gray. Kind of beat up."

My insides lit up like a pinball machine.

"Oh my God," I laughed aloud. "They fucking did it."

"Did what?"

I saved whatever I was writing—probably something unremarkable about Kate Chopin's *The Awakening*—and leapt from my seat. This was me at any given moment in grad school: actual work didn't weigh me down. I dropped it at a moment's notice. I'd gotten very good at tempering the guilt that trailed afterward. My parents had done such a good job instilling a work ethic in me that it took years and years and years of work to uninstall it all, plugging it up with booze and prescription pills and good old-fashioned denial.

"Wait," I could see it dawning on Carrie's face. "You know these people?"

"Know these people? That's Ember Coast down there!"

To her, Ember Coast was one of the million hobbies I did on the side. At their best, they were the young neighbors who'd moved into the newly furnished apartment next door, crawling around the entire complex shirtless, blaring 311 and Incubus, and generally coaxing everyone to have a better time than they were having. At their worst, she felt, they had an almost narcotic hold on me. I dropped everything when those guys showed up.

I ran downstairs, not even bothering to put shoes on. I urged Carrie to do the same.

The doors to the bus pneumatically rushed open. Ethan, the drummer, was wearing a black captain's cap and smiled broadly.

"Ahoy!"

"Holy shit!" I grinned. "You did it."

"You bet your ass we did," Nick was already seated in the bus, smiling broadly from behind oversized sunglasses with messy black scraggles of hair in his face. Nick and I were the closest of the five band members—I could tell that he was already absorbing this as one of his favorite moments in life.

Carrie took a tentative step toward.

"Don't be so shy," Ethan leaned forward with a wide grin.

"This is where the magic happens," Nick added. "Just keep walking. Find a spot."

The bus was completely empty, save for an epic cloudline of pot smoke. Carrie then took a deliberate step back.

"What's up?" I asked in my best don't-make-me-look-like-an-idiot face.

"I'll see you back at home," is all she said to me, smirking.

"No," Sean, the lead singer, ignored her. The doors closed. She was trapped. The spindly lead singer was a bundle of nerves—just like he was on stage. He shut the doors and didn't think twice. Carrie ambled over to me.

"Isn't this the best? Isn't this fantastic?" I asked.

"So this is going to carry you—"

"Across the country, yeah. State to state. I mean, it's got everything."

That, technically, wasn't true.

It was a Holiday Inn airport shuttle bus with wide, curved windows and luggage space. Beyond that, it was a shuttle bus. Not much in the way of décor. As Ethan punched it into reverse, I turned and noticed he was barreling toward a corner of parked cars in my shitty neighborhood.

"Hey, Ethan, we're gonna…"

"Zip it!" Ethan shouted. "I've got five mirrors up here. I don't need a sixth. Got it?"

The buzz was wearing off, and so was my enthusiasm.

"So, where's your first show going to be?"

"On the road?" Nick, the quiet guitarist, considered the question. "Man, I don't know. We have to really get, you know, an actual tour together first."

"Dates, you mean."

"Yeah, concert dates. Gotta get some of them lined up."

"You feeling the energy back there, Carrie?" Ethan smiled broadly, full well knowing she wasn't. "Can't you just feel all the magic? The magic pockets?"

"Yeah, am I blocking your view of anything?"

"No. Is there anyone else we should consider asking to bring along on our maiden voyage of Tempe?"

I laughed immediately, saying yes. I called Matt and told him I'd be there in three minutes.

When Matt staggered out of his apartment, taking baby steps down his staircase with Charlie his dog, it was almost hilarious. He didn't know what he was looking at it. It certainly wasn't a cab; it certainly wasn't leading him to an adventure somewhere. It was just meant to observe and board if you wanted to.

"I was just about to walk Charlie," he said. "It's Sunday night."

"Bring him aboard!" someone shouted.

"But it's bath night for him."

"Rub-a-dub!" Nick shouted.

"I have no idea what I'm doing inside this thing," Matt said, finally, taking a seat across from me. "Is this their tour bus?"

"It's not just *any* tour bus, brother," Nick told him. "This is where the magic is going to happen. Tell him, Nate."

"You know what," Ethan laughed, "I may have to use Paul as rearview mirror, after all. This is the goddamn *cul de sac* from hell."

Once I helped the bus maneuver a seven-point turn out of Matt's neighborhood, Nate and Ethan started describing all their plans for the bus: ripping out the floorboards and installing bunk beds, a flat-panel TV, working sanitation, storage for all their gears underneath, and jam space. I was starting to see it fold all around me in all the ways Carrie never would. Her eyes had gone black.

The minute we disembarked, having been driving around the Tempe Town Lake in an old hotel courtesy shuttle, Matt had had enough. He said his farewells and gave me a confused glance before taking Charlie for a proper walk. Carrie was ready to do the same. When the bus dropped us off, she spun around.

"Is this what you want to be doing with your life?"

"What do you mean?"

"Being part of bands in their twenties who are spending their parents' money to do things before they'll get real jobs?"

I paused. It hurt. "But they're my friends."

I moved to the fridge and reflexively grabbed a Fat Tire.

"They're your friends because they moved in next to you and they're in a band and you want them to really, really like you," she said.

"That's not true."

Carrie has a way of proving she's right without even saying a word.

"Let me guess: you just drove around Tempe on a bus. Has that novelty worn off yet; are you focused again? You have a Master's degree to finish and then what? Have you given any fucking thought to what's next? For us? For a family, maybe?"

Family. The word was like scalding poison. It seared my insides; it shorted out all the electrical cords playing the music that got me through my days. Family was something I kept pushing off in the hope that something magnificent would take its place before any of that nonsense would ever happen.

It was clear from the look on her face that this was a real conversation—one that I couldn't handle while finishing a page on Kate Chopin's *Awakening* or her watching *Grey's Anatomy*.

I slugged back the Fat Tire and slumped into a couch, resigning myself for another few hours of Carrie telling me that I was simply having too much fun and she couldn't do anything about it—even when she was probably completely right.

SHORTLY AFTER WE broke off the engagement—a moment that felt less harrowing and drawn-out than quick and inevitable. Carrie made short order of getting her life together: she called her sister to fly out, planning for the two of them to drive her belongings back to Ohio. A new job was as easy to find for her as it was easy to leave the other. Another job was already waiting for her back in Columbus. Fucking nursing, man. It was like that *Fantastic Beasts* movie where a city block would explode, then a flick of a wand would repair everything just as quickly: boulders arranging themselves into order, rebar snaking into place, glass healing. That's Carrie's life up until that point. We weren't married, so I couldn't do any permanent damage—yet.

This was the best possible thing.

On her moving day, she drove off with her sister and I agreed to "guard" her stuff in her apartment as the moving company grabbed it all. The problem was that I sat amongst all her belongings for ten hours. Yes, ten hours. Not hyperbole. Somewhere across town, the truck broke down or got lost or the driver got high. I don't know. But I sat in Carrie's disassembled apartment for that whole time, terrified to leave it. I had a novel Matt loaned me and a half-dead cell phone. That was it. I paced her rooms, picking at some of the boxes she'd taped up. I peered inside, seeing her memories and, in some cases, hope. Her hopes. I saw things she didn't really want as gifts but kept anyway—cooking gadgets and other things I couldn't afford but bought her. I wandered through it all, like a tomb for another life, and I made fists and seized up. I had no clue who I was. I was angry and ashamed and broken and terrified.

She was my training wheels in life.

When I awoke, it was 7:30 at night and the moving crew showed up. I couldn't wait to hand off everything.

"You don't have to stay, man," one of them gruffly said. "We're good."

I offered to help them. Their contract forbade it.

As they drove off, the giant moving vehicle navigating the tiny angles of the parking complex, I can't explain the explosion of sadness that went off inside me, like when the Genesis Device finally activated in *Star Trek II*. There was no escape. It laid waste to everything. I erupted into tears—deep ones, those ones that shudder out of you. I watched that truck as it receded into a small rectangle, then a square, then a small block of grey, then nothing.

The next morning, I awoke to harsh orange rectangles of sunlight over my coffee table. It was littered with beer cans and a half-eaten pizza. A quarter-full bottle of Sambuca that one of the Ember Coast boys had left. I wasn't in the mood for anyone or anything. I looked at my phone—no missed calls. Full Sunday ahead of me. I wouldn't call and tell my parents that bit of news yet. The day could lead in a thousand directions, but I was pretty sure it'd simply tilt toward drunkenness.

I started it by chugging the Sambuca in the half-dark of the living room, which is a lot like trying to pay your utility bill with Monopoly money. I gagged on it, pissed off that I could've just waited for somewhere to open at ten to get something proper. Because today, I decided: I was entitled to drink.

Look out, world.

Today was different, though. I'd been putting off something—no, someone—for too long now. Our apartment complex was a rogue's gallery not just of amateur meth-makers, musicians, and students like me trying to get by: it also played host to a number of quiet characters who were likely squatting in some of the apartment units around the building. One of them was a tall, beefy black man named Stan Woodrow whose face was always pinched with sadness. Woodrow rarely said hi, nor did he ask how *you* were doing. He asked how your *car* was doing. It made you wonder if Woodrow and your car would be gone the next time you came back down.

I remember parking my Wrangler in the shade one morning, and Woodrow was already *up-and-at-'em,* rooting through the trash cans lining the property. He had a bag and was gingerly putting aluminum items in it. Fresh puke matted one side of the receptacle he was picking through. It didn't seem to bother him one bit.

"Mornin', Sir Paul!" he stood upright in a Tears for Fears shirt.

There was no way in hell he was ever a Tears for Fears fan, but seeing him in a hot neon-pink shirt was amazing.

"How's the old Jeep treating you?"

"She's good, Woodrow."

"She looks like she could use a wash."

"How much you looking to charge?"

Woodrow winced, holding his half-bag of aluminum cans. He poked a tongue through missing teeth, giving me the impression he was both smiling and thinking real hard.

"Ten dollars. I'll clean her better than you've ever had her cleaned."

"Yeah?"

"Yeah."

"Well, fuck, Woodrow," I shook his hand. "You've got

yourself a deal."

The knock was expected.

I just stared at the Sambuca and sighed. I stood, drained what was left, and opened the door. The heat-blast furnace of a morning greeted me, as did Stan Woodrow, dressed in a yellow T-shirt three sizes too large for him.

"Mind if I come in?" he jerked past me.

I hated that about him. I hated how Woodrow looked around my apartment like he was taking a quick mental inventory of everything that was worthwhile in there: vintage telescope; vast collections of albums; CDs; barware; furniture. Surely, some of the stuff I held valuable could have been sold for drugs. Luke would have hated that I invited Woodrow inside, but Luke was living it up as a poet in Prague or something for the summer. I couldn't afford to do anything other than have Stan Woodrow wash my Jeep.

"Hot morning," he slumped into my couch.

"Yeah," I hated being rude to people almost as much as I hated talking about the weather. "It really is."

"Not even eleven yet."

"Well, maybe you ought to get cracking."

"Maybe I should."

We made small talk. He flipped through a James Bond coffee-table book of mine, wondering aloud if they still made the movies. I nodded. He loved taking his son to them before he suddenly died, he said. The movies always came out at Christmas, Woodrow told me. He told me it would've been *Diamonds Are Forever* that they would have seen together, but his son died earlier in 1971. They'd been looking forward to seeing Sean Connery in the role again. He turned the book around and around in his hands, lost in thought.

"Have you seen it?" I asked.

That snapped him out of it.

"What?"

"Did you go see it? That movie?"

"Naw, man," he chuckled. "Haven't seen no Bond movie in forever. Looks like a lot of good ones since."

It went on like this for another ten minutes, where I felt torn between having nothing to do and having nothing to do with Stan Woodrow in my apartment on a Sunday morning.

"Tell you what, Woodrow. Why don't you help yourself to some of the beer in my fridge? I'm going to go grab us some barbecue. Does that sound good?"

He broke into a wide smile.

"Nothing could hit the spot harder. You going to Honey Bear's over there?"

"Yep."

"Aw, yeah, man. Get me two of the brisket sandwiches. Ask for a sack of burnt ends, too."

"A sack of what?"

"Burnt ends," he said. "They sell them to me for about a quarter."

I fished a plastic bucket out from underneath the kitchen sink, along with some dish soap. I planted it right in front of Woodrow.

"I'll walk down and get the BBQ. Why don't you get started?"

"Sounds like a plan, Sir Paul. Just one question."

"Sure."

His eyes narrowed in on a Ziploc bag I kept on a bookshelf:

a crumbled green-grey mess inside.

"Is that weed?"

I laughed. I wouldn't know what do with actual weed if I did have it.

"No, man. That's catnip."

"You sure?" he gave me a sideways glance.

"Positive. It's for Captain."

"Who's the captain?"

"My cat."

"Shit, man. Give that bag here."

I forked the bag over, and he promptly put his snout inside it. Without removing his nose, his eyes drew up to meet mine.

"That's straight-up catnip, nigga. Straight. *Up.*"

"I wasn't lying, Woodrow," I could feel the Sambuca and Carrie's departure and the desperate need to just sleep through the afternoon gripping me. "Now are we doing this?"

"Yeah, yeah, yeah."

"Good. Beer's in the fridge. I'll be back in twenty."

IT WASN'T EVEN NOON and I was convinced Woodrow was dead. The man was lying lengthwise on the asphalt aside my Jeep Wrangler, unnatural. The heat was radiating off the ground at a galactic temperature, but there was Stan Woodrow—pink shirt, flip-flops, white curls of hair—twisted underneath my vehicle. A long rubber hose snaked out from the pool area and filled the bucket, which overflowed with bubbles. At least he'd gotten that part right.

"Woodrow!" I called. "You alive?"

He let out a deep laugh. "I know this looks ridiculous, Sir Paul, but it ain't. I always wash the undercarriage first. Elbow grease."

"This is going to take all day."

Woodrow assembled himself, straightening out his shirt, and downed three-quarters of a Natural Light.

"Where'd you find a Natural Light in my fridge?"

"I didn't," he said, the cold burning his voice. "But I *did* find a ten-dollar bill by the telephone, so I walked down to the corner market. I can't wash your car with that high-octane shit you got up in your fridge. Jesus. Fancy beer."

"Woodrow, do you even have a sponge?"

He looked around, confused. Things were getting worse.

"Let's get you back inside."

Sweat was beading unnaturally around his forehead, and he was blinking in ways that made me think he might pass out. He couldn't focus. As furious as I was, I suggested we go back up to my apartment. The BBQ interested him, which was a good sign. Maybe I could get some food in him. Change his equilibrium. He carefully put his sandwiches and burnt ends out on the table.

After a few bites of the brisket, he sighed and leaned back with a frown on my couch.

"So I got a lead on some clothes."

"A lead? On some clothes?"

"Yeah, brother," he said, pulling out a crinkled piece of paper. "At the bus stop. This guy gave me his address. Has some clothes."

I couldn't believe what I was hearing.

He tried downing his beer and then crinkled the can.

"Mind getting me another one?"

I obeyed and returned with one of my "fancy" Fat Tires, not quite sure where he'd hidden his Natural Lights. In fact, I was starting to get concerned that he'd drunk them all. The morning crept into 100 degrees in no time flat, and by noon, it was unbearable and I had a delirious drunk man on my couch. I gave up on having my Jeep washed and decided to get drunk right along with him. He marveled at iTunes and kept testing it to see if it really had everything. We laughed. We drank.

Then he decided to follow his lead on the clothes.

SOMEWHERE JUST WEST of downtown was a bombed-out section of Phoenix. It all resembled the roof of a beach-house hut, frayed and coming apart. Everything was blasted white in the furnace heat, with all the colors dialed down a level or two. We crawled through one washed-out neighborhood after the next, looking for an address that seemed as elusive as the heat ripples on the horizon. Cinder blocks and coils of barbed wire.

Finally, Woodrow's eyes went wide.

"There."

"Where?" I pumped the brakes.

"Right there, brother," he smiled. "Oh, man. Here we go."

I'd barely stopped the Jeep when he jumped out. He missed a step and staggered a little. Then, he turned and gave me the sort of confident thumbs-up an action-movie supporting character gives before he's immediately gunned down.

"I'll be right back."

I pulled off to the curb, looking around as Woodrow

knocked on the front door of a depressed green bungalow. One of the front windows was missing and replaced with what looked like a parachute, while the screen door practically hung off its hinges. Spanish tiles were flecked around the lot. As he snooped around the house, opening the fence to the backyard, I could feel the beer and heat really vice-gripping my brain.

I'd no sooner flipped my visor down, going through the CDs strapped there, when I saw a pink blur in the corner of my eye.

Woodrow.

He was hard-charging the Jeep, having thrown the house's back fence wide open. Two Dobermans were chasing him.

"Go!" he was screaming. "Go!"

I didn't think twice. I shifted into first and he vaulted onto the Jeep, holding on for life. Gears ground against one another as I struggled to figure out what was going on.

"What the fuck was that about?"

"Don't know," he shook his head.

We drove in silence for a few minutes, coming to an intersection.

"What a goddamn morning," he sighed finally, reached into his pocket, and pulled out a half-eaten brisket sandwich.

THERE WAS A moment near the end of the semester when the entire apartment complex had come alive. Every single patio facing the pool was crammed with dozens of college kids, smoking and drinking and staring up at a desert sky full of stars. The palm fronds around the complex rustled under the

competing music blasting from every cell of that building. I
don't remember the occasion, but everything had locked into
place: perfect weather, sex, booze, whatever. About a dozen of
us were on standing our porch, and even Luke seemed to be
in a good mood, tossing back little glasses of wine with all the
theater majors.

Sean spidered out from the patio of his second-floor
apartment to the ledge. (This was a regular thing.) He landed,
shirtless, with precision and grace onto the precipice of our
patio. He nodded to me, I remember, like Jason Bourne had
just casually knocked everyone out at a Russian consulate.
Everyone went nuts, chanting his name.

"Sean! Sean! Sean!"

Hundreds of voices in the late-spring heat, calling out
for him to jump. Sean turned to us, winked, and leapt. For
a second, I captured him in my brain—his slight frame held
against the starry night and palm trees—as he arced toward the
pool. Seconds later, he was coming up for air. The entire place
erupted in jubilation. You could feel it tremble.

I decided I wanted some of that energy.

I've always been a follower like that, chasing down
secondhand adrenaline.

I jumped to the same precipice, looking down at the pool
for a lot longer than Sean had. I could see the concrete all
around the pool, half-lit from all the shattered lamps in our
parking lot. The pool wasn't entirely illuminated, but I could
see the fists pumping in my direction, the rise of my name
in an encouraging chorus—sirens singing me to shipwreck. I
stared down at Sean, who was beckoning me in. I reached up
and held the stucco frame to steady myself as I stood there,

knees wobbling a little bit. Matt was shaking his head; Luke was wide-eyed. A girl I didn't particularly like came over and swatted me on the ass, causing my right knee to buckle.

"Get going!"

When a hundred people are shouting for you to jump, especially when you're the second one to do it, you should probably jump. But a lot of my sobriety can be found in that single moment right there. When I left Phoenix just a few weeks later, that memory lingered: the thought of me perched on that precipice. No one would remember I'd done it—everyone had been too drunk—and in the end, no one would've remembered if I had gone ahead and jumped in. That's what my life in grad school had all been about. It hadn't mattered that I was there. I spent three years accumulating accidental enemies, debt, alcoholism, loneliness, and had taken more than I'd been given—and I'm not sure anyone was going to remember. I was halfway away from Flagstaff, driving back home to Ohio, when the image of me on that edge emerged.

I didn't jump. But in some ways, I'm still standing there: hunched over, ready, wanting acceptance.

10

MY U-HAUL LUMBERED down the country road, just miles outside my hometown. An early-summer storm brewed over the fields. I almost got sick from the sight of it all. In the span of 1.5 days, I'd graduated Arizona State, quit my job via an email to Christopher, and moved all my shit into a moving truck. Aside from Matt, I didn't tell anyone I was leaving. I was afraid of what I'd become—and I couldn't even pick up the phone to tell anyone that my drinking was turning me into someone I didn't recognize. I wasn't ready for honesty. I wasn't ready for telling people I needed help. I just knew I had to go home.

My parents, of course, were thrilled. Even Carrie swung back into cautious orbit. I was done pretending; I was done playing around. Maybe I'd grown up. Maybe I was ready to settle down. I told myself all these things, and I almost believed them. I'd managed to boomerang right back to where I was trying to escape for twenty-some years: Ohio farmland. All because I couldn't escape the dangerous nobody I'd become. I moved 3,000 miles west to get a degree in something I didn't really believe in, make friends only to alienate them, and completely lose myself while doing it.

BY THE WAY—before I forget—I had one final mission in Arizona. Some people, I'm sure, would do something sentimental before moving back across the country. Visit a favorite restaurant; hug a beloved tree on campus; get a photo with a monument. No. Before I left Arizona for good, I knew I had one last thing to do. After I'd hurriedly boxed up everything and hastily loaded up the U-Haul, I ran over to Woodrow's apartment and left my VHS copy of *Diamonds Are Forever* on his doorstep.

I even made sure it was rewound, too, so it'd just be waiting for him to play.

IT WAS SUPPOSED to be a simple "welcome back" party at Mark's house: my red-headed, movie-making friend from the theater. A few friends, some drinks, another Saturday night in Ohio. Nothing major. It was the start of summer, and I'd only been back a few days. Everything was full of promise on the lake. I'd even secured my old job as a projectionist at Cinema World Plaza 8 again. It seemed fitting, like the logical end to what happens to most people who got Master's degrees in literature: you implode, your illusions fold up shop, you move back home with your parents, and you get your old part-time job back. In fact, not much had changed in the three years since I'd been gone. There'd been no improvements made at the theater. Hell, even Jay was still standing there, ripping tickets.

"*Terminator 3,*" he was shaking his head. "Theater 2. To your right. But trust me: it's no good."

I brought a momentum to Mark's party that he hadn't planned on. I'd expected everything to be heightened, leveled-up. Not so. There was beer in the fridge. I asked his girlfriend where the actual booze was. She dusted off a bottle of tequila that she'd been saving for a special occasion.

"What's more special than this?" I challenged.

She shrugged and decided that margaritas didn't sound half bad.

I drank some of the margarita mix for show, guzzling some of it down as if people would be impressed by it. No one was. Not long after, I wrestled a random girl to the floor, quoting Khan's speech from *Star Trek II.* (Because, you know: *Star Trek.* Why not?) Mark had a pool table and I tried showing off. I talked about how great Arizona was compared to Ohio and how I wished I'd never come home. I blathered on and on and on.

I needed everything to be more than it was.

I needed it to be *nth* degree.

The party wasn't cutting it.

I talked about moving the party to the Old Dutch, which wasn't all that far of a walk. It was within stumbling distance.

I could sense that people were talking about me. They'd gone from having fun with me to observing me, suspiciously, like I was a pod person. I wasn't the same Paul they remembered. The novelty of having me around again had quickly worn off. I was a few shades darker.

And then someone decided to hide my car keys.

I cannot fully explain the sheer rage that began boiling inside me at this moment. When I realized someone had hidden them (it was doubly a mystery how someone had gotten them in the first place, though I suspect it was something along the lines of: "Hey Paul, can I see your car keys?"), I went from bulldozing the party with my *This-needs-to-be-an-11* attitude to full-on anger. It was a whodunit from hell.

I was insulted.

Was this someone's idea of a game?

"Where the fuck are my keys?" I demanded.

My mood had shifted from Fake Khan to Actual Khan. I was officially the villain.

I don't remember much of what followed, but soon enough, I was angrily driving backcountry roads not far from Mark's house. I weaved all over the place. Back in Arizona, this was my normal cruising altitude. I'd gotten from Point A to Point B in far worse condition. The top was off the Jeep, summer-sweet breeze blasting through my hair, Guster's *Lost and Gone*

Forever blaring over the speakers. I knew those roads years ago, and they were coming back to me, emerging like hidden words in steamed glass or song lyrics you hadn't thought of in ages but can sing, line for line.

Soon enough, I had flashing lights behind me.

A "sinking feeling" doesn't quite begin to describe it. It's more like when that massive sinkhole suddenly opened up in Guatemala and swallowed half a city block. For a split-second, my brain considered flooring it and seeing how far I could get through the neighborhoods and backyards with my Wrangler, flaunting all my new off-road skills I'd learned out West. I could park myself in someone's yard, flip the lights off, and wait it out. But, no. I pulled over, full well knowing I was fucked. I knew it with every fiber of my being.

The bullet had been fired, from my very first swallow of Zima back in that closet. It just took its sweet time arriving. And now, years later, here it was.

I pulled over near a local country club, which wasn't exactly festooned with mansions and sprawling estates. More like nice mid-level brick houses lining a narrow stretch of road that wasn't far from the mall. Either way, it was two-thirty in the morning and the entire world was an oscillating gyroscope of reds and blues.

I knew I was so fucked that I opened the door, hands up.

"Okay, okay…" I began, like I'd just led this cop on a cross-country chase and there were fourteen of them, all guns drawn.

"Sir," the cop said. "Please get back into your vehicle."

I complied, but left the door open.

He sauntered close, then sized up the situation.

"You from Arizona?"

"Me? No. Wait. Yes. No. Sort of."

He asked me for my license and registration. I couldn't find the registration straight off, but found a bunch of story ideas I'd scribbled onto Burger King napkins and stuffed into the glove box. Not really helpful at that moment. None of those ideas involved UFOs beaming me out of trouble, either.

So, this is what it's like to get arrested, my brain kept telling me. I was paralyzed. Next up was: *My parents are going to be so upset.*

I think the latter was worse than the former.

Either way, he finally instructed me to step out.

I took in a deep breath, trying to hold in the smell of alcohol—fully aware that whatever paces he was going to put me through, I was going to fail. Just fifteen minutes ago, I was disassembling Mark's apartment, pinning a random girl down on the carpet and screaming, "From hell's heart, I stab at thee!" Now, this police officer was swinging his flashlight this way and that, asking me to do one simple thing: walk in a straight line.

To this day, I'll testify that I rocked that first line. Almost to the point where he was shocked. I remember him being surprised, if not impressed. I figured he might even let me go, like: *Oops. Got the wrong, weaving drunken driver with out-of-state plates.*

"Let's do that again."

I turned back around.

Disaster.

I asked for three do-overs.

There was a breathalyzer involved in there somewhere. I tried to blow around the stick, like I was outsmarting it. The number that came back made him chuckle.

"You do a lot of drinking in college, Carl?"

Carl.

There it was.

Whenever I'm in trouble with the law or at a doctor's office, I'm known as Carl. My first name. The name my parents weirdly abandoned when I was in elementary school. When I'm dying, that's how I'm going to be known. I'm not going to die as "Paul Fuhr." I'm going to be toe-tagged with *Carl Fuhr.*

"Why do you ask that?" I said back at the precinct.

"Because given your BAL, you're able to talk good."

"Talk *well*."

"What?"

"Talk *well*. You don't talk *good*. You talk *well*," I said. "It's like when someone asks you *How are you doing?* You don't ever answer *Doing good*. You answer *Doing well*. I have a Master's in English."

"Oh, good for you."

The next five hours in jail, alone, crawled by.

I WAS COURT-ORDERED to spend that Halloween in an alcohol-awareness program at a hotel adjacent to the movie theater. I could see my workplace, and they could see me. Big Neal and Mark knew I was locked up in the hotel, and it sort of just made me sad to be so close to civilization. Cell phones were forbidden but everyone, including me, sneaked them in. I was getting encouraging texts and the occasional photo of a beer with a middle finger next to it.

Bastards, I'd text back.

My roommates could not be more different from each other: Harald, a tall, barrel-chested German who worked as a senior-level exec for a multinational medical company, had gotten arrested for going 120 mph with an open case of Coors, while my other roommate resembled one of those creepy puppets from the Genesis "Land of Confusion" video. The program's people taped off our rooms at night to make sure none of us broke out. So, my roommates did the next logical thing: they started sizing up how far it'd be to jump out the second-floor window. The creepy puppet dude was wiry and could actually slip through the window but he decided two floors might be too much.

"Your ankles," Harald decided in thick German. "No good."

So we lay there in the dark on two beds and a squeaky cot: three grown men drinking coffee, watching horror movie marathons on cable, and talking about how much we missed drinking. We just needed to get through these next couple of days, and we'd be home free. This sucked, sure, but it could be jail.

Later, there were stories of the girls next door to us scoring coke from the kitchen staff. That just pissed Harald off even more. The next morning, he was working on a new scheme for us: we would crack open the hotel window again, have my movie-theater friends to toss up "a bag of beer" to our floor, and we'd throw money back down.

Even I knew this was fucked up.

Most of my life was a series of ratio-hedging: Was the adventure worth it? Was the juice worth the squeeze?

Once Harald realized I wasn't going to get my friends involved (even though I'm positive any of the box-office kids would've done it for an extra $20), he settled down. Besides, I could kind of feel a little sobriety bubbling inside me. I kind of got it. I'd warmed my hands on the hobo-barrel fire of sobriety for a bit and decided: *This isn't so bad.* There was a guy who talked about getting arrested for being so high, he was driving twenty miles *under* the speed limit. There was another guy who said he had seven such programs to attend, just to see his kids. Another said he didn't even know the name of this awareness program—he had so many court assignments, he couldn't keep track.

My life wasn't so bad.

When I got out, everyone I knew wanted to hear about my time spent in the hotel. I told them it was fine, but I could feel something calcify inside me. I knew I'd gone past that point where I was drinking and it had no consequences. It clearly did. And I felt that maybe I'd be good at giving speeches like the ones I'd heard just hours before, telling twentysomethings that life isn't all Thursday-Saturday night shitshows and regrets and apologetic texts and chasing down who-the-hell-knows-what.

But then Ohio went and made it impossible to get out from under the specter of the DUI.

I had to attend more counseling courses. I had six months without a driver's license. I had a lot of explanations to make about why I couldn't drive places. I couldn't get connected to a sober community in Sandusky, Ohio.

It was worthless, I decided, and so was I.

Who cared?

The rainstorm of self-pity raged inside me. Instead of sharing stories of sobriety in required classes, I was going to share the same bullshit stories on barstools I always had. I'd just talk and talk and talk about nothing. If Ohio wanted me to be an alcoholic, goddammit, then I'd be the best alcoholic anyone had ever seen.

SO THERE I WAS, staring at twenty students in the exact same classroom I'd been in years before. Only this time, I was teaching freshman composition in it. I'd managed to use my brand-new Master's degree to get a teaching job at Firelands College. I'd gotten the job out of sheer luck. Someone had dropped out the week before, and they were desperate. Seemed fitting. It also appealed to the college to have an alumnus teaching courses there.

I tended to award good grades to papers that moved me emotionally, not ones that were well-constructed. Plus, since I liked to grade with glasses of wine, the further down the stack of papers you were as a student, the better the chance you'd get pages and pages and pages of cursive notes from me. Flowery praise. Maybe even a purple speckle of cabernet or two.

One of my students looked way too familiar. She was slumped in her chair, loudly smacked her gum, had raccoon-eyeliner and a knowing smile. It didn't click for days. Then it did: she was one of the girls who'd scored coke from the kitchen line cook at the hotel, sniffing her way through the speeches the next day, dozing off here and there.

It took me four classes to realize we'd been in the same awareness class.

There wasn't exactly a large student population going

to Firelands College so there weren't "college bars" to speak of. There was, however, one at a nearby golf dome. I didn't golf. (Also, true story: the enormous dome blew away in a windstorm and everyone kind of shrugged and kept the bar running.) Either way, I used a credit card nearing its limit and drank whatever I wanted after every class, just to numb the restlessness.

When you're an alcoholic like me, your brain has a volume you can't control. It's cranked up a notch. It's not tuned to music, either—it's dialed into chatter and words and regrets and decisions never made. It's just a constant stream of anxiety piped into your ears. The only thing that washes it clean is that first swallow of syrah, or the belt of warm vodka from the bottle hidden in your gym bag. Nothing ever quiets it entirely.

It was also difficult being about five seconds older than my students and walking them through the strange psychodynamics of, say, the Stanford Prison Experiment. I wanted to be the cool teacher, the guy who sat on backward chairs or on the edge of the desk. I used "fuck" in class a lot, too, which lost its novelty after a while. I felt empty. I had a responsibility with the students that I'd quickly thrown out the window. I invited students to the bars; I invited them to parties. I didn't blur lines—I ignored them altogether. I swore to myself that I could be the *one* college professor who could exist in his own special sphere. (I could revolutionize the way teachers taught!)

I was going to be The Instructor those kids remembered forever.

A few weeks in, I woke up in the community college parking lot after teaching my first class of the day. My hangover made every thought searing and raw, like I was walking on blistered feet. I had gone out to my car to rest, but when I opened my eyes, I realized that I'd managed to miss teaching my second class. I opened my eyes to find some of my students standing there, pointing. They were a little amused, but mostly just pissed off—like a lot of people in my life. I was regularly experiencing the sad, exquisite pain that only closet alcoholics can appreciate. Hearing the world come alive outside your window at 6 a.m. while you're still wide awake, drunk and alone—newspapers thrown onto lawns, cars starting up. Each day I felt less like a human being than a MacGyver gadget, held together with duct tape and bubble gum.

I sat there in my vehicle, ashamed and vulnerable. I felt naked, like in those dreams where you ring up all your groceries and suddenly realize you don't have your wallet. I didn't want to fling the Jeep door open and acknowledge what had happened, but I didn't want to ignore the awkward tension of the moment, either.

So I waved at them.

I was also waving goodbye to teaching as a career.

11

WHEN YOU'RE ARMED with an English degree and a thirsty liver, marriage suddenly seems like a pretty good idea. Carrie and I had been dating for a few months again. She wasn't sold that I'd gotten everything out of my system—and she was right. I always had a delayed sense of fun. When most everyone was settling down in their careers and families, I was still trying to squeeze the last few drops of irresponsibility out of the dishrag. If my life was measured in bars, I was always running up against Last Call.

So I had to act the part of Responsible Adult. I had to make a show of getting out of bed in the morning, doing dishes, looking for jobs. I had to pretend to have some semblance of normalcy about my life. Nothing could be further from the truth. Everything around me was practically melting underfoot and soft to the touch. Carrie, on the other hand, was completely stable: trusting, fixed, rooted, put-together. She knew that I was broken, and I honestly think it kept her coming back. I was a project. As a nurse, she cared for others in a way that baffled me. She could also enjoy a half-glass of wine and leave the rest of it sitting on our kitchen counter. I didn't understand that, in all the ways I didn't understand people who were wired to care for other people as a job.

For me, the wedding reception was about the only thing I cared about. I hadn't even told my parents that the wedding was happening. I was making decisions about flatware and tasting dinners and desserts, but I hadn't summoned up the courage to admit that I was taking the easy way out and marrying Carrie at my lowest, most lost point in life. She wasn't getting a husband—she was getting a burden.

A few weeks before my wedding day, I needed to send an email from my parents' house. When I flipped their laptop open, a Word doc was sitting there. It was only a quarter-complete, but it was enough to see where it was going. It was a letter that my mom was writing to me. It was about how unprepared I was for marriage—how irresponsible and unready and thoughtless I was. I flashed red. I immediately called Carrie and told her what I'd found. She assured me that I wasn't any of the things my mother was calling me in the letter. But deep down, I knew she was wrong. My mom was right. I made a beeline for my parents' liquor cabinet and swallowed a slug of warm whiskey straight from the bottle, settling my nerves.

I was entitled to it.

Frankly, the only thing that mattered to me was me. My alcoholic brain knew exactly how to parasite my fianceé, like one of those face-huggers from *Alien*. I didn't try to or want to—I just did. Even better, she worked late nights at the hospital, which meant I could really let my alcoholism fester, like mushrooms in the dark. After taking a honeymoon through Napa Valley, we filled up our wine cabinet with bottles of expensive stuff. We frequented a quaint little wine shop in the German Village area of Columbus, too, where we rented a tiny brick house amidst cobblestone streets and wrought-iron fences. Across the street was a German cookie place that only opened for Christmastime. It was pretty idyllic. For Carrie, wine was a hobby; for me, it became serious business. And by serious business, I meant I pretended to get interested in it so I could get close to the drinking. I got notebooks; I borrowed books on grape lineages and *terroir* from the library. I got downright academic about my alcohol. I desperately wanted to learn about viticulture, *only* because knowledge over a vice means that you're in control of it. I could even legitimize my drinking by becoming a *sommelier,* I reasoned. There were certifications out there. Someone could rubber-stamp my problem and make it seem almost noble. I knew the taste of different varietals on my tongue. The fat spice of a zinfandel; the lush butter of a syrah; the bright grassiness of a good pinot grigio.

You'd also think that getting married would've tempered some of my drinking habits. Nope. Not in the slightest. I got skilled with corkscrews and wine bottles. I had it down to about six seconds, slicing the foil off and uncorking the bottle. When that first bright wave of chardonnay would hit me, I knew I was home free. The next few hours would be about me steadily sinking into oblivion. If I was lucky, I'd wake up the next day without having emailed anyone two pages of emotional tripe or without ordering $100 worth of used movies and books.[20]

I was starting to collect my wine bottles from the week in a trash bag, wrapping it tight so the glass didn't *clink* too loudly, and driving to a grocery store alley where I'd throw them all away like the Mafia burying a body upstate. Some part of me was deeply in love with the madness. It was like observing my life from a distance, quietly wondering just how bad it could all get.

FOR FUTURE REFERENCE: Ambien and absinthe don't mix. I'd beaten my poor doctor down with enough stories of me not sleeping so he'd finally prescribe me Ambien. Because I'm an alcoholic, I needed a shortcut to sleep. Around that same time, I was ordering bottles of absinthe straight from Europe, back when it was illegal to have it in the States. One bottle had a stalk of wormwood in it. I studied up on the stuff. I bought the accoutrements; I got sugar cubes and the real-deal absinthe spoons. I'd never felt so goddamned refined in my life. It was exotic. I learned how the right amount of water turned it *louche*, as the French called it—a milky-green that meant it was watered down just right.

---

[20] Not going to lie: there is some weird part of me that really enjoyed getting packages addressed to me, containing *exactly* what I'd want to see or read.

I'd put the sugar cube on the spoon, light the sugar cube on fire with a torch, then flip the cube into the glass. It was like the poor man's heroin. There was real showmanship to it, even when I was doing this alone on a Wednesday night when I had work in the morning. I didn't even like the taste of it—the bright anise hitting the back of my throat like I'd been huffing licorice all day. I don't know how many times I'd accidentally knock the burning cube off the spoon and catch our kitchen table on fire—a wide blue flame spreading out in every direction.

I'd pop 10 milligrams of Ambien, just to pump the brakes on my night, which was just about the worst idea imaginable. Once, my wife came into the living room and I was apparently having a full-on conversation with people who weren't there. I remember them—they'd emerged like they were from another dimension. I was living in one of those Victorian novels I half-read in grad school with the coquettes and stiff-lipped prudes. There were parasols and laughter alongside high-minded conversation and nodding.

Lots of nodding.

"What are you doing?"

I mumbled something in return. I just remembered her standing there, amidst my imagined parlor room, not quite sure what to do or think.

I lost count of how many times I'd come to, standing in the corner of a stranger's house or apartment, peeing. Carrie would be screaming at me not only to stop, but to wake the hell up. A couple of times she'd gotten out of bed at three-thirty to visibly shake me out of whatever *Blair Witch* corner-reverie I was in, then take me by hand down to the actual bedroom.

We'd lie back in bed in the dark, minutes later, nothing there but embarrassment and the smell of a carpet cleaner and water thrown on the carpet. The words didn't need to be said, but they were there—big, bright cinematic blocks like the ones from the opening of *North by Northwest,* hanging in the air. They loomed high over the bed: *People know you're an alcoholic.* One Christmas, I drank so much that I successfully pissed off every single person I came into contact with. I made fun of my relatives and their menial-sounding jobs. I went on and on about why *Die Hard* is the best Christmas movie of all time. I angrily pointed out that I missed Arizona so much that I blamed Carrie and her family for ruining my life.

We lay in bed that night, the blackness of those voices and slurred behaviors bubbling between us, and I kept thinking: *It couldn't be that bad.* It couldn't be as bad as the night my parents had a blind wine tasting, and Mark and I ended up across the street at an abandoned house where we downed an exceptional zinfandel on their empty patio—all while Mark swore he saw a ghost up in one of the little windows. We mocked it. We laughed and teased it. The next morning, we recounted the tale to my very unamused parents who told us a family had moved into that house a few weeks prior. It'd been a terrified three-year-old girl in that window.

Yes, I was an alcoholic.

I didn't know what to do with that information. I had people I couldn't let down. People expected me to drink, dammit, and I took that responsibility seriously. But I could also feel the great, inky blackness that was filling up between my wife and me. Every time she found a bottle I'd "mistakenly put in the wrong spot" or every time she forgave me for flirting with one of her friends or every time she found a drunken Facebook exchange with someone that I'd swore I'd deleted, that darkness swelled. It grew, swelled, evolved.

And it eventually consumed everything.

I NEVER ASPIRED to be a parent, but I didn't aspire to be as helpless as a child, either. Thanks to my drinking, that's what I became: just another child for someone else to take care of. I'd love to say I spent hours preparing for the moment: reading manuals, visiting websites, picking people's brains about what it'd be like. There was no curiosity. When my first kid, Elliott, arrived, I can't fully express the sudden rush of acid grief that washed over me. Everything familiar was threatened. All my drinking buddies hoisted shots in celebration, but they may as well have been farewell drinks. Everyone began disappearing. I was bound and determined to beat the system, though. I wasn't going to be one of those parents who ceased to have a life outside putting their kids to bed.

I had zero experience with children—mainly by choice. I'm not one of those people whose insides light up at the sheer sight of a newborn. I'm not programmed that way. I always tended to look the other way when everyone else was fawning over infants and feeling their baby-chicken hair and commenting on dimples and toes. None of it impressed me. In surgical scrubs, I was there for both my sons' births, and I prodded their little bodies with rubber-gloved fingers. Tears flowed involuntarily. But, no lie: my brain was racing through all the realities I couldn't face with either one of them. College tuition, high school trips, clothes, dropping them on their head. Nothing melted inside me like they said it was supposed to. I just felt a sinking feeling, and I knew that I was going to be the worst parent ever.

"I THINK I want to be a stay-at-home dad," I announced over dinner one night.

Carrie blinked, then frowned.

"Why?"

"Because I think it'd really help around here."

This was really just code. It was me telegraphing: *I don't want to go to my shitty editing job anymore.* Or maybe, more succinctly: *I don't want to wear pants anymore.*

The math even kinda-sorta made sense because the entry-level editing job I had brought home *just* enough to equal what a daycare would charge. Being a stay-at-home parent couldn't be all that hard, right? Hell, I might even be good at it. Truth be told, I just didn't want to get up and go to a job. That was too much consistency. As a parent, I could half-ass it in the mornings, shuffling around in pajama bottoms.

It did not go well.

My first memories of being at home with Elliott amount to me curled up in a ball on the couch, PBS Kids in the background, as Elliott jumped in his bouncy seat. If I was lucky, he'd last a full two shows in a row without needing anything from me. I'd drift back into my gray, sleepless hangover. My memories of Elliott's first year are muddy and pixelated, almost like slow-buffering videos. Whenever I was sober enough (or drunk enough) to read books to him, I was only reading words—never paying attention to the stories. That's exactly how I was living my life. I could tell you what was being said, but I couldn't pass a comprehension quiz to save my life.

I was worse than a child. As Elliott grew, I seemed to grow in the opposite direction. I made excuses. I played dumb and I barely told the truth when I was caught. When I forgot to throw out all the little bottles of pinot grigio rolling around in my car's back seat, I'd blame it on an imaginary passenger. I also treated everything and everyone as if they'd evaporate the second I walked away, just like Elliott did when he left a playground. All those close friends he just made? Forgotten. I hurricaned from one bad decision to the next, never once considering that there was a tomorrow.

At a certain point, I was simply terrified to go outside. Everything was a hassle. I couldn't just take Elliott for a walk or a bike ride. He always required military preparation. Wipes, diapers, stroller, sippy cup, snacks, sunscreen for his ears and nose, shade, shoes in case we found a park and wanted to walk around. I took none of this as an opportunity; I looked at none of it as a beautiful thing. I looked at it as shackles. Punishment.

My head would still be throbbing from the night before: electric veins sprouting out from my temples, thanks to whatever crap chardonnay I'd snuck home from the grocery store. No matter what, Elliott was ready to go. His boundless energy against the brick wall of my alcoholism was always too much, but I never took it seriously. Since I was home, it didn't seem much like an actual job to me. In my mind, work required cubicles and cafeterias.

Now the only thing punishing about it all, looking back, is the fact that I didn't immerse myself in any of it. I didn't take advantage of his joy, his wonder, his excitement about the world. I kept him locked in the house, parked in front of the TV. And when I *would* dare to wander the neighborhood in sweatpants, him falling asleep in a stroller, I'd be angry at the universe.

How did my life end up like this?

How did I end up here?

I didn't even want kids.

I'm still sort of surprised that no one questioned whether I'd kidnapped Elliott, given how many times I'd be sitting at a park, watching him with unkempt hair and a ragged beard. Sometimes I'd even have my flask in my pocket (Mark's wedding present to me). At night, when Carrie was working late, I'd crank the baby monitor up as loud as it could go and set it by my ear. And more than once, I still managed to sleep through ear-splitting screams. A few times, I set Elliott to rest in his crib, surveyed the wine situation and decided that the drive to the grocery store for more wasn't too risky. I'd lock up the house, race to the local Kroger, buy a bottle of wine and race back. I'd literally run back upstairs to check to see if Elliott was still up there where I left him—breathing comfortably in his corner.

I eventually decided that this only ends up in one of two ways: he's either right where I left him, or it's the beginning of an NBC crime drama.

I started applying for jobs. Anything and everything. I crafted fourteen versions of my résumé—each one highlighting a different version of me. I had one app that would automatically fire off résumés whenever something matched a profile; I had another app that alerted me whenever a job listing popped up so I could jump on it. If it said "Communications," I was in. The number of jobs requiring someone with an English degree, by the way, wasn't exactly staggering. I spent hours on company websites, setting up profiles and registering myself in every conceivable HR department in Columbus, Ohio. There's no greater despair than pumping résumé after résumé after résumé into the vast black hole of career sites, with no response. I even made a deal with myself: *Successfully send two résumés and you can have a shot of vodka.* Still, I wasn't built for warming baby formula and making applesauce and changing diapers and tickling bellies, so I kept at it until something clicked.

The opening of my resume should've read:

PAUL FUHR

Big talker, short-term thinker. Consistent at being inconsistent. Creative, bitter, mercurial, sarcastic, anxious, insecure, petulant. Articulates ideas well but does not know how to execute them. Seems like he knows what he's doing but actually does not. Resents being managed. Always knows better. Excels in being hungover until noon. Frequently hides in bathroom stalls to count floor tiles while nauseous. Experience spans a wide range of fields and industries because of how quickly and often he leaves jobs.

12

SO, MY SISTER MARRIED Michael, a man twenty years her senior, who'd spent most of his adult life as a ballroom dance instructor. In fact, that's how they improbably met: through dance. Laura had come to know him while he was hosting dance nights at the dinner club my parents frequented. Mike wasn't much taller than me, but he had a football player's build. He was square-shouldered and blunt—no matter which way you looked at him, he seemed to have hidden reserves of strength ready to bowl someone over. He was bald and had heavy-lidded eyes that seemed to maybe have once been fierce, but now seemed a bit distracted. Wandering. Even when he was there, he wasn't really there. That's not to say he wasn't capable of being alive. Oh, quite the contrary. Michael seemed able to harness some otherworldly energy whenever he felt the urge—an electric impulse that possessed him to convert any overheard song into a potential expression of *stand-up-and-dance-now*. Any moment was a chance for him to explode in creative expression.

I don't know how many times we'd be out in public—say, at a Denny's or a Cracker Barrel—and a middling song would come over the speakers and his head would start bobbing, his lidded eyes coming alive. His brain was scrabbling through something—seeing foot schematics, animated twirls, and mental trails of forward momentum, maybe—and he'd pull Laura out of the booth and they'd dance down the aisle in syncopation with the music. I tried ignoring the spectacle that was happening in front of me. Maybe it's just because I refuse to believe my life is a musical.

It's just who Michael was, though. It wasn't wrong. He wanted you to love dancing as much as I want people to desperately love the director's cut of *Almost Famous*. Again, that's all Michael and I wanted in life: connection. Michael stumbled a lot when he wasn't teaching folks dance, but he was in his early fifties and had a lot of sports injuries, he'd told Laura. He tangled words and trailed off with a snuff at the end of his sentences. Michael clearly wasn't the same as he'd been. We were getting the consolation prize version of him. To me, he seemed far removed from the vast succession of awards that lined his shelves at home—but he knew every conceivable style: Salsa, Viennese Waltz, Rumba, West Coast Swing, Jive,

Bolero, Paso Doble. I think Merengue was in there somewhere, too. Whatever the case, my brother-in-law sort of existed in the margins of my busy drunken life, waltzing in here and there (pun intended), but mostly to invite me to whatever dance event they had going on at the dance studio.

The studio itself wasn't bad, though it was hidden inside a ramshackle strip mall way off the beaten path in Sandusky, Ohio. Ironically, my parents' old TV store had occupied one of the spaces just four spots over, which added its own surreality. I was more enamored with the ghost of the old video store that was now a head shop. I desperately wanted to believe I could still smell the bright chemical sheen of fresh VHS cassettes.

As little as I cared about the dance studio or dancing at all, the most beautiful part of it was the culture my sister and Michael had cultivated around it. *Have dance, will have friends.* They had genuine friends—all of them. There was real love in that room. People who had no business being connected to one another—lawyers in their twilight years, NASA engineers, young women looking to learn how to dance for their weddings, grandmothers looking for someone to get frisky with on the floor. It was a nice home-away-from-home, with walls of mirrors and an ergonomic flooring system that actually absorbed the force of your steps. I had to hand it to my sister and Michael: they tried.

Laura had literally pirouetted into this world, looped into it after some crazy night of drinking and dancing—and then connected with Michael enough to go run off to Vegas for a wedding I couldn't afford to attend because I'd, well, drunk our bank account into oblivion. So we watched the wedding from our living room, live-streamed on the Mandalay Bay website, which I hooked up to our HDTV.

As the years wore on, the thing that pissed me off about Mike wasn't that he was a professional shithead. It wasn't even that he was a blowhard one-upper with stories. ("You've climbed K2? Try parachuting Mount Kilimanjaro in your underwear.")[21] He just always knew better than you. He'd already figured it out. Whatever you were trying, he'd done before. Whatever you were thinking, it wasn't worth it. He'd considered all the angles.

He clearly hadn't.

So the question I get a lot now is: *You didn't like Mike from the beginning, did you?*

The answer to that is always "no." That's a leading, bullshit question. It took me a few times to understand why I didn't like him. I had to keep the opinion far underground, too, so that it didn't emerge at inopportune times. But it became clear that Mike was the dreamer and Laura was the realist who could help make Michael's dreams actually expand and grow. My little sister was keeping their whirligig in motion because she genuinely, honestly loved him, but if she didn't keep it in motion, everything would come crashing down.

And about two months after they got married, it struck me that I was having to prepare ahead of time to spend time with Michael. I didn't know if I could handle whatever Yahtzee game of stupid, awkward jokes that would tumble out of his mouth. More than that, if I'd just get ready by getting even drunker, maybe I could lock into his wavelength. No, the real, honest-to-God reason I didn't get along with my sister's hurricane-force husband is because he reminded me exactly of me.

I didn't know he was an alcoholic, but I could sense we

---

[21] Not a true story he shared, but you get the point.

were both orbiting the same, shameful dark star we didn't tell our families about.

We both had the same sloppy stagecraft of bottle-hiding, and we both embellished our pasts to the point where no one could possibly find a fact-based article to prove it, with us shrugging it all off as a misunderstanding. We also had these ambiguous visions for our futures—vast swatches of cloudbanks, pleasant fictions, but we kept saying we had them nonetheless.

My parents are intelligent, so that's what made it so baffling to me: they weren't seeing what I was seeing. It was like watching the world's least secret agent stumble into a clandestine meeting of world-order leaders, knocking all their evil plans off the shelf. But Mike was a unique challenge because his baseline was drunk. He'd answer the phone drunk. He'd grocery-shop drunk. He'd cook drunk. He'd slur instructions to students when they screwed up because Mike accidentally got the footwork wrong. He'd hunch over again, never making eye contact with his dance partner, and start over. It was his baseline and his normal, so no one was really the wiser.

After a few months of occasional sightings, it occurred to me that I was becoming something of a professional alcoholic observer. This was my side job, whether I liked it or not: spotting alcoholics and dispositioning them.

Mike is an alcoholic.

That conclusion hit me early on, but my parents adamantly told me I was wrong. I remember bringing up "alcoholism" and "Mike" with my mom one morning after breakfast, and it was met with the classic burn-the-earth, no-way-in-hell-was-this-true response. *I know alcoholics,* she said, *and Mike is no alcoholic. I've seen them before.* She argued that he was just full of life. And if nothing else, he had a lot of worries and concerns. It all weighed on him, she told me: his kids who didn't talk to him. He had a very different life than we did. We couldn't pass any judgment on his decisions or indecisions or half-hearted attempts to bond with them.

There were only popped seams and half-formed sentences between me and Mike.

Inside, I laughed. My family had turned not talking about our problems into a second job. We were so emotional that no one could touch us—we were radioactive. We couldn't say *I missed you* or *I was sorry* or *I was wrong*. No. That would set the bombs off. But when I said, unwaveringly, that Mike was a straight-up alcoholic who had connected to Laura and her by-comparison stability, everyone rolled their eyes. Hell, this was almost the same narrative as me and Carrie, if I'm being completely honest. I wasn't so far gone that I wasn't a potentially good life partner, though.

The excuses for Mike hurt me, though. At one party, I brought a bottle of Grey Goose and opened it. So had Mike. I paid real close attention that night to what happened. Mike and I toasted to the first shots of that first open bottle, draining them down, and I mentally told myself that the rest would belong to Mike. I had one more shot, then left it be. An hour later, I returned to the scene of the crime and there was the opened bottle of Grey Goose. It was one-quarter full. That was a feat, but kind of unremarkable.

"Nice work," I nodded to Mike—the only other vodka drinker.

"Yeah," he stared right through me.

And that's when I noticed the *second* Grey Goose bottle

in the trash can—*my fucking bottle*—lying there underneath everything. That was my move: half-burying truths. He'd essentially drained two bottles by himself. Alone. In the span of two hours. He used my parents' kitchen island to steady himself most of the time, as he spun ridiculous story after ridiculous story—how he was inches from a million-dollar deal and how he'd been screwed out of a business plan, the details of which crumbled like sand when you asked.

Anyway, I started talking about how I felt like Mike was having a hard weekend every weekend I saw him—and I'd had hard weekends just like that, where you're struggling between Sad and Miserable when you're not dealing with the crushing agony of anxiety—the exhaustion of trying to keep it all twist-tied together. That tension exists for a reason.

Not to get ahead of myself, but when I first got sober, my sister was congratulating me. I was maybe five weeks sober, so she knew I was actually trying. Hell, she'd seen me vomit into sinks and endured me having strange girls in my bedroom while she pretended not to hear what was going on. She'd been through a lot. Midway through the conversation, Mike grabbed the phone:

"Hey!"

"Hey, Mike," I sighed.

"How you doin'?"

"Good." I paused.

"So I hear you're off the wagon."

"*On* it," I corrected him, like a dick. "That's the expression. You get *on* the wagon."

He giggled something unintelligible. My sister screamed something at him in the background.

"I'm just kidding. Just kidding," he apologized for something I didn't understand. "Well, look, I'm real happy you got sober. But listen to me. Listen to me. This is important. Don't get proud. Don't get *fuckin'* proud about it, you got me?"

I sat there, dumbfounded. Mainly I was annoyed that I was getting a lesson from an active alcoholic, but I was also annoyed that he was being so reductive about my sobriety. I'm a sensitive dude (or was), so that stuff hurt.

"I won't be," I lied.

We went five or six rounds on that before he was satisfied and Laura cut him off.

When the call was over, I shut my phone off and stared down and counted carpet threads.

13

MARK WADE SHOWED up to the Credit Dauphine conference room with a shit-eating grin on his face, his graying hair slightly mussed. He'd just turned forty, but you could still see the fire in his eyes from all the shows he performed with his band on the weekends. There was an electrical undercurrent there that fatherhood and office drudgery hadn't yet killed. He was there for a job interview for a manager position on my team. Even though I'd only taken the job at the bank a few months before, I'd risen through the ranks quickly. Now I was an assistant vice president.[22] Getting the job with me would spring Wade from work as an hourly employee. I think I'd met him once or twice before this encounter, and he was a survivor of the dreaded call center.

The mortgage crisis had just happened. The bottom had fallen out on something so complex that I'll never figure it out, no matter how hard Margot Robbie tried to explain it from a bathtub—but it left all the banks with this shell-shocked, anything-goes attitude. If you were in a call center at our bank, you weren't talking to happy people. You were hearing about lawsuits, how someone was going to kill your family in front of you. That's back when the attrition rate at the bank was 50% or something astronomical like that. No one could handle it—not even the basic, seemingly straightforward calls.

Except Mark Wade.

His reputation had preceded him. The war stories were remarkable. He was one of those bank heroes, the legends they whispered about. Wade was one of the few people you could toss the angriest customer call at, and he'd talk them down from the ledge. It did nothing to shake his confidence or rattle his nerves. He soldiered on. That was his reputation. Wade was battle-ready. I needed someone who not only knew what the worst-of-the-worst customer complaints looked like, but what they meant. I had no fucking clue what they meant— their escrow and suspense funds and balloon payments were all hieroglyphics to me. I just knew how to usher the team forward, and I needed someone like Mark to make sense of it for me.

Mark sauntered into the conference room, the rhythm

---

[22] Don't be too impressed: banks throw titles around like party favors.

guitarist of a popular local band, and tossed a rolled up necktie on the desk between us.

"There's my tie," he said.

"I see that," I shook his hand, impressed.

"I forgot the interview was today and not tomorrow."

"But you brought a tie."

"You're goddamn right I did," he smiled broadly.

I filed paperwork to hire him right away. We hit it off immediately as fellow drinkers do, not knowing one another's drinking behaviors at all. We could sense them, though, like how submarines sense deep-wash patterns and barrier reefs and artificial displacements from enemy subs. They don't let off hard sonar pings, but you know something's there. You can feel it.

We started celebrating victories at a shitty Mexican restaurant nearby at lunch, and then I decided to move us over a few blocks to a way shittier Mexican bar on the off-chance that someone from work would see us. Looking back, we were celebrating nothing. We were celebrating case closures. Literally: we closed X amount of escalated mortgage complaints that would, without question, boomerang back to our office with thunder, subpoenas, and legal action in the very next month. But we didn't care. Our narrow job was to close cases and I'd found a drinking buddy in the process.

Wade and I staffed up quickly, and before we knew it, we'd quadrupled the size of our team in six months. They squeezed our team into two training rooms, computers side-by-side one another. We had a blank checkbook. The bank was still washing the blood off the sidewalks from the mortgage crisis, so we could pretty much get away with anything. Wade and I were largely good guys, though. (Mainly because I didn't know how to say "no" to managers.) We have good parents and couldn't sleep at night, knowing we'd fucked someone over. So the people we fucked over were ourselves.

Case in point: business trips.

Wade and I took three fatal business trips together that stand as moments through which I drove across the badlands of alcoholism and lost a great deal of myself while doing it. (I'm convinced Wade is still not completely the same.)

I assumed all drinkers were made equal. When it came to Mark Wade, I couldn't have been more wrong.

LONG BEFORE ADMITTING to being an alcoholic, I had a moment of reckoning. My life was one big stress fracture thanks to drinking. If you held my life up to the light *just right,* you could make out all the hairline cracks spidering in a thousand directions. For me, business trips were a cue to drink and generally misbehave. Airport bars where no one blinked at me ordering beer at 6 a.m. were fantasy lands. So long as I got my work done—said my hellos, recited my talking points, and landed my handshakes—I had a license to drink.

I thought Wade was on that same page.

"Man," he shook his head after the sixth round at some Hooters knockoff in Texas called Twin Peaks, snowdrifts of peanut shells on the floor. "I need to go to bed."

I was trying to order another round and I took his head-shaking as modesty. I knew he'd drink more. His willpower was certainly like when you snap a branch and it's still hanging together by an annoying sliver of bark—a thin skin that just requires a sharp twist.

"Aw, come on," I flagged one of the waitresses with the white shirts knotted near her flat tummy. "Just another one."

Wade narrowed his eyes.

"Look, man," he stared me down. "It's past midnight. No."

When the server came by, I threw the corporate card at her and ordered another round for only myself. Around 4 a.m. in a Hilton Garden Inn in Lewisville, Texas, I woke up on the tiled floor of my bathroom. I'd thrown up in the bathtub, and there were splotches of dried blood leading in from the hallway. When I'd gotten back from the hotel bar, I'd apparently collapsed into the mirrored closet door. There were shards of glass everywhere on the carpet. I'd cut my hand semi-seriously and crawled into the bathroom where I'd passed out.[23]

This was Night #1 of my business trip. I still had two to go. I spent the next few days trying to figure out how to explain the incident. Creative Writing 301 didn't come to my rescue. This was the first time my drinking had spilled into the real world, and I couldn't dream up a way out. When I returned to work, I did seven or eight loops around the office before finding the courage to visit my office admin. I had to explain the expense. This was no accident. There was no explanation, there was no logical way for me to shrug off a room damage fee like this. It was time to come clean.

So, naturally, I lied.

I said I'd lost my balance. I acted embarrassed. Sometimes

---

[23] This is my best guess at what happened.

I get vertigo, I told the admin. It throws off the eardrums—it comes out of nowhere. She knew I was lying. I could see it flash in her eyes, but she nodded anyway. She felt sorry for me. We went through the motions, and she filed a report to make it go away. This was my life: one empty charade after another, with me always depending upon someone to look the other way. Big or small, lies were just a matter of course to get me through the day.

Sadly, people never saw what I wanted them to see exactly when I wanted them to see it. That's not how life worked. In my experience, people always saw exactly what I *didn't* want them to see when I didn't want them to see it. I'm still learning to trust myself because I'm the person I've lied to the most.

AROUND THIS SAME TIME, I agreed to go on a camping trip with some friends from work. One of Wade's friends, Carl, was the tallest and most experienced of the bunch. He was a quiet, reserved man who challenged himself to hike into great wildernesses alone. He knew things Real Men should know. He knew how to pitch camp; he knew how to start fires in subzero temperatures. I remember watching him throw our tent into the Arctic February air in awe, literally thinking: *Our car is four miles away. I'll keep walking if he can't do this.* But Carl persisted and, before I knew it, we had a campsite. We collected wood for the fire, and he was cooking dinner in no time. He's the same kind of guy who runs ultra-marathons and shrugs them off as no big deal. When you're an alcoholic, he's the guy you hang around for a few days, just to feel absolutely terrible about the life you've allowed happen to yourself.

Somewhere along the hike, Carl announced that he'd sneaked a bottle of Canadian Club in his pack. He shouldn't have ever mentioned this. This fact obsessed me for the dozen or so miles we hiked that day. That's all I thought about. He kept asking if the hike was helping to clear my head, and so I lied and said yes. But all I was really thinking about was that fucking bottle of Club. *How much had he brought? Was there enough for me? Could I sneak an extra swig or two without him noticing?*

Hours later, when we were passing the bottle around, thawing our bodies by the fire, I took a longer pull than I should. Same with Round 2. One of our other campers, Nick, actually passed on it. He was too enamored with the stars above to care. I took his drink for him. Next thing I know, I'm being zipped into my sleeping bag by three other grown men.

I never got invited to go camping with them again.

THE FLIGHT TO Florence, South Carolina had been something of a time-travel experiment to Wade. We'd hit the airport bar hard, and he passed out in his seat before takeoff and woke up when we landed at the regional airport. He turned to me with a real expression of annoyance: "When the hell is this thing going to take off?"

"Dude, we just landed."

He immediately resembled the shocked-face emoji.

Hours later, he rested his head against the glass of the rental car.

"I just want to pick all that cotton," Wade mumbled, half-lucid. Fields and fields of cotton rolled by as we cut through the Florence, South Carolina countryside around four in the afternoon. We'd bailed on our scheduled third training session, claiming that we'd need to recalibrate our work for the next day. We didn't. We needed to find a local bar. But not before we got lost trying to find the site where the Air Force had accidentally dropped an atomic bomb in the middle of nowhere.[24]

The night we arrived had gone something like this: we'd carried in all the booze we could, knowing there were no liquor stores around. We made a ton of Jäger bombs with Red Bulls and drank beer in Wade's hotel room, watching the new *A-Team* movie. Somewhere around the point where the tank explodes in midair, Wade checked out and I decided to next-level it. I drank until I couldn't see anymore and stumbled to my room. I forgot where that was, so I padded down to the lobby in my bare feet, slurred my last name to the front desk clerk, and they directed me to my room.

To hear it from Wade, he turned on the shower the next morning and lay on the floor, weeping for five minutes. I wasn't much better. I threw up scrambled eggs, Texas Pete, and grits in the Waffle House bathroom. I came to understand that a truly epic hangover—the sort of searing, bleak stretch in the brain that's not unlike trying to see through a frozen windshield in

---

[24] From Wikipedia: "The 1958 Mars Bluff B-47 nuclear weapon loss incident was an inadvertent nuclear weapon release over Mars Bluff, South Carolina during 1958. The bomb, which lacked the fissile nuclear core, fell over the area causing minor structural damage to buildings below. Six people were injured by the explosion of the bomb's conventional explosive load. The United States Air Force (USAF) was sued by the family of the victims, who received $54,000 (USD), equivalent to $443,647 (USD) in 2015."

winter—always carries with it an element of sad clarity. It's like those stories of soldiers where a bomb goes off right next to them and nothing happens. I suddenly started seeing things I wouldn't normally ever notice. My hangovers unsettled me, bringing me closer to myself than any amount of drinking ever could.

We arrived for another series of training sessions in a building so outdated that I wasn't sure it was even part of our bank. Instead of a computer directory, they used a person with a missing front tooth and a three-ringed binder to locate employees. That person took his time, really relishing the role, too.

"*Dave Lazelle,* you say? Well, let me look…" the man said, taking out the binder and flipping through its laminated pages. "Lazelle…Lazelle…"

I stood in front of yet another conference room, delivered the same speech as the day before and felt gas fumes wafting off my skin. I was sweating through my wrinkled clothes. No one was listening to me—and I certainly wasn't listening to me, reciting ways to close customer complaint cases faster and more efficiently. They all stared at me like a deer in headlights, and I'm sure I wasn't much better. I excused myself midway through, sharp anxiety seizing me, and let Wade do the rest of the dirty work. I barely made it to a bathroom where I dry-heaved for a full ten minutes.

Not long after, Wade pulled me aside.

"You can't do that again," he said.

"What's that? Go to the bathroom?"

He shifted uncomfortably in the hallway, rubbing his three-day stubble. This is not how manager-employee conversations were supposed to go, he knew.

"Everyone can see you're hungover."

"Come on, man. No they can't."

"Are you fucking serious? You're peelin' paint in there. *I* can smell you and I'm half as hungover as you."

If there's one thing I'm good at, it's remorse. I genuinely feel bad about things. It stuck with me. We said our goodbyes to everyone in Florence, and I tried to make it out of there without vomiting again. At the very least, I wanted to make our last impression better than our first, salvaging whatever I could. No one was buying our act. They gave us sad half-glances and half-hearted handshakes.

"Our flight's in, like, forty-five minutes," Wade warned me.

The airport was as small as they get—not much larger than one of those calendar kiosks you see in the mall. It's all waiting rooms and hundred-yard walks to the tarmac where you immediately get onto puddle jumpers. I knew the airport wouldn't be the alcoholic's playground that, say, the Dallas-Fort Worth airport would be. They wouldn't serve drinks on the airplane, either. I could feel the sober wasteland growing around me. We were a half-hour away from actually getting into an aircraft, and we hadn't even returned the rental car. A giant jug of Svedka rattled between us next to the gear shift, and I decided to go Full Cartoon on it. We were at the busiest intersection and I chugged it like a champ, like it was top-shelf Gatorade. Rivulets of vodka streamed from all corners of my mouth. It trailed down my shirt but I didn't care. I was making a statement.

I hated Florence. I hated everyone in it. I hated those dead-eyed employees. I hated that Mark had called me out as a bad manager. I hated that I wasn't the person I thought I was. I hated that I couldn't make it another two hours without a solid buzz.

I drove a little farther, parked out front of the airport—tiny as a roadside rest area—and chucked the half-full Svedka into the first trash can I saw. It bounced out, shattering. I walked away, like this happened every day.

MONTHS LATER, ONE of Wade and I's connecting flights was in Charlotte, which offered us a good ninety minutes at a tequila bar. It was a particular favorite of his—alive and thrumming with life. The drinks were expensive but, hell, if we didn't order dinner, the drinks would be covered by the company. We could live with that. We also quickly realized there was a *second* flight home—the last one out. It was chancy, but we took it; now, we needed a reason to swap our tickets out.

"You take care of our drinks," he instructed, mainly because this would put us over our corporate *per diem,* "and I'll take care of our flights."

I nodded. After all, this was what I was reviewed well at work for: strategy and execution.

Right around the time our next comically oversized margaritas arrived, Wade sauntered back to the table. He forked over a new boarding pass for the next flight out. The airport was suddenly thinning out all around us—the last of the flights washing through. It was disconcerting. The buzz of the bar quickly receded and, suddenly, it was just Wade and me crammed into a booth, alone.

We'd been living off the vibe of the place, not our actual conversation. Wade looked at me with a vaguely lost expression.

"You okay?"

"Yeah," he swallowed down a quarter of the margarita. "Just feel guilty."

"About what?"

"About texting my wife that our flight had been delayed when it really hadn't."

I shrugged it off. Lying to my wife was par for the course, I told him. When it came to booze, I could always find extra minutes and dollars that weren't there.

"Yeah, well," he sipped again, "I don't like lying to Jan. I actually miss my kids."

That stabbed me.

"We're just taking the next flight home," I felt my blood rising—the reflexive swinging-around-in-the-dark stance that my inner drunk took. "It's not like we're taking the flight out tomorrow morning so we can keep drinking, you know."

"Just guilty," he said. "Ninety minutes means I'll miss putting them to bed."

There was a weird silence between us as we stared in different directions and pretended not to be angry with one another. We texted; we checked our email and Facebook; I paid the tab. They were already mopping the tequila bar floor by the time we left.

When we approached the gate, I could see the gate crew recognize Wade, then me. They suddenly went ashen, regarding me like a kid who'd been bullied on the playground.

"Oh, just roll with this," Wade suddenly whispered to me.

"Hello, sir," one of them gingerly took my ticket.

Lots of nods and sad faces. Solemn glances all around.

"I'm so sorry."

"I hope you feel better."

"Get some rest."

"We assigned you a seat near the back."

When we walked down the sky bridge to our plane, I turned, almost pissed.

"What the hell did you tell them, man?"

He shrugged.

"I told them that you shit yourself."

OUR LAST TRIP TOGETHER was in Jacksonville—maybe a week before Oliver, my second child, was born. It was a calculated move, visiting our mortgage brethren down there on such short notice, but we did it. It could only help our names climb the corporate ladder some. We could add value down there. So, we did our little dog-and-pony show with the specialists. We offered suggestions and furrowed our brows, but mostly stalled long enough for Wade and I to get to happy hour.

Somewhere out in the ether, there is a photo of Wade wearing a bib at a beachside Joe's Crab Shack. It was the loneliest Crab Shack on the planet, too. It was one of those test markets where the waitstaff had to erupt into choreographed song routines that seemed ten times more depressing when there were only three tables they were doing it for. It was March and the cold air had knuckles to it. But I stood out there, in full business attire and nice Italian shoes, in the sand. It'd been a long time since I'd seen the ocean. There's nothing sadder than a cold day by the water—it reminded me of Sandusky, hollowed out by winter.

The hotel bar was tiny, but we took it over.

I ordered way more drinks than necessary, including some sort of island-breeze concoction that was on special. It looked like radiator fluid. Hell, it could have been and I wouldn't have cared. By the end of the night, I was promising the bartender a job at our bank, insisting that we could make it work. Wade was nodding, dimly, but not because he agreed—he was nodding as if he was the bit player in the background of a movie where his ten seconds of screen time were almost up. Once his manager (not his friend) paid the bill—his obligation was over.

I hadn't even noticed he'd only ordered one beer at the bar.

ANOTHER BUSINESS TRIP came up a few months later—a routine session where we'd pull a bunch of phone specialists into a room and coach them on how to annotate their calls more quickly in a new customer-service platform. Wade could easily show them how to work three systems at once—noting something here while taking care of something there, all the while saying the right thing to the customer. All of it would be audit-proof, too. This trip was back in Texas—right where I'd collapsed into a closet mirror. I walked over to Wade's desk and told him the good news: *Another business trip.*

He didn't look up from his keyboard for a few seconds, then rolled back away from it. Wade leaned back in his chair, lacing his fingers across his stomach. He looked at me hard.

"Lewisville, huh?"

"Yep. In just a couple of weeks. Looks like they'll need us from, like, a Monday to a Wednesday."

He nodded, understanding. Then he drew in a breath.

"They need *us?*"

"Well, yeah."

"You sure you're going?"

"What do you mean am I going? Of course I'm fucking going. I'll probably see if Chris and Joey can go, too."

"Well, I'm not."

"Because of Chris and Joey?"

"No," he shook his head, dismissing the names of his peers. "Because of *you,* man. I don't think I can survive another business trip."

A solar flare of anger looped up through me.

"What do you mean *no?*"

"I'm not going," he shrugged, standing. "I know these trips are vacations for you, but they're not for me. I pay for these fucking things for weeks afterward. If not from my wife, from my body. I just can't."

I realized, right then and there, that I was being told that I was an alcoholic. From Mark Wade. This guy who owned a half-dozen Fenders and played an infinite amount of bars and rubbed elbows with an equally infinite number of drinkers. And I was being told no. Some part of me even considered whether it was insubordination, but I let it die.

"Are you sure?"

"I'm sure," he nodded, staring me square in the eyes. He didn't want to, but he did. Mark has a way of making you feel the pain that he's going through as he does the right thing. He wore a *goddamn-this-face-hurts* expression, but he was serious.

I nodded, almost fighting back a wave of nausea and, embarrassingly, tears.

I walked back to a job that I wouldn't have for much longer.

14

"I WANT THIS CORD, right here, to go into this part of the receiver, right here, see?" Cole Downs proceeded to try jamming the wrong audio cable into my stereo with the tenacity only a person who'd been drinking since noon can muster. The cable wasn't remotely designed to plug into the spot Cole had chosen, but he kept trying all the same. Still, I was somehow following his logic, furrowing my brow and trying to help.

"Let's think about this," I said a few times, trying to wear my manager's hat. I could certainly strategize my way through this.

Cole worked at the bank and was roughly fifteen years younger than Wade. That's how I solved problems back then: *Go younger*. We'd gotten daydrunk and were holed up in the dark, shitty basement of my house, where if it rained too much, water would pool in all the uneven places. All the *faux*-wood paneling was peeling away from the concrete in great curls.

"I'm telling you," he tried again. "It will work."

"Let me try," I snatched the cable from his hands, trying to do the exact same thing he'd tried.

"No, man," he'd insist. "Let me."

And it'd go on like this for another fifteen minutes.

Finally, I slumped in a papasan with a popped seam. Cole sat on a wooden chair, propped against Mark's pool table that I'd somehow acquired. There were beer cans scattered all around the place—so many so that you'd trip through a forest of aluminum. Spent tea candles were all over the place, too, dripping wax in long bloody streams. We listened to music piped through all the surround-sound speakers I'd hidden in the exposed ceiling. Generally, Cole would just free-associate whatever music came to him: Animal Collective, Sigur Rós, Brian Eno, things I didn't want to hear in that state of mind.

Cole was one of the communications associates on my team, under Mark, and we'd hit it off quickly. He was a stand-up comedian on the side, which, when I heard that, I rolled my eyes. It's kind of like when you hear someone is in a band and they send you their SoundCloud link. You either don't listen or wince the entire time after pushing "Play." You just know your relationship is bound to change because you can't lie about how much you don't like it.

Turns out, Cole is an amazingly funny person—dry, smart, confident, able to work a room.

And at first, I latched onto Cole because he didn't have kids and didn't care that I did. He liked to go out and rip it up. Cole was everything I wanted and needed: a Tesla coil of energy and endless song recommendations. He'd routinely pass out at our house and text his boss Mark that he wasn't going to make it into work in the morning, even though his boss's boss (me) was slogging into the office.

The real reason I latched onto Cole was because he was such a gentle, genuine spirit—someone who wasn't out to hurt anyone. At that point, I didn't trust myself not to ruin someone else or accidentally destroy someone's life without trying. He had this quality about him that was endearing. To this day, when he hears a song or an album that resonates with him, he'll start pestering you about it. Over and over and over again.[25] You'll get texts and instant messages at work about whether you've listened to it. And it's not because Cole's obnoxious or something—no, it's because he's one of those rare people who genuinely wants you to love something as much as he does. Cole is happiest when you're on the exact same emotional wavelength as him.

---

[25] Cole's "tiny" (and complete) list of recommendations to me over the years: The Album Leaf, Alex G, …And You Will Know Us by the Trail of Dead, Animal Collective, The Antlers, Atlas Sound, Beach Fossils, Beach House, Bibio, Blanck Mass, The Books, Brian Eno, Cloud Nothings, Crystal Castles, Cymbals Eat Guitars, Dan Deacon, Deerhunter, Destroyer, Die Antwoord, Diiv, Dune Rats, Explosions in the Sky, Fear of Men, Frankie Rose, French Kicks, Fuck Buttons, Hammock, Here We Go Magic, Hookworms, The Horrors, Hot Chip, I Break Horses, Inventions, Jamie xx, Japandroids, Jefre Cantu-Ledesma, Jon Hopkins, Julianna Barwick, Kurt Vile, Lotus Plaza, Lower Dens, M83, Mikal Cronin, My Bloody Valentine, Mystery Jets, The National, Ought, Panda Bear, Parquet Courts, Pavement, Perfume Genius, The Radio Dept., Real Estate, Rogue Wave, School of Seven Bells, Slowdive, SOAK, Stephen Malkmus & The Jicks, Strand of Oaks, The Streets, A Sunny Day in Glasgow, Swervedriver, Tanlines, This Will Destroy You, Toro Y Moi, Ty Segall, Volcano Choir, The War on Drugs, Washed Out, Wavves, Waxahatchee, Wild Nothing, Wolf Parade, WU LYF, Yo La Tengo, Youth Lagoon, and Yuck.

"Paul."

I snapped awake. Ethereal shoegaze music was fluttering between speakers, and Cole's head was bobbing dreamily to it.

"What?"

"You're falling asleep."

"No I wasn't."

"Come on, man."

I wasn't so much interested in the music as having Cole near. There was comfort in having someone as drunk as me right next to my side. The music lulled me right back to sleep.

"Paul!"

And it'd continue like this well into the night.

ONCE, THERE WAS a crew of about five or six workers who arrived right on the button at eight o'clock in the morning, tearing out all our house's windows and replacing them with new ones. It was one of the few grown-up decisions Carrie and I had made as a married couple—adding equity to a hundred-year-old house—and there I was, listening to them bang on the door, trying to get in for their scheduled appointment. Cole snapped to attention last. Beer cans were everywhere. Carrie had long since left for work, and I was barely aware of the knocking, as if it was coming from another room. My brain did that quick Holy Shit math, even fogged with drunkenness, that allows you to spring into motion. So they proceeded to tear the windows out, one by one—sawing and hacking and cutting—and the wind blasted through the place. But Cole and

I didn't care. Cole cracked open a beer and so did I, guzzling it down. I drank until I felt human enough to drive us to a place that might serve around nine o'clock in the morning.

"YOU NEVER FOLLOW through," he casually said, sipping warm beer from one of those hard-plastic Coca-Cola cups that pizza places use.

"Usually gets colder by about eleven," the old lady said from behind the bar. It was her means of an apology, although she was more dismayed two people showed up not for the breakfast bar but for the actual bar at nine. She'd clearly made an exception and connected nozzles to the draft beer for us. Warm Miller Lite at nine-thirty a.m.

"What do you mean I don't follow through?"

Nothing hurt my alcoholic ego like a casual slight—it was a sliver under the skin. I was under the impression that I had it all figured out and people pretty much adored how well-organized I was. Nothing was remotely close to that.

"What about my comedy show last week?"

"I told you Oliver was sick."

"Yeah, but I have them every Thursday."

Got me there.

"My birthday campout?"

Ugh. Nothing turned my stomach more than the thought of camping with a bunch of coworkers in the middle of Kentucky farm-country, firing off guns and drinking until the first daylight leaks across the horizon. But, of course, drunkenly I'd said yes—because when you're drinking and everyone else is saying yes, you can't *not* get caught up in agreeable momentum. You commit without even thinking twice.

I'd even peppered him that morning of the campout with a few *maybe I-will/maybe I-won't-make-it* text messages.

"Right."

He listed off at least a dozen recent instances of things I'd committed to, but failed to appear at—all minor offenses in my brain, but they were clearly major in his. I was sort of blown away by how many there were—and then I got defensive. And then I got angry at myself. I was constantly putting myself out there and then never following through. The idea of something sounded infinitely better than the actual *doing*—especially as an alcoholic.

I sat there on my threadbare stool as they fired up the pizza ovens, feeling even worse about myself than before with the hangover.

"It's just that I can't plan anything with you, man," he said. "Kind of hard to make a friendship with someone who, when it comes down to it, never shows up as your friend."

That was right around the time Carrie called, angrily, to ask if two drunk guys, including her husband, had left a window-replacement crew alone at her house.

COLE ONCE HAD a wedding reception to attend near my wife's hometown, so we'd driven him there as a favor. I secretly leapt for joy, knowing that I'd have a built-in excuse to drink. I delivered him to that reception, but not before toasting him with a tall boy of Miller Lite in the church parking lot. I downed mine in two giant gulps, ignoring the cold gasoline burn from my throat down into my belly. Cole was more mindful with his, sipping it and coming up with foam on his upper lip.

"I can't drink this whole fucking thing," he laughed at the absurdity of it, then realized with horror that I'd already downed mine.

I expected him to be impressed. Instead, I saw a flicker of pity in his eyes, like I was a rope-trick cowboy who'd wandered out onto a Coachella stage. I shrugged, said goodbye to Cole, and drank the rest of his beer. I mentally figured out how much I could drink without being wasted to the point where Carrie (or Carrie's parents) wouldn't let me drive to get Cole, or me actually being too fucked-up to get him at all.

Later that night, Cole emerged from the reception hall looking like a depressed mannequin. Worse than that, Drunk Cole was sort of like having three aliens remote-controlling separate sections of his body, pretending to be a human adult. He seemed to move in competing directions at once.

"Cole," I shouted from the window of my car. "I'm over here."

He looked around the parking lot, then wandered in the complete opposite direction of my vehicle. After getting him into the car, he slumped into his seat and spouted off some gibberish about the wedding. Something about making someone mad and forgetting to say goodbye to someone else.

"Fuck it," he waved at the reception hall.

"All right."

I put the car in reverse and he started tossing the interior of my car, looking for something.

"What'd you lose?"

"My beer. Where's my beer?"

"What beer? Did you bring a beer out with you?"

"No," he switched the interior light on. "The beer from before."

"From earlier? When I dropped you off?"

"Yeah."

"I drank it."

Cole's eyes went black. *"What?"*

"I drank it," I shrugged.

He took this betrayal the only way he knew how: unplugging my iPhone from my stereo and replacing it with his. Seconds later, we were listening to Aphex Twin while I proceeded to get us lost deep in the country. My phone was dying and, to make matters even worse, the car was down to the last fuel cell on the dashboard. Nothing looked familiar. I drove up and down pitch-black country roads which, in daylight, already looked identical. I saw deer eyes glowing from the side of the road in my high beams as desperation started sinking in. It was too late for Carrie to pick up the phone, so she wasn't answering my frantic calls. We drove around and around in circles—the glow of a distant town many miles away.

Panic percolated the alcohol in my body. I could feel it burning through my veins, and I was getting dizzier by the second. My mouth was going dry, and I wished I *had* hidden Cole's beer from before.

"I think we're lost, man," I said.

No response from Cole.

"Did you hear me?"

Seconds later, Cole's head slumped onto my shoulder. He

was completely passed out. The seatbelt only did so much as he sort of bobbed around in the passenger seat. Whenever I made a turn, he turned with it. He may as well have been dead. The night was crashing down all around me: the unfamiliar surroundings, the ghost of my buzz, the gas light. Cole wasn't helping.

I suddenly jammed the wheel hard to the left, throwing Cole's body to the right. There was an audible smack as his head connected with the passenger-side window. It didn't wake him up. He just groaned and leaned forward, his head suspended over his knees.

I turned to the road outlined in the high beams in front of me. The narrowness of the night was familiar—how I was always cutting it too close for comfort. And yet, some distant part of me didn't recognize that, so much as it recognized that I loved the rush of not knowing how I was going to make it out on the other side. I yearned for moments like that: the barely-controlled chaos of a night where everything was somehow miraculously held in place, but constantly threatening to spin apart at any given second.

I drove, listening to Cole snore, and hoped for the best.

WHEN YOUR FRIENDS begin getting younger and younger, you start not recognizing yourself in them. You're in unsettling territory. Everything looks and sounds like it should, but everything's just slightly off. It's like you're in the foreign version of your life's TV show, not the real one. You don't have as much to connect with. Your jokes are a little too obscure, but not by much. Just enough. Your points of references get blank looks. You don't feel young—you feel twice as old. And that's because you're shaving a few layers deeper than you should, whittling the wood too finely. When everyone around you is in their twenties and you're in your mid-thirties, you don't have a lot of common ground beyond drinking. No one around me had signed mortgage documents yet. No one was engaged, much less married. Diaper-changing was a foreign, repulsive concept. All the responsibilities I was avoiding by hanging out with people like Cole, were all things that were still a decade down the road.

Even surrounded by Cole and his friends at a table for bar trivia night, I'd have pangs of emptiness. I drank them away. I was the oldest guy there.

I needed to get away.

I MADE A REAL production out of attending one of Cole's comedy performances, making sure he knew I was coming well in advance. I even hit him with countless texts, reminding him. I showed up early. I bought him beers. I dropped hints suggesting that it wasn't easy getting out of the house, even though it wasn't any problem at all. This would balance out the ledger, I figured. Cole was performing in one of the worst imaginable stand-up locations ever: in the front window of a hipster hot dog restaurant under a single light on a Sunday night. They'd literally removed the four-seat table there in the window and crammed some makeshift stereo equipment in its place along with a microphone stand.

The restaurant was tiny as it was—a shoebox with a bar that didn't quiet its televisions nor the chatter of the kitchen just a few paces from the stand-up comedians. People shouted over the jokes and held loud conversations with themselves. And yet, Cole sat at the edge of the bar, nursing a drink and scribbling things down on a crinkled napkin. I didn't watch the comics, really, nor was I listening to them. I couldn't stomach the agony of watching their jokes evaporate into the silent, laughless crowd. More than that, my heart was beating a mile a minute, waiting for Cole to take to the microphone. I was genuinely nervous for him. I was sweating there, well into the fourth hipster craft-brew they had on tap.

I wanted to protect Cole from the crowd, thinking they were more like the dagger-pit trap of a jungle adventure, just waiting for him to plummet into them. The closer it got to Cole's set, the more I needed to drink. The adrenaline was burning off my buzz. Finally, he took the stage after three hilariously unfunny comedians, introduced himself, and proceeded to kill. One joke after the next, he had the room. He even managed to seamlessly work the conversations other people were having at the bar into the set. It was nothing short of miraculous.

I used to recall this moment before a big presentation, trying to summon an ounce of Cole's easy confidence behind a microphone. Even if a joke wasn't going over well, you could see his brain already moving on to something else. He wasn't mourning its death or getting caught in some sad spiral of self-pity. Cole simply moved on. *Oh well,* he shrugged with a grin. *That didn't work.* To the next joke. And the one after that. And he told them with precision. He didn't stammer; he wasn't nervously flustered. He was there, live and present—a command over all the people eating hot dogs slathered with mango chutney.

More than anything, he just did it. I'll never forget that: the easy manner in which he set a goal and accomplished it. Simply by showing up and being there.

And when it was over, it was over.

Later, when I reminded him I'd been there that night, he cut me off.

"I get it. You're here."

But I really wasn't.

15

I WAS RUNNING out of excuses at work. There at the bank, change is a way of life. You usually get fresh starts twice a year with a new set of managers. But even then, people start to talk. It's not like with every organizational change comes a tidal shift where titles and responsibilities and performance, like shells and rocks, are churned into vanishing clouds. I'd been moved out of management and was now a low-level communications officer in a group of marketing people who really, really, really wanted to work in an ad agency. Marketing people, if you don't know this already, can be insane. Batshit insane. I'm not just saying this to get a rise out of you (or them). Ask a marketing person for yourself and they'll tell you: their wiring is off. Everything they say carries a sense of belligerent entitlement to it. That's because they know their worlds are built on decisions and impressions—not hard numbers or facts. Some high-level executive said "I really like this campaign" two years before, and entire departments sprouted out of that. Smart people get out and move on to the next thing; the not-so-smart people stay, but they get meaner and more aggressive, like a territorial dog fed once every week. They hold meetings because they're enamored with the idea of meetings. They stare at each other across conference room tables and debate adjectives. And when you're working in the marketing arm of a bank, everyone is fighting over taglines and stray bits of copy that appear on mortgage statements or those inserts that appear alongside your credit card bills. There weren't even campaigns. Not at my level, at least, there weren't. It's like a dozen farmers on the same half-acre of land.

In a huge company, you can hide. I've never been one to do that but when you cease to care, you start to pray for invisibility. I did the least required; I did just enough to not get noticed. I'd contribute an edit to a sentence of copy and see it red-marked into oblivion by three managers who knew better than me. So I showed up to work more hungover by the day, sometimes sleeping it off in the parking lot. My work got sloppier. I'd write something, turn it in and go home for the day. I took days off without warning. I called in sick. I even called in Really Sick once by intimating that my doctor didn't like the look of my lab results. (He didn't, but the truth of the matter was that he was frowning at my liver enzymes, not my white blood cell count.)

Like I said, I was running out of excuses.

So I quit.

I felt cornered by nothing except my own alcoholism. I honestly felt it was the only way out: quitting. Not furtively looking for more work or maybe a position in a different department—just living off savings and thinking another job would magically appear.[26]

CARRIE WAS IN full-on panic mode. She was the only one between the two of us who seemed to understand that you can't keep cashing out retirement savings or living off credit cards. To me, that's just how people got by when their jobs didn't work out. She immediately drew up a budget using construction paper and our kids' crayons, and nowhere on it was "entertainment" or "booze." I was mortified. I argued with her that we'd get by—that I'd get a job.

"There's an order to these things," she hissed. "You can't just keep quitting jobs because you don't like the people you work with."

Truth be told, I felt special. I felt above everyone and everything—I was going to survive this Tunguska event, even if every other goddamn sign told me I wouldn't. I could feel the air pressure giving way, see the fuselage ripping apart, the fire boiling from the seams—but I didn't care. I knew that good things came to people like me.

Or so I thought.

No job came. For the next couple of days, I was baffled that no one called me to interview for the jobs I applied for on

---

[26] Spoiler alert: it didn't.

Indeed.com. I'd somehow forgotten just how hard it'd been to find a job in the first place. Getting my shitty editing job had taken every bit of a year—especially with me massaging the details of my resume out a little, to explain some of the missing time and details. Even the references weren't connected to previous jobs. And the bank job had come down like divine providence—a job interview out of the blue, followed by a battery of other interviews before eventually getting promotion after promotion after promotion.

Drinking hadn't just made me feel invincible—it erased the memory of agony.

Before I knew it, there was a red *For Sale* sign being hammered in our front yard. We simply couldn't afford to live where we lived. Hell, we couldn't afford anywhere. Every few hours, Carrie would break down crying and not tell me why. The neighbors were all shocked, mock-joking with us: "Was it something we said?" (If they really wanted the answer, it rested in the recycling bin that I drug to the street every Tuesday morning: a truly jaw-dropping collection of plastic pints and beer bottles, strewn with boxed chardonnays and budget zinfandels. Maybe a bottle of olive oil.)

I had to do something drastic.

I had to make a change.

I had to pull the rip cord.

At four-thirty a.m., bleary-eyed on Facebook, I sent a message to an old friend who still lived in Phoenix and was hiring.

It was a flare fired in the dark—and one that would catch my entire ocean, now flooded with gasoline, on fire.

THREE

You abuse the ones who love you,
You abuse the ones who won't.
If you ever had a real heart,
I don't think you'd know where to start.
'Cause I think I'm coming down.
I think I'm coming down.
I think I'm coming down.

Yeah, I think I'm coming down.

—Dum Dum Girls

16

HIGHWAY 17 RIBBONS across the high desert of northern Arizona—a gray scribble of road through scrub-brush, vast green-orange swaths of pine and oyster-colored Kaibab Limestone. The two-hour stretch between Flagstaff and Phoenix is something I've often played through my head: the way the road curls and loops back in on itself, teasing the desert beyond. You get hints of it, but never all at once. The San Francisco Peaks dominate the landscape in your rearview

mirror—peppered with trees, salted with snow—and keep
quiet watch against the perfect-blue sky.

When the highway finally emerges into the Verde Valley,
it opens up on the sort of sweeping spectacle that's reserved
for John Ford movies from the 1930s. Civilization is sparse,
scattered and sun-blasted, flanked high by the Mogollon Rim.
17 suddenly cuts steep and sharp into the valley, reaching
forward into an almost interminable line. It yawns so far that it
looks impossibly long, like you'll never make it there yourself.
You can't imagine ever making it that far toward the horizon,
where it begins yet another climb before getting swallowed
into the dark folds of another mountain range.

Clearly, I'd romanticized the drive for years after landing
back in Ohio—the special kind of self-torture reserved for
people who don't understand that they never actually made
the decisions that landed them where they were. I simply
couldn't do the math on how I'd been pulled back into Ohio's
black gravity well. I couldn't escape it. Now, years later, I was
driving Carrie's Alero back into the heart of the valley, the same
one she'd bought for herself when graduating nursing school,
feeling both victorious and ashamed.

I could feel it tugging at my thoughts—the dull sense that
I was forcing all this to happen. I was awkwardly jamming this
puzzle piece into place. It'd already been three long days of
driving from Columbus—hours spent alone with my thoughts
and Spotify, whenever the signal was strong enough. Very
often, there'd be long stretches of bleached emptiness where
I'd hear nothing at all. I'd be driving through some windswept
corner of Oklahoma when Spotify would start pixelating, as if
someone was stealing the track, block by block, and retreating

with it. The songs wouldn't just vanish without warning—they'd die slow, cancerous deaths, disappearing into a garbled wash.

This is precisely how I felt about my life at that moment.

Then it'd just be me for miles, hurtling toward a life I'd neither expected nor deserved.

When Highway 17 broke through the tree line and angled down into the valley, I was exhausted. The monotony of the drive had gotten to me. I flipped on the cruise control and reached behind me, where my red Arc'teryx bag (the same one I'd bought in Flagstaff back in grad school, actually) was stuffed behind the passenger seat, along with three oversized luggage bags that belonged to Carrie. I'd crammed three screw-top Miller Lite cans into the bag at the last gas station. They were rewards for the end of the road.

This, of course, made no sense.

It's not like there weren't gas stations or liquor stores at my destination—nor was I at the "end of the road." I'd convinced myself otherwise, but the dark part of myself knew what they were really for. No, the alcoholic in me had already it worked out that the three aluminum cans of Miller Lite would be just what I needed to finish off the drive.

I shakily unzipped the bag, like a nervous teenager fumbling at a bra. I jerked it open partway and reached inside, feeling the cold, beaded sweat on the cans. I plucked out one of the cans, then jammed it between my legs. I considered what I was about to do. I'd never actively drunk while driving before. This was new territory. I'd driven drunk, sure, but never in broad daylight and never while behind the wheel.

I convinced myself this was a toast to new beginnings, that I was celebrating my arrival back in Arizona.

I twisted off the screw-top lid, carefully setting it down in the cup holder to my right. I didn't want to spill anything. I made sure there were no cars around (which was sort of easy, since the other line of traffic was a quarter-mile away on the opposite side), gingerly put the beer to my lips, then downed three-quarters of it. The beer was cold, bracing. I felt an immediate rush and not entirely from the beer—it was sort of liberating driving into the valley, where I'd imagined being so many times before, and drinking out in the open. I felt free. I made sure my speed was right where it needed to be, then finished the rest. My throat burned for a few seconds before melting into that familiar warmth, creeping up my shoulder blades and loosening up my thoughts.

This was my normal.

I screwed the lid back on and slipped the can back into the bag, reaching for a second one.

I HAD NO IDEA how long I'd be out in Phoenix before the house sold or before my family could move out to join me. At the end of the three beers, I wasn't guessing long, but alcoholics have a magical sort of short-term optimism. It was a gamble, but we were hopeful. In the interim, I had zero plan. None. The short-term plan was to hole up in a motel for a bit, then hope some friends would eventually help me out. If nothing else, I'd have to make new friends. After all, things always worked out for me, I kept telling myself.

In the meantime, I landed on a Saturday evening at a Quality Suites in Tempe, Arizona. My new job started on Monday. It was a sad, broken motel with a ramshackle courtyard littered with palm bark. The pool attracted teenagers who clearly weren't even staying at the motel, where they'd smoke pot while swimming and occasionally looking to see if anyone from the front office was paying attention. No one was.

The motel was the kind of place you stayed if you were running away from home, cheating on your husband, or doing meth. There were lots of doors halfway open, giving glimpses into other worlds: people yelling at each other in Spanish, kids peeking out while adults were passed out on their bed. I paid for a full week up front, carting my bags into a room that reeked of industrial disinfectant. There were so many awful, competing smells that they sort of cancelled each other out. I immediately got used to it, pulled out my computer and hooked up to the super-slow complimentary Wi-Fi. My room key kept not working and the front desk insisted it was because I was sticking the key in my wallet with my other credit cards, which would demagnetize the hotel key.

Whatever.

My room was a modest-sized living room, a kitchenette with a sink that groaned when you turned it on, a bathroom with some rusted fixtures, and a cramped bedroom. The only saving grace of the bedroom was that it looked directly out on the parking lot, so I could see if anyone was breaking into the Alero, should I care to watch while I did nothing. There was a large black stain in the doorway, so heavily scrubbed that the checkered carpeting was almost a shiny, solid surface. I couldn't help but think that the room was where someone had answered a knock at the door, then gotten capped in the head by a jealous lover.

The first night there, I FaceTimed with the kids, my thoughts more taken with the palm trees and the smell of sand.

This was home, I told myself.

The three Miller Lites were gone well before I'd reached Tempe. Once I shut FaceTime off, I considered how I'd spend my Saturday night alone.

DIRECTLY ACROSS THE street was one of those fake Mexican eateries that tries so hard to look authentic: ceramic red tile; thatched roof; fake adobe façade. The neon signs beckoned to me as I crossed Scottsdale Road. It was a furnace outside and the wisps of high cirrus caught fire in the early sunset. As I walked in, I decided this place was going to be my anchor. It'd be my home base of operations. The hotel suite wouldn't work—I needed an endless selection of poison to calm my anxiety. The first blast of air conditioning rattled me—it was at least a forty-degree difference inside. It was packed, Saturday night and all, but I managed to squeeze in at the bar.

The trick I normally pull when people strike up conversation with me at a bar is that I pretend I have no idea where I am. It's my default: to lie. It's easier to make something up than explain the whole situation: I'd quit my corporate job for no reason; I'd been unemployed for three months; our savings had dried up; I'd moved 3,000 miles away to secure a job for my family; I was waiting for them to come out; I was an alcoholic who'd caused all the terrible weather in his life.

I tried ordering a draft Kiltlifter, a local brew remembered from my grad college days, but they had just cashed the keg minutes before I arrived. (A fucking red flag from the universe.) So I ordered a bottle of Miller Lite instead and a side shot of Jameson. I didn't even like Jameson. I just ordered it because the guy next to me had ordered one, and I pointed at his glass and said, "And one of those, too," when I ordered the beer. It seemed so suave to me, but it was really just the equivalent of me ordering a Number 4 Meal at Burger King because no one really likes to order a Whopper combo meal by name.

I waited for someone to ask me where I was from, so I could make up a variation of why I was in the bar—business trip, reclusive author, press junket for a movie—but no one asked. No one cared. I studied my iPhone, texted friends. Big Neal sent me questions I didn't feel like answering; Cole sent me memes; Wade sent me "ha," which meant he wasn't really into hearing from me.

I reached my cruising altitude, alone around other people, paid the tab with money I didn't have and stumbled back to my motel. I couldn't bear the thought of returning to a room without the pillow of more alcohol. That was unbearable. Anxiety pooled around my thoughts, so I wandered over to the gas station. I plucked a six-pack of Fat Tire from the cooler and shuffled to the corner where they kept a narrow shelf of wine. I grabbed a dusty liter of Barefoot chardonnay by its neck and went to the counter.

"Need a corkscrew?" the pimply kid asked.

"God," I nodded, feeling myself flush with thanks. "You're a lifesaver."

I drunkenly tried giving him a tip for being so kind and thoughtful.

"Please. I insist."

I kept trying to give the kid a moist, wrinkled dollar bill. He regarded me like I was a TV channel that wasn't quite coming in clearly.

Minutes later, I was in my room, fumbling with the budget corkscrew. I jammed it into the bottle and the metal bent as I levered it against the glass. The cork was old and brittle, kind of crumbling as I yanked it free. The wine came out in a sour blast. I took one of the plastic shrink-wrapped water cups and poured it three-quarters of the way full. I braced myself and swallowed the sweet gasoline down. I really didn't want to taste any of it—I just wanted it to burn out the thoughts of everything at home. That's all I was trying to do in Phoenix: flamethrow back all the realities that kept crawling into view. I didn't want to think of what I was missing back in Ohio—the house sale, the cost of moving everyone out, all the unknowns.

I flipped Facebook on and switched my status to "Lives in Tempe, Arizona."

I was in Arizona, yes, but I certainly wasn't living.

SUNDAY WAS RECONNAISSANCE. I woke up around eleven. Right around the time that housekeeping was knocking on doors. I could tell they were practiced at knocking harder than nice hotels. They probably did a lot of mid-morning evictions. Part of me wondered how much fear those housekeeping ladies operated under—just how tuned-out and disconnected they'd have to be after all the horrific things they'd seen and discovered.

There's nothing more beautiful to me than those first

seconds when you open your hotel room door: the hard reset refreshing everything inside.

I'd lucked into a job at the *Arizona Republic* or, rather, its parent company, Gannett. Andrea, my friend from my days at the shady non-profit, was now a senior-level marketing person there. We'd kept in contact and three months after I'd left Credit Dauphine, she miraculously had a position open under her. To hear it from her, the person she'd hired had failed their background check with flying colors. So this felt like it was meant to be. But my drive down from Flagstaff had taught me otherwise—that this time was different. Something was off. I couldn't put my finger on it, but I dimly knew that my time in Phoenix had a shelf life.

I drove around, trying to get my bearings again. It came back to me quickly, but Tempe had grown and changed quickly. There were new subdivisions and strip malls and shopping districts at nearly every turn. It wasn't unlike weeds along sidewalks, sprouting up after being left alone too long. This wasn't my town anymore. I'd left it behind years before and now it all belonged to someone else. Towns like Phoenix don't really care about history.

I mapped out my drive to work, clocking it. I met Sean, the same guy who launched himself from my balcony, at a poolside bar where he was performing. His shirt was soaked through with sweat. I had at least four beers and a shot at the cabana bar, treating people I didn't know to drinks. I split the bill across two credit cards so my wife wouldn't notice. It was a treat after figuring out where I'd be showing up the following day. It was another reward.

I showed up to work that Monday with the sort of hangover

that's so bad you don't actually feel it. It constantly feels like that wet sheet of ice that remains standing in place after you lower your car window. It's temporary—a mask that could slide off at any second. I was holding it together the best I could, having drunk less than usual the night before. The lack of sleep burned behind my eyeballs as I stepped into the lobby. I was corralled with the other new hires into a conference room for orientation. It was all I could do to act the part of a human being and not erupt into a bunch of foam snakes when the HR person asked me questions.

I kept telling myself what I had told Andrea in a text message: *I'm going to be a rock star employee.*

She'd texted back: *I'm not worried.*

She should've been.

17

THE JOB VERY quickly turned out to be pretty mindless work, just short of data entry work or maybe ringing up groceries. It was nothing that I'd been sold on, but it was a job and a pretty good-paying one at that. The role was "Consumer Engagement Manager," but the actual job was creating junk mail and spam for all the newspapers Gannett ran. The newspaper market was steadily evaporating: decades-long columnists laid off, full departments unceremoniously shuttered, entire offices closed. Tiny little areas like mine were doing everything we could to keep subscribers before they realized they could get their news for free somewhere else. True sadness is touring the emptied-out mazes of old art departments and news bullpens, all derelict ships sitting in broad daylight. They kept the lights on above, but no one was around.

My job was to remind grandparents that they could buy digital versions of the newspapers they liked holding in their hands. It was hopeless from the start. But we had surgical demographic data delivered to my team: unnervingly specific information about our subscribers—their likely interests, hobbies, salaries—all sorted by ZIP code.

You never really think about all the work that goes into crafting mailers and junk-mail messages that people never read. For the most part, people never even make it past the subject line. It all usually just caused people to unsubscribe from the mailing lists. I told myself that the job would straighten out— that this was all temporary. This is what naturally happens to married people with kids when they're alone—you're circling the airport, waiting to land. But I was grateful. I was in a high-rise office again, overlooking all of downtown Phoenix.

I felt important. Below me was the NBC affiliate studio where they shot the local news. The wide-angled conference rooms looked down on rooftops where air-conditioning fans fought and wheeled against the heat. It was the sort of workplace that yielded good Instagram photos.

I made fast friends with my coworkers: all of them in their early twenties, mostly right out of college. This was their first job, their first foray into the working world. It was all as new to them as it was curiously exciting: cubicle life, instant-messaging in-jokes back and forth, swiping a badge to get into the building, the quiet ways in which being in the lower rungs of a career can kill you—the not-knowing, the worry of making the cut, the lack of information. I realized I'd taken a step back in life—a considerable one—but I'd rebound, I told myself. This was like the hard reset of hotel rooms. It'd refresh my life.

THE DOOR TO MY ROOM was cracked open when I got back to the motel. I double-checked the number to make sure it was actually my room. Maybe I'd forgotten. No, it was 233. I stood on the landing there on the second floor, sort of frozen in the heat. The bright smell of Clorox or maybe meth caught me as I stood there. Finally, I trudged toward the door, half-expecting some of those pool teenagers to be fucking around in my room. Or maybe a meth-head rooting around my drawers and medicine bag for something they could sell.

I nudged the door open with my shoe.

The first thing I saw was the ridiculously large bottle of chardonnay (my second in under three days) sitting on the sink. It was half-empty. (That was my handiwork, no one else's.)

Nothing was missing. Some of my clothes were neatly folded on the bed. In fact, it was nicer than when I'd been there. Someone had taken care of everything while I was gone, tidying up the place.[27] I called the front desk and told them that someone had broken into my room. The front desk clerk told me that the cleaning woman had probably just forgotten to shut my door. There were no police reports; there was not even a visit to my room from management. Nothing. This was the Quality Suites. I'd rather something had been stolen. I would have had more closure that way—I wouldn't have the

---

[27]This was a pattern completely wasted on me.

faint sense that someone had blustered through my room and found nothing of value.

A few days later, I stuffed some of my work shirts into one of the plastic dry-cleaning bags and brought it to the front desk. It'd be easier to have them press it. Plus, I was goddamn lazy.

The woman at the front desk looked at the bag like I was offering her a biohazard.

"Do you know that I don't think we've ever had someone use this service?" she said.

"Really?"

She nodded. "I've been here three years, too."

My clothes came back the next day. One of my shirts was missing.

I didn't report it.

It didn't matter. Phoenix was taking me apart slowly, one shirt at a time.

TWO WEEKS ALONE is enough time to get you acclimated to a job, but it's not enough time to distract you from the fact that something's missing. My kids were being watched by a nanny we couldn't afford. Carrie was going insane trying to transition out of her job, keep the house clean enough for potential buyers to tour it and decide they didn't want it, and keeping the kids' eating and sleeping schedules together. Time alone in Phoenix started to feel like the lower depths of the movie *Inception*—the deeper I went, the more time crawled to a syrup. I felt every second pass by.

So I drank more.

My life as a grad student had more structure than this existence I was trying to mete out. It consisted of waking up, washing four Ibuprofen down with the last warm gulp of beer, eating a breakfast sandwich on the way into work, staring at a computer screen for eight hours, and returning to a shitty motel room. Repeat. I didn't have Jesus; I didn't have friends; I didn't have a real routine. My family was a phantom limb that throbbed at inconvenient times. I'd be sitting in some marketing meeting, and I'd feel my thoughts telescope out to Ohio.

Once, I was on a call with the publisher of an Oregon newspaper, which was in my marketing zone. He was a soft-spoken, browbeaten man who you instantly felt sorry for. This was his life. He'd spent decades carving out this career for himself—having gotten to know everything about Eugene, Oregon. Someone at my level shouldn't be talking to someone at his, but that speaks volumes about how awful things were in the newspaper world. He was willing to try anything and talk to anyone. He was an old-school guy, someone who probably grew up delivering the very same paper he was now the head of. We were discussing a new campaign I'd come up with: junk mail and spam with a twist. Mine would have heart. It'd have the stories of their two outdoors photographers on them. Maybe even a map of the Oregon hiking trails or sights. I'd thrown a ton of ideas at him in an email, which he'd taken to. Now, on the phone, I was a different person.

"So, what are you thinking? Bios of the photographers? Quotes? That sort of thing?"

"Yeah, uh-huh," I nodded, absently scribbling on a notepad. "Something with quotes."

"Tri-fold? Full-color? Something bigger?"

"I'm thinking probably interviewing the photographers and getting a few quotes."

Silence.

Mild panic settled in and I snapped back into the conversation. My brain was jangled—full of loose, sour voltage.

"For the email campaign," I tried to salvage it, "I was thinking of a map. Dotted lines all over, showing where you can go to sightsee."

"Talk to me about this campaign," he put the word in air quotes. "Is this going to be a phased approach? Several emails? Different ones targeted to different subsections of subscribers?"

Very often, I'll realize I'm in the middle of talking to someone and feel out-of-body about it. My brain goes blank. I stand outside myself. This guy could've been talking to a hologram of myself and he would've had better luck getting good answers.

"That's right," I lied.

"About which part?"

I was losing him. My brain was on fire from the night before. My cell phone was blowing up with frantic texts from my wife saying our youngest, Oliver, had a fever and someone had inquired about looking at the house but she couldn't do it because she had a sick kid on her hands. I was worried when my next drink would be.

It was also eleven in the morning.

"It'll be an email with a map and—"

"Wait. I thought this was a campaign."

"Well, it is."

"A campaign is more than just an email," he was losing confidence in me, the air coming fast out of the balloon. "So, are you saying this is just an email?"

"No, we'll have a printed thing, too."

"A printed thing."

"That's right. A mailer. We'll do postcards, probably."

"With quotes."

"Right."

"And a map of hiking trails."

"Yes."

"Yes about what? Which part?"

"The trails."

"But not the quotes?"

I was so disconnected from the conversation that I was mentally floating high above Phoenix, looking down on the circuit-board symmetry of it all. I wasn't talking to a man who'd run a newspaper for the last two decades, whose name was firmly on the masthead and his photograph was austere and kind. I was hearing a voice that was taking on familiar tones: disbelief, doubt. I was thinking about how I could sneak off to the gourmet pizza place I'd discovered and slam a pint at noon. That'd set me right.

"Paul?"

"Right. Yeah. Quotes and a map."

There were some other words said. Mostly pleasantries that brought the conversation back down to earth so we could at least end on a semi-professional note. Panic was starting to rise in me, delayed, like blood that seeps from a deep paper cut. The gravity of the phone call was starting to dawn on me. This is the sort of thing I should've prepared for—I shouldn't have assumed I was going to rock the conversation simply because I'd proposed ideas in an email. There's a big difference between throwing ideas down and convincing someone that you're truly going to deliver on those ideas. It wasn't any different than me sitting in the Wonder Bar back in Milan, deep into my seventh beer, and telling anyone within earshot that I'd be a screenwriter someday.

Both of us knew I wasn't going to deliver on anything I'd gotten his attention with a week earlier in the email.

"Don't worry. I've got this," I lied.

"Okay, Paul," he said.

I never spoke to him again.

A half hour later, I was hunched over the bar of a shitty Mexican restaurant near work, guzzling Corona as fast as I could.

Back when I worked at the theater, if you didn't clean the projectors regularly, the tiniest piece of dirt would scratch the film. Sometimes, you didn't really notice it. There'd just be this thin vertical line, that you kinda/sorta got used to while you were watching the movie. And it only got worse if you didn't clean the projector. If you were a lazy projectionist like me, sending that movie back through dirty sprockets over and over again, the scratches only got worse. If you weren't careful, those thin black lines grew into fat green ones and, eventually, wide yellow squiggles. Cyans, magentas, golds. That's when you knew you'd cut deep into the emulsion. The film couldn't ever be seen the same way again. That's exactly how I felt about my life, sitting there at a bar when I should've been at my desk.

I was cutting in deep now, and people were going to start noticing.

18

I AGREED TO DOG-SIT for one of my new coworkers while she and her boyfriend went away over Labor Day. I knew nothing about dogs, but they were a reprieve from two weeks at the Quality Inn. It was a four-day job in north Phoenix on the third floor of a fairly nice apartment complex. I couldn't say no. We were bleeding money with me at the motel, and I could stay at someone's house, free of charge, and enjoy their giant-screen television. The boyfriend, Dale, was about my height but had about fifty pounds of muscle on him and not a brain cell in his body. He spent hours in the gym but I'm convinced he only worked on his arms. Two hours in the gym in the morning, one hour at night. He was so dumb that he was almost gleefully open about it. Except he had zero personality. He was a dial tone of a human being. He sort-of enjoyed going through life acting like he *was just this side of having* had blunt-force head trauma in his youth. Truth be told, he was on a wide range of pills and powders that were impossibly well-organized in the kitchen cabinet. There were protein shakes and bottles and vials and tinctures and needles and elastic bands and everything in between. It was a pharmacy, right next to their shelves of Cheez-Its and Doritos.

He lovingly put everything into a duffel bag, one bottle at a time and made them travel-safe, lining it all with crumpled newspapers and rolled-up shirts. After giving me the tour of the place, telling me I had pretty much free rein until they got back. So long as Apollo and Rocky got their walks in, I was golden.

"You're doing us a solid here," he said.

"Sure, no problem. I'm really happy to help."

My coworker Robin, who I barely knew, had a screeching personality and one too many racist jokes for my liking. She was overweight and all sassy-pants, where everything she said was spoken like she'd just popped a chewing gum bubble. She mistook sass for being clever or decent. She brayed when she laughed, and usually at someone else's expense.

One morning, she took one look at me and screwed up her face in disgust.

"You dress yourself in the dark this morning? God."

Maybe my pants weren't pressed, but it's not like she wasn't wearing a black circus tent herself to work. Still, a free place to stay for four days was a free place to stay for four days. I'd sit down across from her, thinking a cold war had broken out, but then she'd suddenly invite me to come over to check out all the racist memes she was sharing on Facebook. She and one of my other meta-human coworkers would huddle in her cube, giggling over texts the other one was receiving. Whenever one of them scored a dick pic, she drew a hash mark on the dry-erase board in her cube. They were collectively up to eight, last I saw.

"And don't go snoopin'."

"Hahaha," I laughed. "I won't."

"I mean it," Dale narrowed his eyes. "I know where everything is in this place."

I had no fucking clue what he was talking about, but he seemed real certain that I wasn't to go searching through their shit.

So, Robin and Dale left for their extended weekend, giving me no instructions beyond "Here are their leashes." I carted all my luggage up the three flights of stone stairs into their apartment. I imagined what it'd be like if this was my new home, finally having settled after the few weeks of agony. The dogs were yapping and the Wi-Fi was incredibly slow. Robin watched reality TV; she didn't use the Internet, so they didn't pay for an expensive service. It was a slow morphine drip from website to website.

I stocked the fridge with a mini-keg of Heineken, a six-pack of Fat Tire, two bottles of wine, and a pint of whiskey. For a long weekend. I didn't really like the hard stuff all that much—beer and wine got me through just fine. But whiskey had started to sound good to me. Something in my cells was telling me it was the next logical step. Liquor always cut the parachute cords too quick and I'd be hurtling down to blackness before I knew it. I wanted the slow, gauzy burn of wine where the thoughts get dimmer and more ambitious at the same time.

That night, I successfully walked the dogs around the apartment complex, being careful not to have them make eye contact with other dogs. (This was apparently a big no-no because Apollo really didn't like other dogs—or people for that matter.) They tugged me around the complex for a good twenty minutes, and I thought of it as the only real obligation I had over that extended weekend. I deftly navigated them away from other dogs and people, the leashes wrapped so tight around my hand, my fingertips were white. I was terrified of losing them, like they were heavy helium balloons.

After I did the bare minimum with them, I climbed back up the three flights of stairs and looked down at the pool. It just seemed like too much work to get into my swimsuit and go back down into the early morning sun. A woman in her thirties was down there, though. She just seemed to have it all together—sun hat, sensible pool wear, sunglasses, coffee mug, two magazines. She'd found a nice swath of shadow near the water. It'd be dark for another two hours in that corner, easy, and she just seemed so fucking relaxed. It bothered me. How could someone be that put together and at ease with themselves? I was always filled with misdirected, nervous energy that carried me into places that didn't matter. I would've been a hell of a Y2K huckster.

I watched her from the balcony for a few minutes: the

way she casually drank her coffee, the manner in which she occasionally stood up and dipped her feet into the pool, then returned to her magazines.

It was beautiful.

It was about ten in the morning. I'd been in town for less than a month and I'd already curried several invites. My friend from elementary school, Tom Schenk, had graduated from the Marines to an IT job in Peoria, just north of where I was. He wanted to get together for some craft beers at a microbrewery he knew of. Some of my other coworkers were very sweet and kept inviting me out to their various, overbooked weekends: hard Sunday brunches, rooftop wine, hot yoga. One of the dads of the Ember Coast kids, himself clean and sober, was constantly reaching out for me to come over for dinner.

Expectations and appointments were like cancer to me. They blackened the time that lay ahead of me. That's all these were: diseased futures. I didn't want that. I wanted to watch movies on their tremendously large television and fade out into oblivion.

I was drinking before noon. I had the sort of depression that gives you a sense of entitled belligerence: *I'm allowed to do this.* Also, it excuses how terrible you feel about it all. You're constantly bargaining with yourself: *You're wasting your entire day and hiding out, but it's okay. You need to.*

After declining all the invites via Facebook or text message, disappointing a half-dozen people in less than five minutes, I shuttered the blinds and cracked open another beer.

I took the dogs for another walk, paced around the apartment a bit, checked my phone to see if there was any house news from Ohio and laid on the couch.

I SOMETIMES IMAGINE THAT an astronaut, who wakes up after his first night orbiting the earth, feels the exact same way alcoholic people do when they pass out in the middle of the day. They're disoriented, surrounded by perpetual night. It was nine o'clock. The air-conditioning was on, but in Phoenix, you can still sense the heat radiating outside. You can feel it on a different, subatomic level. You just know it's hot. Even in the dark with strange surroundings, I knew it was hot somewhere. I could also feel myself buoyed by beer bottles. I felt calm.

I groggily stood and saw Apollo and Rocky by the door. They shit all over the carpet. I'd missed their evening walk by about three hours.

I decided I'd scrub the carpets later.

I wandered to the fridge, grabbed a slice of cold pizza and another beer.

I checked my phone. Four missed calls and two missed FaceTime messages.

One last haunting text from Carrie:

Elliott and Oliver just wanted to say goodnight but you didn't answer.

WHEN ROBIN AND Dale returned, they offered to let me stay in the spare bedroom until I went back home for a friend's wedding. That was another seven days of no rent. My parents had sprung for a plane ticket for me to see the family, get the house in better shape to show potential buyers—and to simply be there. Most of my friends were quietly plotting an "Aren't you sure you'd prefer it back here?" campaign, too. I could feel a distant part of my brain relax. One less thing to worry about.

Robin was out buying groceries for the week. I gave her two twenties.

"I can't thank you enough," I told Dale, who was frowning at his laptop.

"You didn't use this, did you?" he asked.

"Your laptop? Me? No."

"Man," he gave the laptop a few sidelong glances, then me a distrustful one. "I told you not to go snooping."

"I didn't. I have my own computer."

He got quiet, which is just about the worst thing you could do to me at the time. When I was an active alcoholic, everything needed to be telegraphed and spelled out like in subtitled movies. No emotions or agendas went unchecked. No one could speak in code. It was all out in the open. I needed to know why he was so angry.

"You go through my collection, too?"

"Your what?"

He slammed the lid to his laptop.

"My fucking collection," he leaned forward. "You know what the fuck I'm talking about. Don't fuckin' pretend. You snooped."

A cartoonist couldn't possibly sketch a more imposing villain in the shape of this guy—all bulging circles, broad strokes across the shoulders, wide posture. Clench your fist and that's what he looked like—all bound and seized with anger.

"I didn't."

"Sure you did," he threw the laptop across the room to the other couch. In his anger, I'm pretty sure he didn't even care there was another piece of furniture to catch it. "Come with me. We're going to look together."

"What?"

I felt that cold emptiness of guilt—except I wasn't guilty of anything.

He turned to me, narrowing his eyes.

"Now."

I followed him into their bedroom—the one place where I hadn't gone the entire time I was there. I'd been warned before, so I'd avoided it.

Several paces ahead, the human fist stopped.

"Aw, what the fuck is *this?*"

I seized too, waiting for him to whirl around, swinging. Something was off about him—or, maybe, this was just his default factory setting. Either way, I didn't like being alone with him. Rage was simmering just below the surface with this guy. His face was growing a shade of red you only see in comic books. He was gritting his teeth when I saw what he was pointing at. There was dog shit around the bed, encircling it like little Asian votive candles or something.

"So you didn't walk the dogs either?"

"No, man, I walked them…"

"Don't fuckin' lie to me," he was seething.

"But I'm not."

I was just broken inside, just vulnerable enough, that I honestly felt like I was about to cry.

"So you're telling me that I'm lookin' at fuckin' dog shit

around my fuckin' bed," he was doing some real deductive reasoning now, "and they don't shit when they've been walked. But I'm seeing dog shit here."

"That's what I'm saying."

He stood there for a real five seconds, sizing me up, blankness in his eyes. It's like he was an old pinball machine on "TILT." Finally, he was distracted by something else.

"Snooping."

"What's that?"

He pointed over my shoulder to his entertainment center. It was a sparsely populated collection of books—mostly weightlifting manuals and sports memoirs—with a shelf dedicated to DVDs. Nothing unusual about the shelf. In fact, from that side of the room, I recognized quite a few of the spines: *Anchorman. Step Brothers. Old School.*

"You been watching my movies?"

"No, man," I said.

Half the time when I was drinking, I had no idea if I was telling the truth at any given second. I just said whatever came to mind first. That's because I was usually being asked direct questions that someone (mainly my wife) wasn't going to like the real answer to.

He walked over to inspect the DVD shelf.

When I got close, I noticed some other titles strewn among the recognizable ones. Hot pinks and bright purples. It suddenly occurred to me that there were just as many porn DVDs in there as Will Ferrell comedies.

In Diana Jones. The Bare Bitch Project. Bi-tanic.

"They're out of place."

Thankfully, Robin came home with bags of groceries, and I

assumed he'd just snap out of his quiet, accusatory rage. I knew that it would all go back to normal. I just couldn't be alone with him. It'd be fine.

"You know what this motherfucker did?" he jerked his thumb in my direction as we both emerged from her bedroom.

Robin was setting down a bag, trying to do the math on what was going on.

"What's that?"

"He didn't walk Apollo or Rocky," he said. "There's shit everywhere. Fucker also watched some of my porn. Used my laptop, too."

She immediately leveled a hard gaze at me.

I didn't even know what to do.

He sauntered over to the fridge and opened it.

"I bet you even drank my beer," he said, opening the door and letting out a laugh. "Sure enough. You fuckin' drank almost all my Fat Tire."

"I bought that Fat Tire."

"Fat Tire is Dale's favorite beer," Robin said quietly, as if she was equally disappointed in me for a lie I wasn't telling. "I bought that for him before I left."

She hadn't.

But I needed a place to stay.

So I took the anger.

I apologized for everything.

I scrubbed the dog shit off their bedroom carpet. He inspected it once, looking at it from all angles, and frowned saying he could still see spots, so I did it twice. I lied and said I used his laptop. I also copped to watching a DVD that I'd never watch in a million years.

Just to get another couple nights of sleep without having to pay for it.

THE NEXT FEW nights were relatively normal. I was getting amped for my return trip to Columbus. I was drinking less. I was waking up earlier. I was firing on all cylinders at work. I was engaged on conference calls, making people laugh, and remembering facts faster than my brain normally processed them. I was actually playing the part of someone Andrea would be proud to hire. Facts and figures weren't reluctantly given to me by my brain—they were just there. Operating on sleep and not booze, I felt like a new man.

My flight left on a Thursday morning at 7:33 a.m. from Sky Harbor, so I had to get up ridiculously early. Dale and Robin had gotten into a fight when I'd gone out for happy hour. When I rolled in, she was sitting in the blue glow of *The Real Housewives,* gorging on a half-gallon of ice cream. Tears sparkled on her cheeks.

"What's wrong?"

"I don't want to talk about it."

Fair enough, I thought, whirling back to the spare bedroom.

But then Robin started in about how Dale thought she was cheating on him, and with a bunch of guys at the same time. Dale found a site called Plenty of Fish on her laptop. It was ridiculous to hear her say it.

"He was making fun of me because it was a free site and not a pay one," she was blubbering.

And then she started off telling me the reverse was actually true: she'd found some suspicious emails he'd been sending from his Facebook account. He'd made lots of recent calls to weird contacts in his phone to names she didn't recognize, typically at like 2 or 3 in the morning. She found some random boob photos saved on his computer in a folder (I shit you not) called "Private."

It was a mess.

I listened for about twenty minutes, then did my best imitation of someone who cared, and went back to the bedroom. I packed up all my belongings.

It was about ten o'clock. I was starting to wind down for the night. Texted the kids, told them how excited I was to see them. How I'd packed prickly pear candy for them. I was ready for five o'clock to roll around and claim me. I'd drive straight to the airport with all my belongings and hopefully have a new solution figured out when I got there.

Somewhere around midnight, I started getting angry texts from Dale. One after the other, coming in quick succession.

What the fuck dude
Im gonna kill you
I hate u
You r dead
Fucken when i find u
Bitch
She told me evrything
U R
Dead

I had no idea what any of this meant, but I could feel the terror rising in my throat. It was like a heat-seeking missile was arcing toward me in the desert dark. I had to get the hell out of there—fast. I took my luggage down the flights of stairs to my car. It was still ninety outside, and the air was almost solid. I climbed into the Alero, wondering where the hell I was going to go for the five hours I had to waste before my flight.

Five hours was both too short and too long, I told myself.

Plus, I had two flights back to Ohio, not one.

I could certainly catch up on sleep somewhere in the mix there.

I drove toward the airport, finding a hole-in-the-wall bar called Abuelita's. It was the real deal: no one greeted you when you walked in the door; no one really gave a shit that you were there. There was a rumor that this place stayed open well past its closing hours. I put that rumor to the test. I put away drink after drink by myself, scrolling through Facebook on my phone next to a lawn maintenance worker who was heading straight to his job after his early-morning tequila and Sols. He spoke broken English but just enough English to ask me if I wanted a shot. *My treat,* he kept saying, throwing crumpled fives across the bar. The bartender was sleepy and almost animatronic—I kept looking to see if there was a copper slot she was running along on the floor. There was no music—just the sound of people living in between the spaces; drinking in the margins.

The place closed around 3:45 in the morning without much pomp and circumstance. It seemed to close when she decided everyone had finally had enough. I'd reached cruising altitude, but now I was careening back to the earth without options. Panic rose inside me. I knew that I'd been in a hermetically sealed bubble in this bar—this off-the-grid watering hole in the barrio. When I left, four Mexicans crammed into a pickup truck, landscaping gear in the back, and drove off for parts unknown.

I was alone.

I climbed into the Alero, heart beating overtime at the thought of me not being able to gently come back down. So I leaned the seat all the way back, set my iPhone alarm for five-thirty, and got about an hour of sleep there in the parking lot. I woke up at the sound of the FedEx jets lumbering to life before the passenger jet routes—the low rumble of giant engines against the hot desert air. I woke up drunker than I'd liked, but the thought of going home excused my situation. I was sitting in a hobo parking lot at five-thirty in the morning, with a modern hobo's amount of carry-on luggage crammed into the car.

I rubbed my eyes and thought: *I can drink early at the airport. That will get me through.*

Seriously: that was the carrot on the end of the stick. Not the adrenaline rush of flying home to see my family. I was too goddamn spent to focus on that. No, that first Bloody Mary before Security would set me right.

WHEN I CAME home, Oliver didn't recognize me. I'd only been gone a little more than a month. You notice imperceptible things that have changed while you've been gone for that long: the way books are stacked; the way dishes are arranged. Everything in the house was sale-ready, not one hair out of place. Oliver stared at me for a while, barely a year old, trying to figure out how I fit into his life. He wasn't quite sure.

Neither was I.

Carrie also liked to add that I was missing out on so many things about Oliver's development, which didn't help me at all.

While I was in Ohio, my boss Andrea texted me: *You're more than welcome to stay with us. We have room.* I'd obviously told her the whole sad-sack story of how the house wasn't selling, how I was sort of stuck between two worlds, and the Robin-Dale debacle.

I think part of her was simply afraid I wouldn't come back to work, but I remember it being an incredibly kind, selfless gesture—one that was completely wasted on me. I figured that if I accepted the offer, I'd only be there for maybe a couple of weeks. A month, tops. I was convinced our house *had* to sell— it just couldn't sit there in a nice neighborhood with a *For Sale* sign hammered in the yard—so I figured this was yet another meant-to-be signal from the universe. I kept *just* getting by, hanging on by my teeth. Andrea was *supposed* to do this. After all, that's what generous friends did: they let closet alcoholics into their home to stay, rent-free, for indefinite periods of time where their disease could fester and grow like mold.

My visit to Ohio was like trying to work with hot mercury. I wasn't really there. Wine, however, was. I may as well have been 3,000 miles away again. I slept more than I should. Happy breakfasts went on below without me while I slept in. The trip was over as quickly as it began. Wine robbed me of memories, but it also helped blunt the fighting Carrie threw at me over our situation, and it carried me back off to the airport in a haze.

19

PULLING OUR ELEVEN-YEAR-OLD Alero into the neighborhood, I immediately knew I was out of place. The car was missing a line of weather stripping on the passenger side, part of the dashboard was wrinkled from the sun, and it had four bald tires. Warner Ranch was all low-slung bungalows and family homes made of stucco and Spanish tile, along nice, orderly streets. Some people even had horses on their lots. People came every other day to leaf-blow the neighborhood. My car was the only one parked out front. Andrea drove a Lexus, and her husband Shawn drove a Range Rover. I drove the sort of car that gets blown up in the background of a *Transformers* movie.

The house was a two-story ranch with a wide entryway and adobe tile throughout.

"Here's your room," Andrea showed me. "It's not much."

It wasn't their spare bedroom so much as a modest library and closet, connected to its own bathroom. Shawn's collection of art manuals and journals lined the wall just beneath the windows. There was an inflatable camping mattress on the floor with a few folded sheets waiting for me. It dominated three-quarters of the room.

"It's perfect."

I could feel it settling in on me. I didn't want to bother either one of them; I wanted to be as unobtrusive as possible. I wanted to give them the illusion that I wasn't there. So I made myself a hermit. I barely came out of that room. And when I wasn't there, I was out at the bar down the street—an awful chain restaurant called the Tilted Kilt with busty servers clad in fake Scottish kilts. They had playing cards with their names and faces on them. But I also didn't want to wake Andrea or Shawn, so I'd stay for an extra two rounds to ensure they were fast asleep by the time I got home.

I turned my bathroom into a sad alcoholic laboratory: bottles of empty wine and beer and booze quickly crowded the pipework under the sink. I'd wait until Shawn and Andrea had both left for work on the morning of Trash Day, then I'd collect all the bottles around the house. I needed two large trash bags to get everything. I was even careful of the bottles' clinking so the neighbors didn't hear. If there was already another bag in the trash can, I'd be careful to set that one on top. The way bottles of wine strike one another sets off something inside me, like a tuning fork, unlike glass soda bottles. I know and understand their weight and their promise. I know, without looking, when two wine bottles hit one another in someone's grocery cart.

In that tiny room, in the upstairs of a ranch house in Tempe, Arizona, is where my alcoholism kicked into a new level. It was already a black speck of mold—tiny and unnoticeable—but now, it was given the perfect conditions to proliferate and spread in the dark. My alcoholism had long since caused leaks inside me, but now they'd grown steady and constant, causing the walls and foundation to sag and swell from places unseen. I allowed my loneliness to excuse my drinking, which, in turn, made it worse. That spore of mold grew into green-black constellations—patterns of self-loathing that reached out along the walls and undersides.

I smuggled bottles of wine and pints of vodka into their house in my work bag, heading straight upstairs to my room where I'd commit the cycle all over again. I called in sick to work via email to the person whose house I was staying in. I'd heard her setting about her day, hours earlier, getting ready for the gym. My hangovers weren't even hangovers anymore—they were just atomic-blast zones where nothing survived. My brain was a sort of irradiated wasteland where hopes and aspirations tingled down from the sky as ash. I couldn't get off the inflatable mattress, and even when I did, I felt like the ground was the same sort of pliable surface. Everything felt shapeless around me. My head burned, punishing. My face muscles were fixed in a permanent scowl.

On weekends, I'd sleep until well after noon. Andrea's

parents would come over, hoping for a glimpse of the sick homeless person they'd taken under their wing. I'd hear them whispering downstairs, careful not to wake me, but wondering who the hell I was. I felt like if they'd have flung the bedroom door open, they'd have been horrified at the sight of all the clothes strewn about the place, the twisted sheets, the bottles haphazardly left around the room. It'd be like the scene of a sci-fi movie where the astronauts find a derelict spacecraft, slashing through the dark with their searchlights. Signs of the virus were everywhere, having rapidly grown out of control and contaminating every square inch.

I was a biohazard. I was the opening of an *X-Files* episode. I wrote gibberish emails, I wrote nonsense Facebook status updates at 3 a.m., I scribbled ideas for stories that I'd never write on the back of liquor store receipts. I tapped out sad signals into the universe and hoped for a ping back.

THREE MONTHS INTO my extended stay, I discovered that our Ohio realtor hadn't listed our house correctly. If someone was looking for a house in our neighborhood, they wouldn't find it. It was like listing a house as "Detroit" when it's really "Grosse Pointe." I discovered that on a Saturday when my roommates were away overseas. I opened my bedroom door and let some of the virus spill out into the living room and kitchen. Empty beer bottles collected on the countertops, and the bottle cap tray overflowed. It wasn't even noon yet, as I stared in disbelief at our Ohio house listing; I could feel a sharp angle of anxiety slant through me.

I called Carrie to explain the situation. I figured I'd have to explain it, but she understood immediately and broke down crying. It would reset the timer on everything, this one careless mistake. Fifteen minutes and two beers later, I was laying into our realtor—a well-intentioned Vietnam combat veteran. I cracked open another beer as I talked to him. I could feel the drunken momentum really kicking in—that violent moment where present drunkenness connects with the previous night's drunkenness, like two railcars coupling on a downward mountain pass.

It's not like he didn't get it, either. This was entitled drinking, though. The worst kind. I made my point four times, and when I hung up, I was out of beer. I didn't want to crack into my housemates' bottles of wine, either. Their wine collection didn't look like the sort of stuff I could easily replace with bottles from World Market. Their bottles looked expensive and manicured—rows of old-vine zinfandels; fine syrahs; one cabernet even had a signed label.

It was Halloween, right around the time when the weather finally seems to crack in Phoenix. I'd been getting text invites to parties; reminders of things I probably said "Sure!" to. I'm a serial committer, saying "yes" to all kinds of things I figured I could cancel on later. Truth be told, alcoholics like me love the ideas of things more than the actual things themselves.

The hope my family coming out to Arizona and the whole plan working out as I'd hope, was dwindling. I'd passed the point in time at which the company would pay for relocation; I'd also come to realize that my drinking was only getting worse, not better. I couldn't bear to face the reality that none of it was working out. That said, this was a call to arms. Bad news entitled me to bring my brain to manageable levels—I needed something to settle out the scrambled signal.

I drove to the nearest Total Wine—essentially, a Costco for booze—and parked. Across the lot, the sliding glass doors of an IKEA were swallowing families in whole. Total Wine was about to do the same thing to me. I had a nice beer buzz going as I stepped into the warehouse. Instead of a plastic Smirnoff, I went for a full bottle of Ketel One. Instead of a six-pack of Miller Lite, I carefully assembled my own six-pack of beer from the craft selection: thick IPAs, light Japanese lagers, even one lager with a Tabasco pepper at the bottom. I rounded out the order with a bottle of budget cabernet.

I brought them all to the counter, tried to play it off like I wasn't buying this shit for a Saturday spent alone. The clerk had an issue ringing up one of the singles, so she had to call over a manager. I could feel the shame and the eyeballs of the people piling up in line behind me. It was all clearly for me: a disheveled thirtysomething in shorts, Crocs, and an ill-fitting T-shirt. I don't think I'd brushed my hair in two days. Buying it with money we didn't have.

I cared enough to wish I didn't care about what other people thought.

I went back to the car, hurriedly unscrewed the Ketel One cap and took a quick slug there in the parking lot. If you're used to warm vodka, chances are good that you're an alcoholic. I was getting used to room-temperature booze in the way that some people get used to spicy food over the years. You don't just jump into enjoying habaneros—you work up to them. The Ketel One didn't have that faint kerosene taste that I was used to, but it didn't help me not gag, either.

I drove the mile back to the house with my bounty, parked myself on their nice leather couch, and watched a Bond movie. I knew every beat, every line. I felt myself slipping into the movie's cadence and my eyes were growing heavy. Next thing I knew, there was another volley of voicemails and photo texts from my kids in their Halloween costumes—the curse of a three-hour time difference. Bruised twilight outside the windows. That's when it hit me.

Something had woken me up.

There it was again. At the front door.

I could hear it—voices outside, murmuring.

A knock. Several knocks.

More voices.

Then it dawned on me: Halloween.

The entire neighborhood was out and about for trick-or-treat. Parents and their kids were going from house to house. I peeked through the keyhole and saw a fishbowled view of several parents and their costumed children at my door. Of course, I'd left the porch light on. I couldn't exactly snap it off. I panicked. More knocking. The doorbell rang.

I hit the floor and crawled to the couch, like I was evading laser motion sensors. I didn't want anyone seeing me through the glass.

I sat there on the floor for a while, quiet, hugging my knees. I uncorked the cheap cabernet and glugged a full half glass out of the neck, my lips touching the torn, ragged foil. I listened to the children outside the door, expectant and hopeful, and I began to cry there in the dark. I thought of Elliott and Oliver. Crying was a reflex those days, but this came from somewhere a little deeper.

I knew it was over.

THE MORNING I put my two weeks' notice in, I hadn't slept the night before. I hadn't given it a whole ton of thought—I just knew I had to do it. I didn't consult anyone; I didn't ask Carrie. I was running on two sugar-free Red Bulls and pure force of will. Driving into work, a news alert told me that that there'd been a shooting at an elementary school in Connecticut. Unfortunate. Shootings in random places, sadly, weren't all that surprising. Someone getting shot at an elementary school sounded awful, though. Working at a newspaper, you're plunged into a world that's one pace ahead—it's sort of like how sunrise touches Maine earlier than the rest of the country. That's how working in the media industry is. You have a fifteen-minute head start on everyone else. You read the raw feeds, all the stories clogging the arteries before they get shaped into the ones that will make the front page.

By the time mid-morning rolled around in Phoenix, it became clear that the shooting in Newtown was far more insidious. I sat there, not doing any work, and feeling my emptiness grow. I was detached from my surroundings. Robin didn't even bother me as she cussed out some poor customer service rep from Zappo's. I looked around my cube. There was a piece of construction paper with Elliott's handprints on it in paint. *Even though we're far apart, you're always in my heart.*

I couldn't stop reading news updates as they ticked by on the Gannett news feed—each detail grimmer and uglier than the last. It was like watching something quickly die on a vine.

I couldn't stop reading. I didn't even cry; I didn't have it in me. It was eleven in the morning, just barely lunchtime. I had the sort of job where I could toss a bunch of emails in other people's directions and then it'd take at least an hour for them to respond to the volley. Plenty of time. I pocketed some Dentyne Ice and dazedly took the elevator down to the lobby. I sneaked through the deliveries-only section of the Hyatt next door and was greeted with a blast of hot, ripe garbage. Minutes later, I was guzzling draft beers at a pizza place next to the movie theater. It was a ballsy move, given that any of my coworkers could roll in at any second for legitimate lunch.

I had to give it to the bartenders: they didn't even flinch. They just nodded when I asked for the beer, sliding it across the bar. I generally found myself only as ashamed as my bartenders' glances. If they cocked an eyebrow, I knew I was in trouble. But if they didn't care, I didn't care. That was my barometer. If someone wanted to drink at eleven o'clock in the morning, this pizza place wasn't going to turn down my Visa card. I drank the brown ale way too quickly and ordered another one. Newtown was all over the TVs hanging above the bar, looking down on me, taunting.

"Want another?"

I nodded. It was 11:20.

Live, CNN reported.

I drank the third beer so quickly that I was already pulling out my credit card, as if to cut the cord on myself and slow the disaster that was happening. I had to stop.

I started doing math story problems in my head. Long-range ones. When they showed the black-and-white photo of Adam Lanza—looking like a sketch someone draws of a wide-eyed skeleton-monster they saw at Lover's Lane—I was repulsed. But my brain reeled at the thought of how his life, and these innocent little children's lives, could possibly intersect. That morning, those children had been hustled into their clothes, their parents herding them out the doors onto school buses, maybe telling them they were running late. The parents, if they were anything like me, wanted them out of the house on time. There was plenty of time to, later that night, play whatever game they wanted.

And here comes Adam Lanza, carrying on a sideways trajectory, guns in tow, ready to cross lines on the universe's *x/y* axis with them. None of it made sense to me—the dark geometry that binds everyone together. How we're all just unilluminated lines in the black, racing toward no destination in particular. We're just moving. And our children certainly don't have destinations in mind. They're used to sitting in a classroom, not being ushered into closets while a madman goes on a rampage.

"Horrible, right?" the hipster bartender with gauged ears shook his head, crossing his arms.

"Unbelievable."

"You got kids?"

"In Ohio."

"Oh. You just visiting?"

The question reverberated through me like the time Nate Jennings dared me to touch an electric fence in fifth grade. I didn't feel anything for three full seconds before the jolt knocked my feet out from under me. I didn't even have time to process it. The question hit me the same way. I didn't feel it at first, then every cell was immediately on fire from the beer and self-pity and loneliness.

"Yes," I decided, telling the truth for the first time in a year. "I'm just visiting."

LONG STORY SHORT: they didn't want to lose me as an employee. Andrea was incredibly nice like that. But it was time to clear out the alcoholic burrow I'd built for myself in their spare office for the last four months. I was probably like that little piece of corn that gets stuck in your teeth. They were finally getting rid of me. Andrea arranged for me to transfer from the *Arizona Republic* to the *Cincinnati Enquirer* building—another flagship newspaper for the company. From Phoenix, the commute seemed (in my head) little more than just an hour's drive. I could handle that.

I had to go home.

I remember calling Carrie and telling her everything was off in Phoenix. I was coming home. The Columbus-to-Cincinnati commute would work out. It had to. And if it didn't, something else would. Thoughts came to me like bubbles in a lava lamp— separating, then glomming onto one another. I planned it so that I'd be home on Christmas Eve.

I cleared out the bedroom, finding vodka bottles I'd hidden in a dresser under clothes that weren't even mine. Some of the bottles were still a quarter-full, which was like finding a twenty-dollar bill in a jacket you haven't worn in a year. I slugged those down and tossed them in my trash bag. When everyone was gone, I tied off the bag and tossed it into the back of the Alero. Since I was leaving, I didn't want anyone rooting through the trash and discovering that they'd had a full-blown alcoholic in their house for the last few months. I was surgical (or so I thought) about the trash situation. When I threw the bags behind gas stations, I nervously looked for surveillance cameras, partly because my brain was jangled with booze and conspiracy. No one was watching.

SO I LEFT Arizona for Ohio.
Again.
With a hangover.
Again.

BEFORE I KNEW IT, I was in a wide-open stretch of countryside that just seemed "off." The further I drove, the weirder it got. Dead, bone-white trees were twisted and pitched at odd angles. The highway was eerily empty. Even the sunset looked diseased. I'd quickly discover I was skirting the edge of Joplin, Missouri—a city all but erased by an F5 tornado just a few months before.

Everything looked exactly like how I felt: ruined by something random and beyond my control. I believed a tornado had touched down in my own life, bringing with it twist-cap bottles of wine and plastic pints of cheap vodka. The city simply wasn't there and, thanks to drinking, neither was I. Like the people of Joplin, I was no stranger to loss. I'd lost good friends, casual acquaintances, trust, freelance jobs, actual jobs, arguments, memories, choices, confidence, and everything in between. Losing things just comes with the territory when you're an alcoholic. You actually get used to it. You don't look back on things in the exact same way you stop looking forward to anything. Loss was also never my fault. Ever. I was convinced that—like the people of Joplin—I never saw the disaster coming.

You could fill the Grand Canyon with the number of grievances I had against the universe. Life wasn't delivering what I thought I was owed. I drank because of unexpected bills, being unemployed, and all the people who suddenly turned their back on me. One morning, I remember opening the fridge and a half-gallon of orange juice toppled out, spilling everywhere. I was furious, as if the juice had shifted during flight or something. I drank over that, too. Soon enough, I was only happy when I was miserable and I only felt right when I felt wronged.

It's never been hard for me to feel sorry for myself—it's a reflex. What's worse is that I didn't have a checkered childhood where my parents fought all the time; it wasn't like I was ignored, or I needed anything. You hear about creative people who had terrible upbringings, which sag down on them like water-damaged ceiling tiles. I'm quite the opposite. I've just always been really talented at feeling personally slighted by the universe. Drinking only made that worse. Now, I honestly shudder to think how exhausting of a human being I was to be around.

It was always about me—and in many ways, it still is. I used to lie awake at night wondering how many people would attend my funeral or, worse, whether someone would get the service playlist right.[28] Until very recently, I don't think I'd ever stopped to ask another person how they were doing—and genuinely care. If I asked, it was only to buffer the time before I could launch into my latest round of problems.

Can you believe that person stopped talking to me?

Can you believe they said I drank too much?

Can you believe I haven't gotten a job yet?

I couldn't do the math that maybe, just maybe, I had some small part in what was going on in my life. Other people's feelings were secondary to me. In the moment, I genuinely did care. But drinking is good at filling you up with a temporary glow for other people's well-being, before it quickly evaporates like those details of a good dream right when you wake up. Same thing with my closest friends and family. They never got the version of me that cared—they only got the muddied VHS tape version, recorded over dozens of times, that barely resembled someone who cared.

I constantly blamed other people and things. I held grudges, I was passive-aggressive, I proudly showed off text-message exchanges where I felt like I'd won an argument. Never once did I think about how empty and shallow I was. After all, I wasn't being judgmental—I was right, goddammit. People were sounding boards. Nothing more. I needed witnesses and nods. I desperately needed other people to understand just how poorly the universe was treating me. One time, my parents had

---

[28] For the mordibly curious, there are probably only three songs I'd request to be played at my funeral, even if it's tomorrow or ages from now: "Find the River" by R.E.M. because it's my favorite song, Bing Crosby's Christmas song "Mele Kalikimaka" because I want everyone to sit through it wondering what the hell is going on, and "Live and Let Die" by Wings.

scheduled service on my car, and it was going to take an hour longer than scheduled. I couldn't deal with that. So I left my car there and walked the three miles home just to demonstrate how put out I was by my parents and the auto shop. Ironically, if anyone acted the same way around me, you'd never hear the end of it. I'd cut you out of my social circle, no questions asked. Except maybe, "Can you believe how self-absorbed he is?"

Being judgmental was second nature, mainly because I was insecure and empty all the time. Whenever I played the victim, I always focused on how bad everything was—never about the good things. I ignored the facts: we had a house, we had healthy kids, and my wife had a steady job. I just took everything for granted in the way that I assume Tyler Perry will keep on making terrible movies. I was more focused on how unfair it was that liquor stores were closed on Sundays.

I'm embarrassed to say I'm still not above self-pity. Not in the slightest. I can feel sorry for myself if I accidentally kick over my cat's food bowl or miss a green light. I'm no victim, though. Absolutely not. Alcoholism didn't suddenly choose me. Maybe I'm victim to a bad genetic lottery, poor circumstances, or a perfect storm of both—but that doesn't matter. Going down that road doesn't help anything. Whenever I play the victim card, I'm at the center of my own sad little tornado, constantly baffled as to why I'm always running for cover. I lose sight that I'm the root cause of most problems.

I'm the tornado.

And if I'm not honest about who and what I am, I'm just sound and fury, signifying nothing.

20

MY EVENTUAL COMMUTE was two hours, door to door. Think that over for a second: four hours every day in your car, five days a week, just for a job. At the time, though, it made complete sense to me. Maybe *this* was how it was supposed to be. Maybe I first had to lasso the job in Phoenix, suffer through all of that, and then do it in Cincinnati.

For the first time in months, I saw my kids when I woke up in the morning. The *For Sale* sign was gone from the front yard. Things were relatively calm. The entire house seemed to breathe a sigh of relief. (It shouldn't have, but still.) It was just the calm-before-storm silence. In all the same ways that a burning house from across a field looks like a painting and not a burning house, my addiction was consuming me but no one really noticed.

I attacked the drive to Cincinnati like I was heading to any other job. I packed my lunch and drove two full hours, watching the landscape as it shifted from nothingness to strip malls to winding high hills. Finally, it opened up to downtown: a crowded collection of skyscrapers competing for attention alongside the Ohio River. I found my building's parking garage and entered it with absolutely no guidance on the day before New Year's Eve. There was no one to show me around, no little-old-lady HR rep to show me where the coffee pot was. Little did I know that this parking garage would be the stage for the worst parts of my alcoholism. Most everyone was on vacation, so the entire floor was empty.

The *Cincinnati Enquirer* building seemed somewhat more stately than the *Republic*. It had that old-school air of "newspaper" everywhere you turned. Its lobby was black granite and high-ceilinged windows. Framed, oversized prints of its best covers lined the walls. Plush leather furniture. I found my way to the 22nd floor, where I was to report. The person I was reporting to, of course, was Andrea—who was 3,000 miles away and gone on vacation, too. I found myself in a low-cubicle-walled area of artists and creative types, graphic designers and sketch makers.

One girl named Sarah, barely out of her teens, got it.

"It's not like we're curing cancer here," Sarah would say a few weeks later, imploring anyone and everyone to go to happy hour with her. She breezed past the design easels and graphic design kiosks. "We're creating junk mail and spam, y'all."

In that first week, Sarah and I made fast friends, and she took me across the street to a little-visited pub for lunch. It was all wood-paneled and low-lit. There was a little horseshoe of a bar, and we plopped down there. We were the only people in the place, but she seemed to have a hall pass on life. She also knew everyone. They slid her free drinks and recounted how crazy the previous weekend had gotten, apologizing to her. I had no idea what was going on.

I asked for a food menu; she asked for a Bullitt and Coke. I ordered a Miller Lite, just to show that I was semi-serious about my job.

It was eleven-thirty, after all.

"All newspaper people drink," she shrugged as she hunched over her drink. "Our reporters? Fucked-up by nine, man. They've been writing all night. Drinking the whole time, too."

She also explained that this wasn't Ohio, not really. This was Kentucky. It was a drinking person's state. Cincinnati didn't belong to Ohio.

I loved this girl immediately.

Maybe I *was* in the right business.

So long as I could do my writing, so long as I could control my drinking, everything would be okay. I could harness it, level up, become great.

I SOON FELT at home in the vanishing atmosphere of the newspaper world. You could feel it everywhere you turned at the *Enquirer*. Everything was temporary. Everything. Oxygen was leaking from places unseen. Nobody was investing in anything—conversations, projects, people. There were more paddocks of cubes and empty bullpens. Conference rooms gone unused. The sales numbers bore it out: the digital ads weren't working, physical ads were done, no one wanted anything to do with what we were calling "digital account activation." No grandmother cared about reading her news on an iPad. But that's what we were selling.

Just beyond the windows of the *Enquirer* was a maze of empty brick apartment buildings and gutted-out office buildings. Whenever it rained, everything looked black. I used to stare out the window of a lonely conference room at a corner, wondering what lives went on in those apartments and offices back when they were occupied. From that high-up angle, I could see all the narrow slants of alleys and open windows where wind, rain, and leaves blew in. It was like death outside—and that's how working for the newspaper world felt. All the roots were drying up. There was nothing to sustain it.

Drinking, I was convinced, was the only way to get through the experience. I'd told myself the job would be temporary until I found something else, but it is shocking how a four-hour commute and being drunk half the time really took the wind out of your ambitions.

That's all I did.

I was removed from everyone and everything. My Phoenix coworkers didn't arrive on the scene for a full three hours after I rolled into Cincinnati (yay, time difference!) though the people immediately around me went to and fro. They had purpose. They had lives; they had soccer practices to take kids to; they had dinner dates they had to make it home to. I felt dislocated in time and space, like I was there and yet I wasn't. People didn't really talk to me because—well, why would they? I was just some guy who had a cube. I was like a time-traveling observer, invisible to the world. I didn't even have a nameplate.

The job was so ridiculously easy that I couldn't tell if it was beneath me, that I was completely missing the mark and others were covering for me, or whether my drinking was making things seem easier than they were, like how rearview-mirror glass adds distance. Probably all three. I feel like I drove two hours to turn on my computer, do three hours of loading documents to SharePoint sites, approve marketing work that I couldn't actually reject, sit on calls where I didn't contribute anything, then drive back home. I knew I added no value. People would comment on how stark my cubicle was—I had no plants, no photographs, nothing personal at all. Maybe it's because on some microscopic level, I could sense that none of this would last.

At a certain point, I was waking up at six o'clock in the morning in a blind stagger, picking clothes up off the floor and shrugging them on in the dark. I didn't have any job beyond getting passably dressed—no one was paying that close attention to me at work—and getting in a vehicle to drive two hours. I'd wake up on the way. At first, a McDonald's sausage biscuit sandwich with cheese and an orange juice seemed to get me through. But then I discovered a new trick: buying a six-pack of Miller Lite for the drive down to Cincinnati. I'd plug my earbuds in and listen to Adam Carolla's podcast as mile after boring mile of Ohio countryside scrolled past. I'd unscrew the cap carefully, slam the beer, then force the cap back onto the bottle with my palm. I'd set each beer back in the six-pack container carefully. I didn't want to spill anything. By about Beer #3, I could handle the drive. I was even in fairly good spirits, like a reanimated corpse. You're dead but, hey, you've got enough voodoo in your veins to keep you dancing.

Sometimes I'd roll past the *Enquirer* altogether and make a trip across the river. This amounted to an extra five minutes out of my day. Just over the Ohio border, as Sarah had pointed out, was a row of sketchy liquor stores and bars that stayed open 24 hours. Some of them were even drive-thrus. It was insane. I went on a fact-finding mission one morning, just to see if Sarah was bullshitting me.

She was not.

There, along the low-level waterline of the Ohio River were about a half-dozen liquor stores, all open and doing plenty of business on a Tuesday morning before eight. I pulled in, not quite sure how to feel. Right next to the store was a Dunkin' Donuts where someone responsible was just getting coffee and donut holes. Me? I was stepping out with a beer buzz tempering a hangover from hell. I wandered into the air-conditioned store, looking at row after row of booze. The owners didn't bat an eyelash. I felt like I needed to play-act or excuse why I was there—make up some story about why I was investigating the coolers of beer. It didn't matter, nor did they care.

I wasn't alone, either.

I was surrounded by people—mostly vacant-eyed middle-aged women picking through the travel-sized samplers of tequila and Kahlua. A few truck drivers scratching unkempt beards at the prices of whiskey. I went for a six pack of Michelob Ultra and a pint of Smirnoff. I slid it across the counter and they didn't even care. They just rang it up. No shame in the transaction. All this did was make me feel normal. If they'd have raised one eyebrow or made some snarky comment, I'd have run away, never to return. Not that place. That was normal. That's what they were there for.

Soon enough, this would become my routine: shooting past work and landing in one of the half-dozen liquor stores to get whatever it was that I thought I needed, just over the border. It stretched my drinking life out even thinner, like a piece of gum between two fingers. I was a thread, drooping at the center, threatening to come apart.

I drove back to the parking garage and found the highest, emptiest spot. Usually the seventh floor. No one went up there. That's where I'd eventually shoot myself in the head, I once jokingly told myself. The joke came so fast and furious that it didn't occur to me that it was suicide I was thinking about. The point is: I was now driving my in-laws' Bonneville. I'd destroyed the Alero with all the wear-and-tear I put on it. Carrie had purchased that Alero with her own hard-earned dollars from her first hospital job. Cash. She was supposed to have traded it in for something nicer. Nope. Just like everything else, I was the cancer that robbed her of that opportunity, and now I was driving a charity sedan from her parents just to get me to a paycheck two hours away.

It was madness.

The parking garage was something of a Rubik's Cube or maybe one of those Hogwarts hallways where the staircases swing at their own angles and by their own volition. It was easy to go up one ramp before suddenly realizing it wasn't the way you were supposed to go. I found my quiet little corner on the seventh floor where I'd put the Bonneville in park, run to my desk upstairs, flip my computer on to see no messages waiting for me, then I'd go *back* down to the car where my Kentucky booze and beer were waiting. I put my earbuds in. I flipped on a white-noise app, leaned my seat back, and cranked it up. I took a hit from Smirnoff and felt my brain clamp down into forced rest. Occasionally, Andrea would call early, asking me if I was at my desk (to which I'd just say I'd stepped out—technically true). But most times, I slept in that garage until nine or ten, right when my Arizona coworkers arrived 2,000 miles away.

They didn't notice the difference. I always made sure I was online a few minutes earlier: an expectant green dot, available on instant-messaging.

And then my day would proceed as all the previous ones. The ballet of generating marketing ideas that didn't matter: having them accepted, ushering them from artist to graphic designer to production designer to print, never seeing one bit of impact. When something of mine was finished, I didn't even want to hold it. It was just an envelope with the newspaper logo on it. Junk mail. Inside were clever ideas and words—*my* clever ideas and words—but I couldn't bring myself to read any of them.

None of it was real.

I sat at my desk and when the rush of nausea would hit me, I'd bring my work bag to the bathroom with me. I'd sit in a stall, hang that bag on the garment hook, unzip it, and pull out the bottle of Smirnoff. I'd take a thick slug and screw the cap back on. I could immediately feel myself brighten a bit. I'd very often run into the head of HR—a thin, prim-and-proper woman who used carefully chosen words, right outside her office after I hit the bottle. Instead of having her worry about me, I'd be charming as fuck and use carefully chosen words of my own. I'd ask her all kinds of questions about her family, remembering names I shouldn't and recalling things they were getting into. She was super impressed. I knew that after our interaction, she'd go back and report to Andrea how delightful I'd been. It's all what my job was: appearing that I wasn't falling apart. Perception was everything. I swallowed my Tic Tacs and breathed a sigh of relief.

I prepared for another day of creating spam, driving, and not seeing my children.

I FOUND THIS hole-in-the-wall bar in Cincinnati called Tina's that was just about as unpretentious and no-frills as it gets. It was just far enough from the office—four blocks away—that very few coworkers ever made their way to it. I visited the bar at odd hours. Two-thirty was perfect. Thin crowd. Daydrinkers need only apply. From there, you could see the actual *WKRP in Cincinnati* tower. The bar reeked of whiskey and cinnamon.[29] There was a "chili meter" right when you opened the first door—a cartoonish barometer telling you exactly how hot their chili was today. No matter when I had it, it was 90% cinnamon soup with a few beans in it. I lived on it.

When you're an alcoholic, you cross a terrible invisible line where you become a regular. It's usually the third or fourth time when a bartender recognizes your patterns. They lock onto your habits and cater to them. Beers you didn't yet order, magically

---

[29] "Cincinnati-style chili" uses cinnamon.

appear in front of you. I hated it. I wanted anonymity, dammit, not recognition. Still, Tina's would have to do. I wasn't about to spend my afternoons wandering the Queen City, hopping from bar to bar trying to be invisible. I ordered a shot of Jameson and a Miller Lite. Classy. I was playing Words With Friends with some former high school acquaintance who seemed hell-bent on using cheat-apps to score 130 points on me. When I saw him use the word PORPHYRITIC, I knew he didn't know what it meant. I raised the shot glass to my lips. We were both cheaters, I guessed: him at Words With Friends, me at life.

My right hand trembled.

In fact, it shook so bad that half the whiskey spilled out.

I set the glass down, alarmed. Only the half-conscious guy to my right noticed, but I was embarrassed that anyone noticed at all. He winked, then looked away. It'd be one thing if he'd had simply nodded, as if understanding.

No, he had to fucking wink.

I tried again: no dice.

Well, this is no good, I thought.

I hunched over the bar and slurped the whiskey without picking it up off the table, like that was a perfectly normal thing to do. I then grabbed the beer and slammed it as fast as I could. Seconds later, I had the stamina to pick up the shot glass and finish it. The beer straightened me out.

Still, I was scared. I knew something was happening.

Inside, I was officially coming undone.

TO THIS DAY, I can't believe I was never arrested for a DUI on the way to or from Cincinnati. It's one of those things that would make even the staunchest atheist on the planet reconsider their position on the universe. By just about every mathematical equation, I should've been caught. Again. Somehow, I escaped the drunken geometry and algebra that guaranteed me ending up in some rural-town jail cell between Cincinnati and Columbus. Nope. Not once. I wasn't even closely tailed by a police officer for any stomach-churning amount of time. I'd just hit cruise control in the Bonneville and go.

By this point, home life was a sliver of what it should have been. I didn't have room for Carrie. I had no use for a wife, and I was of no use to her. My children sounded like garden rakes being dragged against sidewalks. I was living between the moments where anyone at home was awake or asleep. It was always dark outside—and such was my life inside, as well.

"PAUL, WHAT DO you think?"

When you're an alcoholic, your life is pretty much just on autopilot. That's your default setting. You cruise, you finish other people's sentences, you nod in agreement to show that you've been listening when you really have no fucking clue what's going on. So when someone catches you off guard, say, in a conference room surrounded by twenty-five other marketing people, it's disconcerting. It was nine o'clock on a Monday morning in February, and the windows were frosted so hard that I could barely make out the giant Bengals stadium just beyond our 22nd-floor vantage point. A tall row of windows opened up onto the sweeping panorama of riverfront where I'd been just thirty minutes before, scoring more vodka and beer.

I'd attended this meeting at least a dozen times before, but no one had ever called on me. I was a prop. I was just someone sitting in a chair. I wasn't supposed to say anything. The decorative plant in the corner had more effect in the room than me. The table was surrounded by the company's marketing geniuses—the last gasp of newspaper salvation—and they showed up to meetings late, talked about nothing, laughed about late newspapers that were delivered to sales kiosks. We were past the end days of newspapers—and they knew it. They were coasting.

Danielle, the head marketing executive, was a stout egomaniac whose face was 90% teeth. She had an unenviable job: stop the bleeding. No one was advertising in newspapers anymore, but she shrugged off all this. She treated it all with a plastic smile and belligerent confidence. The people around that table were the reason the *Enquirer* still existed. She threw just enough buzzwords and sass around to curtail the fact that she was captaining a sinking ship.

So when she asked me what I thought, I almost collapsed.

"About?"

"Taking notes here."

My entire body relaxed from a full-on seize.

"Sure."

I checked to make sure I'd even brought a writing instrument to the meeting. Thank God I had. I'd scribbled a bunch of gibberish in the margins of my notepad the day before—ideas of stories, a character flaw I thought would be interesting for a side character, a few screenplay titles I thought might be clever.

Dime's Dozen. An HBO drama series called *Speakeasy* about a mysterious hole-in-the-wall Prohibition-era basement with weird supernatural accidents. *Halcyon.*

"Paul?"

I was starting to have real episodes like this. Real jump-cut moments in life where I'd be missing time. Ten, fifteen seconds where I'd be out of my head and then everyone would be staring at me, expectant and curious.

"You get that?"

"Of course," I nodded, pretending to scribble.

That satisfied the dozen people in the room—but not me. I looked down in horror at my piece of paper and realized my hand was completely shaking. I couldn't write—and this is what I did for a living. Holding a pencil felt foreign to me. Not like a *oh-these-are-chopsticks-this-is-cute* sort of way, either. I didn't fucking know how to use a pencil. My brain wasn't transferring what they were saying into cogent sentences. I made scribbles and gestures, but that was it. I couldn't process the motor function of writing. I nodded and furrowed my brow, acting like I was taking down all their ideas for saving the newspaper world: asking famous actors from Kentucky to be part of their ad campaigns, tightening the demographic algorithms, going after fiftysomethings in a specific affluent neighborhood.

I stood up. Everyone ignored me for a few seconds, but when I staggered a few steps, they knew something was wrong.

I made no excuse.

I just staggered toward the conference room door. Someone stood, motioning: *Should I go check on him?* Danielle shook her head: *Not with him. He might have the flu or something.* I didn't even process the fact that I'd just dramatically left a roomful of the most important media executives in the biggest conference room in Cincinnati. I didn't care. My heart was beating in my throat; my brain was fuzzy and garbled. I kept feeling an icy rope of anxiety rise up between my shoulder blades.

I CALLED 911 on myself.

If you've never had a panic attack, I envy you. A panic attack doesn't feel like you think a panic attack should feel. It doesn't announce itself. It doesn't feel like a lack of sleep, like when you're overwhelmed with projects at work or when a wire's gotten crossed in your brain. You see it in movies: the walls closing in, lights getting bright, people and noises getting more pronounced. True panic doesn't rise inside you. It *is* you. It's like you suddenly feel like you're in a high-rise building and the building around you has vanished, deleted by some careless Photoshop editor. You're just hanging there in midair.

I walked around the perimeter of the *Enquirer* building, increasingly convinced that I was having a stroke. I knew it. It's why part of my face was numb; this was why my thoughts were jumbled; this was why I couldn't write. When I stumbled back in the grand *Enquirer* lobby, I mumbled something to the front-desk clerk and instructed her to call 911.

"What's wrong?" she regarded me with suspicion.

"Me."

"*You're* the emergency?"

"Would you just fucking call 911?"

I normally never cuss at strangers—especially when I'm

stabbing a cell phone at that person. I couldn't even dial 911. If I could've, I would've. But when you can't articulate what's wrong—when you tell the front desk of a national newspaper that you're the emergency, lots of unnecessary things happen. You get pushed down to an oversized couch and the entire lobby is cleared out. Police start to show up. You see them as your breath sharpens. You're taking in oxygen in short, sharp blasts. Everything registers on a different playing field. A fire ladder truck and an emergency SWAT vehicle and an ambulance all pull up outside in record minutes. They jump out—an army of Cincinnati's finest, waiting to see if Paul Fuhr, mid-thirties alcoholic, was a threat to national security.

Distantly, I felt important. I'd also somehow managed to call Carrie right before all the action happened, setting the phone down on the table in front of me. All she could do was listen to them attend to me—helpless.

"What's your name?"

I managed that much.

Lead Guy was the most level-headed. He used a notepad and scribbled stuff down. Everyone else was wearing bomb-padded equipment. They cut open my shirt and revealed nothing but a doughy belly. They took vitals. I could see the disbelief in some of their eyes that they'd been called to the *Enquirer* for *this*. They were really hoping for something to write home about—a reporter who'd gotten some facts wrong, maybe, and was now threatening suicide by taking out everyone with C-4.

"What's the matter, Carl?"

Carl. There it was.

I could see some of my "coworkers" peering around the corner.

"I just don't feel like being here anymore."

This got Lead Guy's attention.

"Oh, really? And what does that mean, Carl?"

"I just don't want to be here."

I broke down crying.

I had a lot going on at home. I had a lot going on here. I had of people I was disappointing. I'd poisoned a lot of wells. I was sick.

End of story: I just didn't want to be here anymore.

I imagined getting in the Bonneville after that moment, so ashamed, and getting onto I-71, cranking R.E.M., downing as much vodka as I could, and then ramming it right into an eighteen-wheeler.

Maybe that'd do the trick.

But I'd need to write a note—and I couldn't write.

That legitimately stopped that thought of suicide in its tracks: the fact that I couldn't write or type.

My fingers tingled like they'd touched a low-voltage fence. The EMTs told me I'd feel that way for a while—something about oxygen. It was a good sign, they said.

I closed my eyes.

It sure didn't feel like a good sign.

21

BEING AT HOME around children was sort of like how I imagine what happens when a bomb goes off too close to someone's head in a war zone. For days later, there's a ringing—the sound of cells dying, frequencies you'll never hear again. Brown noise. I had absolutely zero room in my head for it. Alcoholism was filling it all up. My kids ran around the place, threw toys around, screamed, dog-eared my favorite books, drew circles on the walls with colored pencils.

I had zero patience for anyone and anything.

I started to simply not drive to Cincinnati. I'd wake up, roll over, and log into my laptop from Columbus. I'd nudge the trackpad every twenty minutes or so to appear like I was online, then go back to sleep. And the shocking thing: no one really noticed. No one had bothered to assign me a work phone number in Cincinnati because, well, I didn't really exist as an employee. That's what people thought of me back then. And rightly so. If my boss asked me to give her a call, I rerouted my cell phone so that it emulated a 513 area code (Cincinnati) so she thought I was calling from the office.

The charades were exhausting.

Alcoholism was bleeding into every part of my life like how coffee stains a napkin—it slowly creeps into every fiber, soaking it up.

On my worst days "working from home," I'd lie there in bed, having full-on conversations with publishers and print directors in my boxers with the covers up to my chin. I'd go to the liquor store where the Russians would follow me around with their eyes, knowing I'd just come right up to the counter where my Smirnoff pint was waiting. I made a big show of pretending to look for other stuff when the pint was right there waiting for me. Then I'd go back to "work," feeling a little better, but only in the way that someone who's been shot in the shoulder feels after surviving a gunman's massacre in a shopping mall. The worst was surely yet to come.

A FEW WEEKS LATER, after my boss Andrea was getting

feedback that I wasn't actually showing up to the office, she arranged to fly to Cincinnati. I'd grown to absolutely dread moments where I had to be present, impress people, and stick the landings. Especially when I was still sweating out the last night's cabernet. There I was again, standing in an epic conference room in the high-rise office I worked in. The same long-paneled windows opened up on a sweeping view of downtown: a panorama of flowered hills, bombed-out brick warehouses, and upscale restaurants dotting the riverfront. About a dozen publishing execs and marketing specialists sat around a long table, waiting for a presentation on demographics to hit for a new marketing campaign.

I figured I would have had a new job by then, but I was too drunk, lazy, or on the road to find one. Working in the newspaper industry was a lot like rearranging deck chairs on the *Titanic*: we were all kidding ourselves that any of our meetings mattered. But it was my job. I had to deliver. *This is exactly how we sell digital newspaper subscriptions to senior citizens,* I began showing off my PowerPoint deck. *Here is all the expensive research we've done. Here are all the ZIP codes we should target. Here are examples of the messaging we should use.* I'd spent weeks on making the slides pretty, but I'd done zero work on the speech. I figured I'd just wing it, like I did everything, and trust adrenaline and luck.

I went for broke.

I just made shit up.

And as I spoke, people started nodding. They were buying it. I couldn't believe it. And that's when it happened: about sixty seconds in, I mentally folded up shop. I could feel it uncoil inside me like a broken spring. It was probably how stand-up comedians felt when they crashed after having an incredible opening salvo of jokes. I could see it in their eyes: pride bleeding into pity. Andrea looked down. She couldn't bear to see her employee going down so quickly and, worse, so willingly.

My face, hardened into an alcoholic scowl, just took it all in.

"**WE HAVE A** problem with Oliver's daycare," Carrie said one afternoon. I was focused more on the fact that I hadn't quite hidden the bottle of cabernet well enough—I could see it poking out from the opposite wall and couch. She'd gotten home too early for me to bury it in a closet.

I truly didn't care what she said, so much as I hoped she didn't turn her head ninety degrees to the right. That was very much my life at that point: just hoping I could keep the illusion together, like a kids' sock-puppet show at a library.

"We have a problem with Oliver's daycare" is something I could deal with. If I'd passed out with my computer on my lap and Facebook Messenger open, all bets were off if she wanted to talk. Whenever that happened, I generally had a lot of explaining to do.

"What's wrong?"

I just figured the prices were going up. Small adjustments.

"They said you were drunk."

I didn't know what "my blood ran cold" meant until that second. My brain tried catching up.

"When?"

"This morning."

Again, this could've been true on any given morning at that point.

"I wasn't drunk…"

"I don't care. They smelled alcohol."

"Okay."

"It wasn't the first time. Apparently, they've smelled it before. Allison smelled it."

"Who's Allison? The big one?"

"The pregnant one."

"Oh."

"You opened your mouth and about bowled her over."

It pissed me off. I knew exactly which one she was talking about now, and I swore I'd hit enough breath mints beforehand. I guess not.

This just flooded me with battery-acid shame, but it was leaking so steadily these days, it didn't awaken anything more than an "I'm working on it."

I WAS RUNNING out of beer and booze earlier and earlier—especially on my work-from-home days. So then it became a countdown between when Carrie wound down for the evening versus when I could sneak out. I couldn't just say I was going for a quick trip to the grocery store. I spent half my life in the car at that point, so it didn't make any sense. So I pretended I wanted to go for a night bike ride.

I got so drunk one night at home that it went from ten to two in the morning in the span of what felt like two Spotify songs. I was wobbly, but not in any shape to stagger into a bar for another jolt. No, this called for a grocery store. I wasn't in any shape to drive, either. So I took my bike out of the garage, rode it down the main drag in our neighborhood—a stretch where it's nothing but check-cashing places and a shady Wendy's—and disappeared down the bike path. Within seconds, I realized my mistake. There were no bike trail lights. It was pitch-black. I rolled down into the dark, hearing nothing but the clacking of my spokes and the wind rushing through my hair. I got to the bottom of the hill and stopped. I grabbed my iPhone and turned on the light.

I swear this is true: When I turned it on, a man was standing there, maybe five feet away.

There was no way I could've known he was standing there. I maybe would've hit him if I hadn't stopped. He was just standing there in the center of the path, an old black man with distant eyes and a netted bag over a shoulder. He didn't even seem surprised.

I was so shocked I didn't even respond.

I just clambered up the hill, pumping my pedals and listening to them grind.

I turned over my shoulder and saw him recede into the dark.

That might be me one day, I thought.

AT SOME POINT, I'd simply given up on my appearance. It was hard enough getting through the day, let alone doing something more than picking up clothes from the bedroom floor, checking them for wrinkles and slipping them on. The same went for my personal hygiene. I'd been putting off getting my wisdom teeth taken out for years, too, and I could feel that coming down the line, too. It loomed large on the schedule. I cancelled twice, and simply didn't show up the third time. The fourth time, the dentist's office left me two messages, checking to make sure I'd be showing up for the appointment. Something locked into place in my brain and I agreed, yes, I'd be there. I knew I wouldn't be able to drink that much the night before. The appointment was seven-thirty in the morning.

The night before, though, I had a six-pack of Great Lakes Christmas Ale. And I'd forgotten that I'd purchased them in the first place, which, to an alcoholic, is the best sort of amnesia imaginable. The six-pack was sitting there, perfectly staged in my fridge. This was something like the Holy Grail of beers for a Midwesterner like me, too: the simple sight of the artwork of the little trolley car filled with ornaments was enough to send a light jolt through my body. At the time, it was hard to find. I'd met people through Craigslist to get the beer, buying it in a shady parking lot. It was also 11% or 12%. (Not that it mattered.) It was spiced perfectly—a perfume of cinnamon and cardamom and nutmeg. This wasn't beer—this was as perfect an accompaniment to a fireplace as Venetian blinds in a house facing west.

I tore into the first beer, all alone in the house, and put on some indie band Cole recommended at full blast. Three beers in, I was madly texting people how much I missed them and Facebook-messaged others I hadn't ever spoken with. I was a man untethered. It wasn't until my fifth Christmas Ale that I could feel the caramel glow inside my veins begin to remind me that I had an obligation in the morning. I drank the sixth one just to put the memory of that obligation out of my brain. I staggered upstairs to our room, barely made it into the bed, and set my phone alarm.

Miraculously, I woke up on time and drove myself to the dental office wearing the same clothes. Oddly enough, I didn't even feel horrible. I didn't have the hooded eyes or the *don't-fucking-talk-to-me* buzz in my brain. In fact, I had that hurricane-center clarity of mind that comes when your hangover hasn't quite hit yet. Everything's sky-blue and dead calm. I was making jokes with the desk clerk who put on a fake smile because she knew I'd also been a no-show recently and I probably smelled of booze.

"Carl?" they called my name.

I rolled my eyes and walked in the back, kind of forgetting what was about to happen.

This was serious dental work. This wasn't a cleaning.

I lay down on the chair, slowly coming to realize that I hadn't given this the amount of respect and consideration I owed it.

"So, do you know what we're getting into here this morning?" the humorless hygienist said, sounding as bored as I was terrified.

I nodded, which meant I'd be finding out even less than I should about the next hour or so.

My heart began beating quickly, and she instructed me to pull out my iPhone and play music, if I wanted. Naturally, it was at 10% power, but I put my earbuds in anyway. I pretended to ignore the pricks of novocaine at all four corners of my gums, pretending not to feel their icy work going to town as a live Bruce Hornsby track came on.

And that's also the very second that the hangover hit.

The brutal wave of Christmas Ale came sweeping into that room as I lay there alone. The hygienist and dentist were waiting in the other room for the novocaine to kick in. I could feel my airway swelling. I couldn't breathe as easily as I did just a minute beforehand. I sat at an odd angle as I considered bolting from the room as the hangover oozed into an *X-Files* black oil taking over my body. My fingers tingled; sweat prickled on my skin; a genuine headache anviled its way into the center of my thoughts.

The dentist returned in time to catch me getting a second wind at pretending I was fine. Out came the silver dentistry equipment, laid out on a thin tray. I imagined that in twenty years, it'd be in a museum with "cruel, unusual tools of the dental trade" as a caption. They began their work; I could feel it and hear it with Dolby Surround Sound as they cracked and sawed and pulled and yanked at my wisdom teeth. They were doing real paleontology in my head. Messy bone-finding. All the while, bits of bone and smoke choked me. I also realized, with horror, that my esophagus was shrinking.

I couldn't choke back any air. I felt like I was drowning or, worse yet, being waterboarded.

I coughed and sputtered. They immediately recoiled, not expecting me to sit up straight. I banged my head on the light, sending it in another direction.

I was wheezing, icy panic rising, desperate to catch some air.

"Calm down," the dentist said evenly. "Just breathe. It's okay."

Seconds later, flush with embarrassment, I realized it was

all in my head.

"Should we continue?"

I nodded, feeling a tear slide out of my right eye.

I'D INVITED EVERYONE I knew to my son's fourth birthday party: our parents, brothers, sisters, neighbors, work friends, Facebook friends, assorted acquaintances, countless cousins and, most importantly, all my drinking buddies. I'd gone all-out and rented one of those bounce castles that someone called an "inflatable babysitter." Half the backyard was taken up by the thing. While my wife had busied herself with all the actual details of the birthday itself (you know: the cake, gift bags, food), I was worried about what kind of beer I should stock up on. I even solicited requests from people ahead of time. Most everyone gave me puzzled looks and crinkled brows. I asked my wife if we should have some wine on hand. She reminded me that it was a four-year-old's birthday party. I nodded and mentally noted that I'd probably need to get a bottle or two of chardonnay then. I packed an entire cooler full of cans and bottles of beer and lovingly covered it with ice. My role in the party planning was complete.

At some point during that same party, I found myself inside that castle, bouncing little kids in every direction as beer raced through my bloodstream. Some of the kids tumbled out, desperate to escape. I didn't care—I'd reached my normal cruising altitude. I'd put down four or five beers before noon. (It was a party, so public morning drinking was okay, I told myself.) As I bounced, I dimly realized I'd put myself on display for everyone to see: a thirtysomething dad who was drunkenly jumping around inside a red-yellow-blue castle. I clambered out and quickly offered some of the parents around me something to drink. If they drank, it'd make me feel better. *No thanks,* most of them insisted. *The water is fine.* I shrugged and grabbed another cold one, downing it.

That was pretty much my life as a parent in a snapshot. At home, I made sure alcohol was all around me, so I could easily taproot into it. If it was my house, I could do whatever the hell I wanted. But when you have kids, you're automatically invited to other people's houses for any number of playdates and parties. I wasn't the popular one—my kids were. It's kind of like when you're young and other kids come over, just to play with your cool toys and computer games—not necessarily you.

So when the parental obligations started mounting, I was forced to start making temporary connections with people I barely knew—or even wanted to. At other parents' houses, I had to strategize more. I burned brainpower rationalizing whose parties I could attend and whose parties I couldn't. When you're as deep in the bottle as me, you automatically find yourself surrounded by other parents who were prone to drinking. I could bring a six-pack of beer, and no one would bat an eyelash.

Getting invited to a kid's birthday party because they're simply friends with your kid at daycare? That's tricky business. I had to mentally gear myself up for the two-hour arc of games, birthday singing, and party favors by getting Just Drunk Enough that I could survive. Not enough drinks and I'd be feeling time crawl by the second; one drink too many and I'd be excitedly talking about *Fringe* with a slight slur.

My drinking problem wasn't a secret. It was usually on full display—either in overly excited conversations or with a hangover burning in my eyes. I wasn't doing the math, regarding the fact that we weren't getting invitations back to visit.

A modest diagram of my drinking:

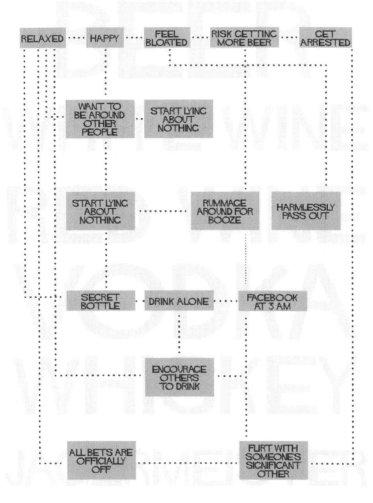

22

ONE DAY WHEN I was pretending to be in Cincinnati, I was actually crushing my job. I was mobilizing all sorts of marketing initiatives. People were listening to me. Some of my ideas had gained traction. One of my concepts was something that celebrated Rochester, New York's "food scene"—it resembled a restaurant menu and was being passed around the office as the best thing the design team had ever done. I was getting zero credit, but it gave me satisfaction. I knew what I was doing.

I was lying in bed, listening to a conference call where my

coworkers went on about their failed campaigns in the *Daily News Leader* in Murfreesboro and the *Argus Leader* in Sioux Falls. Places that didn't actually exist to me. I didn't think there were actual newspaper offices in those towns. They were fiction—like my life in Cincinnati.

An hour later, I woke up and the line was dead.

I'm positive I was snoring on the call.

I COULDN'T KEEP it together—the whirligig of my life was just too much. I'd weaved too complex a spiderweb for myself. The mileage had literally gotten to me: it destroyed one car and was now threatening to destroy my sanity. It was eating at me. I was convinced it was the job that was driving my alcoholism, not anything else. I was leaving a trail of McDonald's wrappers, side-of-the-road vomit, and blistering headaches. The Cincinnati skyline always seemed to emerge like that castle spire from the end of the *Never-Ending Story* on that asteroid. There it was: against all odds, still intact.

I pulled into the parking garage with the borrowed Bonneville, looking down at the Miller Lite six-pack in its bag. Four of them were drained. Two more held promise. I pulled into a spot near the edge of the garage, rolled down the windows and closed my eyes, listening to the rain falling against brick.

Tomorrow was the day, I knew.

THERE ARE CORRECT, graceful, elegant ways to quit your job. In fact, "quit" is a hard term. Let's go with "transition." When you build up enough hurricane-strength gusto to transition between jobs, you should probably have another one in the pipeline. The two jobs should sort of overlap, gentlemanly. Not me. I guessed that one of the two or three job leads I had in the works would come to be—one being a communications director for a community center, another being a medical transcription consultant. I had no experience in either field, but I had just enough juice running beneath my skin to convince me that I was a lock for either one. I just needed to get free from this shitty job. It'd turned on me. It was like the piece of fruit I'd been savoring for weeks—staring at its perfect form in the bowl—and then when I picked it up, it was soft and supple and rotted.

The job had betrayed me.

It was two-thirty on a spring afternoon when it happened; it was too nice to be working anyway. I paced around my empty house, empty Labatt bottles lining the countertops. When I'd see a half-drunk one, I'd finish it off. I paced and paced, waiting for the right time. I was furious. I sat down at my corporate laptop and decided to write an eloquent *Fuck you* letter.

The words just flowed. After all, remember: for me, there's nothing better than drunken entitlement.

Dear Andrea,

I don't know when or how or why this job turned into such a joke. Maybe it was from the beginning and I just didn't see it. I have no idea. But you're kidding yourself if you think anything we do matters here. None of this is real. We write junk mail and spam, for God's sake. It's nonsense. Furthermore, you've created an environment where I don't trust you—and no one else does, either. You want our gossip and all of our secrets. You want to be in control. You can't see that you're not in control at all. You don't see that you're chasing all of your good employees away, including me. I'm no prize pig, but I'm far from your worst employee. Me leaving is going to be costly. Good luck finding someone with my experience and skill set.

Consider this my notice. **Effective immediately.**

No one tells you that there's a genuine narcotic thrill to quitting your job in a blaze of glory—copying everyone in sight. When I sent the email, I cc:'d the entire HR department, directors, assistant vice presidents, random distribution lists and low-level associates. I even copied a random person I'd met on my first day, as if I needed a witness. It was a scorched-earth campaign. I then boxed everything up, drinking the whole time, and taped it down. It was so incredibly satisfying. I sat there, proud, as I stared at the laptop in its box. Then I realized I forgot to throw the power cord in there. So I unpacked everything, tossed in the cord and re-packed everything. I tossed my badge in there, too, for good measure. I boxed everything up and stared it down against the kitchen counter.

I texted a few coworkers a bleary-eyed "Goodbye" and passed out.

23

WELL, IF YOU'VE read this far, you probably assumed (correctly) this was where it was all heading: rehab. I was almost expecting to fail the initial treatment facility screening, too. I wasn't as bad as an "alcoholic." Like, I'd tell them how much I was drinking and they'd go: *Ehhhh. Just drink lots of water and Gatorade. You'll be fine.*

Not so.

"You certainly qualify for treatment," the woman on the

other end of the phone intoned.

I felt like I'd won the lottery at the same time that I'd failed a written exam entirely populated with James Bond trivia. I couldn't believe my horrible luck. I'd spent at least two weeks reading up on alcohol detox which, by the way, didn't help. If you spend any real amount of time reading about detox when you're an alcoholic, you'll never stop drinking. The potential, common side effects read like something out of a Michael Crichton novel where a pandemic tears the country apart: gastrointestinal problems, violent mood swings, tremors, insomnia, disorientation. Truth be told, every time I eased my foot off the drinking accelerator, I could feel the anxiety and panic start to rise inside me, so I kept drinking.

"We have a bed for you," they told me. "It'll be ready tomorrow."

We exchanged pleasantries, and she told me she'd expect me the following day. Carrie arranged to use her lunch break to take me to the facility. We didn't talk much about the whole, well, *going-to-rehab* thing. We both agreed this was the best thing for me—especially since my attempts at getting sober involved sleepless nights, hearing voices, and basement-dark anxiety. The night before rehab, I was splayed out on the floor, trying to get warm with a baby blanket twisted around my ankles.

I shut off my cell phone. I'd been sending all kinds of late-night Facebook messages I didn't remember sending.

Garbled self-arguments about R.E.M.

Movie clips.

Almost Famous quotes.

Posts like *Music saved my life this year.*

Underneath it, embroidered into all my posts was the subtitle: *Help me. Please help me.* That afternoon, while I was curled up on the couch, I got a message from my friend Shawn. I'd told him—and only him—that I was going to rehab. He quickly sent me something that wasn't self-effacing or a meme. He sent me the following (which I saved):

Sober Paul will be the Best Paul. You're doing this for Carrie and your kids. That makes you a hero. I look up to you and so will your kids. You'll be better for this. See you on the other side of this, brother.

"IT LOOKED DIFFERENT on the website" is all I said.

Carrie had to agree at the sight of the place, which pained her. On the Parkside website, the facility actually looked like a sprawling estate with an impressive brick façade, regal white columns, and expansive, rolling yards—all of it tucked neatly beyond the eaves of maples and evergreens. Photoshop, however, is fucking amazing. Carrie had been impressed, which isn't easy to do, since she's a nurse. Then again, maybe it was the lack of sleep and desperation that shaded my opinion. To me, Parkside appeared like the picture of serenity: a secure, strong brick structure sitting high atop a hill. Well-manicured shrubbery. Beautifully kept lawns.

Alas, the website wasn't even remotely close to reality as we sat in the car, with my overnight bag between my feet. The zipper wouldn't close because it was jammed with nearly every shirt and pair of shorts I owned. I'd thrown everything in seconds before we'd driven over.

"Well," Carrie said, shifting the car into park. "Here we go."

WHEN I CHECKED in, I was officially "Carl F." No one cared about the "Paul" part there, let alone my last name. Certainly not the puffy-faced receptionist who was paying more than a little attention to the TV in the waiting room over my shoulder. It was an old fat TV set grabbing free channels from the air. There were a few future patients littered around the place—bunched and balled up on the threadbare furniture, waiting to be admitted. I sat there, sizing up everyone, wishing I was drunker than I was. I'd managed to squeeze in two Labatt Blues before Carrie picked me up, but I didn't really feel any lift.

There was a woman in her thirties wearing sweatpants and stretching across two chairs, fast asleep, her head resting in an older woman's, probably her mother's, lap. The mother stroked her daughter's hair like she was five years old.

I was jealous and angry and terrified.

I wanted my mom.

I WAS USHERED into Intake by a girl in blue scrubs with a faded snake tattoo on the base of her neck. I was in something of an interrogation room with low ceilings and even lower lighting. The girl took my vitals and frowned when she gave me a breath alcohol test. She jabbed me with needles, taking blood samples. Already, time seemed to be slipping away from me.

The dour director of the facility came in and scribbled lots of notes and dropped words like "anhedonia." He didn't expect me to know what the word meant; I immediately felt super-intelligent and above the place. *I'll be out of here in no time,* I told myself. He wasn't impressed in the slightest nor was his stone-faced assistant next to him. She told me a number of times that I was doing the right thing, but I didn't believe her.

I knew exactly how I'd gotten there, but not how long I'd have to stay. Carrie couldn't get a straight answer out of anyone, which scared me. I could see it in her eyes: the sinking-in realization that I could be a prisoner of Parkside for weeks on end.

"But he needs to look for a job."

"Treatment is individualized," the counselor said.

"What does that mean?"

"It's different for everyone."

"But what if someone calls him for an interview?"

This didn't compute with either of them. I liked that Carrie was doing all the talking, because I was pretty sure I'd just start crying by the second sentence.

"It's just going to take however long it takes for him," he said, like I wasn't even in the room.

"But what about music?"

"What about it?"

"He likes music. His iPod helps calm him down."

"We've been doing this for a long time," the assistant said evenly. "Music isn't part of the program."

"What about books?"

"No. No books. He can have a notepad and a pen."

"So you can't tell me how long he's going to be here?"

"No."

Then, I followed a hulking orderly into the bathroom and

peed on a strip of paper for him. No drugs in my system. He was faintly disappointed. When I returned to Intake, a man wearing rubber gloves had removed all my unfolded clothes and was properly re-folding them, gingerly setting each one down on the bench. He was feeling around for things that weren't in there. *It's part of my job,* he was saying. I was embarrassed that I couldn't even fold clothes right. I felt like I was in grade school, raw and exposed.

The man tried to make small talk about the weather. None of it seemed real to me. I nodded, agreed the weather exists and tried to focus on something else.

I broke down, sobbing uncontrollably.

I couldn't even fold clothes right.

THE FIRST PERSON I met in rehab was a girl named Aubrey, who was barely out of her teens. She passed me on the stairs as I was being shown to my room by the girl with the faded snake tattoo. Aubrey was pale and had close-cropped jet-black hair and wore a sweatshirt several sizes too large. She seemed to want to disappear into the shirt when she was introduced to me. She was shy and couldn't make eye contact. Aubrey looked like a clown without circus makeup, which is to say that she wasn't used to being dressed down.

"I'm Aubrey," she offered.

"I'm Paul."

"Carl," the girl with the snake tattoo corrected me.

"No, actually, it's Paul."

Both of them were immediately confused.

"Are we done?" she asked the girl with the tattoo.

"Actually, no. Dr. Sapra needs your paperwork. I'll run down with you. I'll be right back, Carl."

They both disappeared.

The second person I met was named Moochy—an old black gentleman with a freckled face and an easy, tired smile. He said his name without irony, shame, or any sense that it was anything but his God-given name. He seemed to zero in on new people like a heat-seeking missile from 1980s action movies.

"What's your name?" Moochy challenged.

I told him but Moochy was already onto a familiar line of questioning.

"What you in for?"

Moochy was in his late fifties, hunched over like a blighted tree by a forgotten roadside. He was cloaked in tattered pajama pants and a flannel robe. He had hooded eyes and a perpetual smirk. Moochy had been allowed to ask whatever question he pleased for far too long. There was a filtered cigarette tucked behind one ear, and he seemed content to guard the top of the stairwell. Maybe he was the gatekeeper, I thought.

"Alcohol," I shrugged. "Just alcohol."

"Just alcohol, huh?"

Moochy let out a thin, watery laugh. He aimed a gnarled wooden cane at me, and there was suddenly no difference between the man or the cane. They'd both clearly seen better days.

"You'd better watch it with that."

"Watch what?"

"*Just alcohol*," Moochy turned the phrase over and over on

his chapped lips.

"That's what I'm in for."

"There ain't no *just* about it," he said. "Moochy's been around these rooms for years. Alcohol's just as bad as anything else. Don't matter if it's by itself or dancing with the devil."

I got an odd charge from the man, especially since he talked about himself in the third person.

"What are you in for?"

Moochy smiled. "You learn quick."

"How's that?"

"The only currency you got in here," he said, "is being polite. Be polite, take the pills they give you, and pretend you're interested in other people, brother."

"Well, what are you here for?"

"Heroin," he said, with barely a millisecond between his answer and my question. It's an answer that's always locked in the chamber, ready to fire.

My eyes must have went wide because he nodded, as if he was shocked, too.

"Twenty-five years, brother, yeah," he said.

I couldn't see it in Moochy's eyes, though. There is no telltale sign of heroin use. I couldn't see anything like squiggled frequencies on an oscilloscope. I was just staring at an old black man in ratty pajamas, resting all his forward weight on a weathered cane.

"How long have you been in here?"

"State put me in here thirteen days ago," he smiled. "Lucky thirteen. Moochy don't keep track of time no more, though. Could be fourteen. Ain't no fifteen days, though. That's for goddamn sure."

I laughed nervously, mainly because I couldn't believe I was standing there.

"Carl your real name?"

I almost wanted to say no, simply because Moochy seemed excited by the prospect that I might not be who I said I was.

"Yeah. That's my name."

"You sure?"

"Why would I lie?"

"Why *wouldn't* you lie? You're an addict."

I shifted uncomfortably in place.

"Don't get defensive on me, brother," Moochy said. "All I'm saying is that if you aren't lying outside, you'll be lying in here. That's what they really teach you in here. How to become a liar. It's the only way to get out. Say *yes* if you mean *no, no* if you mean *yes, more* if you mean *some, some* if you mean *always*."

I stood there, seeing Aubrey haunt the stairwell again.

"Everyone's a liar here, Mr. Carl. Moochy knows."

The tattooed girl returned, a bit more frazzled than before. She skipped every other step to collect me, looking as weary as the facility, or maybe like she was operating on outdated software: overworked processors, little memory, constantly running cooling fan.

"Ready, Carl?"

"Paul."

"Right," she said. "Let's show you your room."

"See you, Moochy."

Moochy grinned.

"I'll be here. Moochy's always here."

Halfway down the long, narrow corridor, I turned to the girl.

"His real name isn't Moochy, is it?"

"Not even close."

THE DOOR CREAKED open to reveal a cramped two-bedroom suite. The ceiling was freckled with water damage, and the floor had more stains than carpet. Forgotten furniture was strewn about the place. I saw two feet stretched over the edge of the spare bed. Faint snoring.

"Your roommate is sleeping."

"I'm just glad he's not dead," I joked.

She didn't find it funny.

My name was scrawled in hot pink on a dry-erase board next to my room, where greasy light leaks in from the tiny window. The name *Josh C.* is scribbled on the spare bedroom wall.

"He just arrived this morning, too," she continued.

I just nod.

"I'm sure you guys'll be fast friends."

"THIS IS GONNA make you feel snowy," the med assistant promised me, handing me one small paper cup with two pills inside and another cup with just enough water to not choke on the pills.

"Snowy," I repeated.

Aubrey breezed past with two girls in tow, offering me a

faint smile.

"You bought the ticket," she laughed, seeing that I'm light-years out of my element. "Might as well take the ride."

I swallowed the meds.

Ativan dialed everything down from a 9 or a 10 to a 3 or a 4. Not quite a 1 or a 2. Just enough to make me feel translucent yet not invisible. I could feel my brain getting gauzy as I shambled around Parkside, getting my bearings. The facility was a two-story U-shaped building with a common area at the center. If a building could have bad posture and could slouch in its seat, Parkside would. It wasn't nice, but it wasn't embarrassed by itself, either.

Not everyone wanted to engage with eye contact there. In fact, most people seemed like they couldn't. I felt overdressed in my cargo shorts and U.S.S. *Enterprise* T-shirt. The place was filled with dead-eyed zombies padding around in flip-flops and bathrobes. Middle-aged men, teenaged girls, grandmothers. There was the occasional hello, but most everyone was content to be disconnected from one another, lounging around the common room and staring into the middle distance.

I ventured outside. It was one of those Octobers in Ohio that didn't know it was October. It was humid, and the sky was newspaper grey. There were maybe a half-dozen people milling around a small, crowded patio. Everyone was furiously smoking. Parkside didn't seem awake yet even though it was four in the afternoon.

"You can't go there," someone immediately said.

I turned. It was the orderly who gave me my drug test, smoking.

"Where?"

"Anywhere past that line," he pointed behind me with his cigarette.

I was confined to a patio area roughly the size of my old office at Arizona State (that I shared with Lynn). Beyond it were looping pathways leading into some silvery ash trees. The creek advertised on the website was nothing more than a concrete culvert, now drained and under maintenance. Tanned, burly men were hosing it down, getting ready to paint it or something. In the meantime, it was an ugly brown scar.

"The whole time?"

"Not until you get a green band," he shrugged. "You aren't through detox yet."

"But I don't feel like I'm in detox."

"That means the drugs are working."

I considered this. I don't smoke and I could already start to feel Parkside getting smaller.

"I'm going to go back to my room."

The orderly nodded distantly, not caring.

THE LADYBUG WAS unassuming, scuttling across the wall in quiet zig-zags and the occasional flutter of wings. Its movements were oddly hypnotic. I followed it with my eyes, watching as it crossed from the windowsill, up along the wall, and then above me on the ceiling.

I felt as though there was a weight in the pit of my stomach, pinning me to the ratty mattress as I traced the insect's path. The ladybug made it as far as the light fixture, then plopped to the floor. For a few seconds, I couldn't sort the ladybug from the stained carpet, then I saw it. It was crawling around aimlessly. It hesitated, stopping.

I narrowed my eyes.

The ladybug seemed to shudder and then, improbably, grow. There were flashes of muscle and pink sinew, glistening under its wings. It swelled. The insect undulated and in a matter of seconds, tripled in size. I tried to move but couldn't.

The ladybug exploded like a grotesque Transformer, unpacking itself into the size of a small dog. Its legs had thick spines and shivering hair. The insect's eyes lock with mine. When it does, the entire carapace flashes bright purple, and the ladybug races across the floor toward me, mandibles gaping wide.

I tried to scream but the insect was already stuffing itself inside me, burrowing down my throat, suffocating me.

I awakened with a double jolt: once to discover the ladybug wasn't real; next, to find my roommate standing in the doorway, drowsily leaning against the frame.

"Did I wake you?" I asked. My throat felt like fabric.

My roommate was younger than me, late twenties, and maybe a hundred pounds. His face was stubbled, and his eyes drifted from one corner of the room to the other. The spires of a huge chest tattoo crept out from his T-shirt and sprouted out over his clavicle.

"Huh?"

"Did I wake you? Was I screaming?"

I wiped a sheen of sweat from my forehead, pushing myself up from the bed. The box spring creaked relief.

"Dude, I don't even know where I am right now?"

"Is that a question?"

"Huh?"

"You're in my doorway."

"That's the rumor," he nodded. "Yeah?"

The kid spoke as if every sentence was crooked, bent upward toward a question mark. It was like a screensaver had gone off in the kid's head, and I'd just nudged his brain awake.

I rubbed my eyes. *Snowy,* I thought.

"I guess neither of us are really here."

"Where's here?"

I paused. "Parkside."

"Hotel?"

"Does this look like a fuckin' hotel?"

He squinted. "Motel?"

"What?"

"I'm just fuckin' with you. I know where I am."

He was twitchy, constantly moving around. Now that I'd jostled the screensaver, the kid wouldn't stop moving. He was made of bees. He scratched his neck, then brushed his nose, then squirmed. He also didn't seem to notice he was barefoot.

"Wanna go outside?"

"I was just there," I said sullenly.

"You sure you don't want to go?"

I could still feel the cloud of Ativan, the foggy weight of it in my shoes.

"Sure. I'll go."

"I'm always waking up in places like this. Kind of a talent?"

"That doesn't seem like much of a talent."

The kid felt around in his jeans pockets. I watched him with a detached amusement, considering he was something like an amnesiac. The childlike wonder was missing, though. Instead, there was something blank behind his eyes. The kid found a pack of cigarettes in his pocket, shakily putting one between his lips.

"I'm Josh."

There was a pause.

"I'm Paul."

He shrugged backward, toward the name on my door. "Says Carl?"

"I'm Paul."

"Don't believe everything you read, right?"

"**THIS IS LIKE** the worst summer camp ever," I told Josh. He laughed hard, but his eyes still darted around as he huddled his body together, like he was bracing himself against a cold wind that wasn't there. It was sunny and almost seventy. Josh told me his story in less than sixty seconds. Booze was pretty much just the background of his story. Pills were the real problem.

"Summer camp," he laughed. "That's what this place is, yeah?"

I looked around at everyone on the patio. All I saw were thousand-mile stares, unkept promises, and arrest warrants everywhere I looked. Tattoos and tempers.

"You're kind of scared?" he asked.

A kid even younger than Josh leaned in and shook my hand.

"Mike," he introduced himself.

"Paul."

Mike was tall and lanky, with sunken eyes. He was so thin

that guessing his weight would be like measuring the weight of shadows. He had a kind smile, though, which is how I judge people. I can tell a lot about someone through their smile. He tried introducing me to some of the people around us on the smoking patio, but that's like being introduced to a roomful of strangers and being expected to take a test later. I just nodded and grunted my name. Mike was young but seemed to have a hold over everyone—one he wasn't even aware of. He'd done the deal for a while, you could just tell. There was a U2 video ages ago where the band was surrounded by slow-motion explosions and carnage, even though they were moving in real time. It reminded me of Mike. All of it was swirling around him in the background—all the chaos and confusion. None of it fazed him. I locked onto that confidence immediately, wanting it.

"This place is nothing like *Crazy Heart*," I told Mike.

"That a book?"

"No," I felt the conversation going down the drain. "Movie."

"Good one?"

"No. I mean, yes. Has Jeff Bridges. Has a part about rehab."

"A part about rehab."

"Yeah."

"Hmmm."

"I was just saying this place is nothing like that movie."

I also knew I wasn't like the people around me, I thought. I didn't belong out there on the smoking patio where I didn't smoke. Workers were still scrubbing out the concrete creek.

"What's your D.O.C.?" Josh asked me.

"D.O.C.?"

"Drug of Choice."

"Alcohol," I said. "Just alcohol."

"There you go again," Moochy said in passing, shaking his head.

"What's yours?" I asked.

"Pills."

"Oh yeah?"

"Fuck yes. Benzos, brother."

"Yours?" I asked Mike.

"Heroin," he shrugged.

Josh nodded.

"Oh, you a fan?" Mike asked, half-mocking.

"Not really," Josh said. "I'm a garbage-can junky, man. I'll do anything you got."

I was hopelessly out of my element. I didn't belong at Parkside with them. They were the types of people you read about in magazines. There were countless profile pieces on the social dropouts standing around me. I wasn't one of them. The longer I stayed here, the longer their disease infected me.

"I see," I kept my hands in my pockets.

I was immediately a loner, orbiting Josh only because I didn't want to go back to our room. If I did, I'm not sure if I'd wake up in time for a meeting. If I didn't, one of the orderlies would start banging down the door, which they enjoyed doing. I also didn't want more nightmare ladybugs raining down on me, either.

To our left, sitting alone and scribbling in a notepad, was Aubrey. Writing was the only thing we were allowed to do there. No paperback novels, no music, nothing else. She wasn't like the others, I thought. I recognized her as a kindred spirit, but the distant kind—I desperately wanted to connect with someone there, so I invented a history for her. Then it dawned on me that everyone there had invented histories, so it didn't matter what I came up with for her.

I'd be right no matter what.

IT WAS NO accident the chalkboard dominated the common area. It had everything scheduled out for the day, carefully scrawled, in half-hour increments. At first, I was insulted by its size. Then it hit me: not everyone has their days dictated, organized, arranged. And that's probably why everyone stole glances at it throughout the morning. It just becomes second nature. Patients gather unconsciously, collecting wordlessly in front of it before sessions.

Spirituality. Breakfast. Group therapy. Fellowship. Lunch. Guest speaker. Free time. Counselor. Med eval. More free time. Dinner. Free time. Evening therapy. Free time. Sleep.

Always free time.

The chalkboard glared down at me before the first session: Group.

Some people liked it. They truly enjoyed the ushering, the direction, the mindless *go-here* of it all. Patients started to file into the common area, as if called by an alien beacon to Devil's Tower, like in *Close Encounters*. There were also no clocks in Parkside, so orderlies rapped on the doors of the few stragglers, studying laminated notepads with our faces printed on them.

"I don't really think I'm an alcoholic," an older, gray-skinned woman shrugged in my first group session. There were a few dozen of us sitting in a semicircle. She crossed her arms and shifted uncomfortably in her chair. "I just think my husband got tired of my shit."

"You don't come here in the same way a parent doesn't go to a PTA meeting to see if they have children," the counselor countered. "Let's try that again."

The lady refused to admit anything. It was a game of tug and war.

I stiffened. They were getting closer to me, and I didn't want to speak. I'd make something up if I had to. That was how I'd gotten through life that far. The longer it took to get around to me, too, the more elaborate the lie and my backstory was going to be. Up to then, that's how my brain worked: the lies were all just bubbling there, waiting.

When the discussion wound its way to Aubrey, she told a story about living online. How Facebook was her friend, how it was all like being in love with love, how she was just another stupid girl with a Tumblr page, how she loved to fill herself up with benzodiazepines and then preach nothings on Twitter. How the Internet was a cemetery where nothing ever really dies and that she loved haunting it, digging things up.

I tried not to make eye contact, but my heart was full. Not like I was in love or anything. Just the sheer fact that I'd found a connection. Maybe it was the Ativan. Maybe not.

The guy next to her was a creaky door of a human being. He had see-through teeth and was really proud of being able to turn "seven dollars into seventy" in a week. He knew that when he got out of Parkside, he'd go right back to using, he said. He was absolutely certain of that. "I know who I am and who I'm not," he said.

I sort of envied him.

I WAITED IN the common room for my daily med eval, not knowing if it was three in the morning or seven. I wanted to be first, so I didn't have to wait in a line. There were a few cushions missing next to me on the couch and some kitty-litter gravel was scattered on the linoleum below. It reeked of Clorox and I-don't-want-to-know. The TV was playing a muddy VHS of some Dan Aykroyd comedy from the Eighties. One of the orderlies took a key from around his neck and jammed it into the wall of telephones, turning it. People suddenly swarmed the phones.

Mike breezed by. "Phones are life."

I still had the white bracelet, which meant I wasn't allowed to call anyone, even though I desperately wanted to connect with home. I wanted to hear if my luck had miraculously changed on the outside. Maybe companies were calling me, wanting an interview. As I waited, I sat and listened to the hushed conversations wash around me, one after the other. Tense apologies. Delicate schedulings of daycares and appointments. Tears. Whispered rumors of hidden stashes of caffeine somewhere in the center. One guy pulled an athletic sock from his back pocket and wrapped it over the receiver, then talked through that. *Germs*, he explained matter-of-factly.

"Carl F.," the doctor called me.

He didn't even bother getting out of his office. I meandered over. I'd gotten down the timing of rehab. There was no need for urgency.

The doctor didn't make eye contact. He was a prop, a paper

mill, asking me a series of questions.

"Any cravings?" he asked.

"Donuts," I admitted.

He stared at me blankly.

It was an honest response. I had been craving donuts.

"No," he said. "For alcohol."

"Then, no."

He scribbled a few notes, then dismissed me.

Next.

I GAVE MORE blood. I found Aubrey standing in front of the chalkboard, one arm tucked under the other, swirling decaf tea in a Styrofoam cup. She studied the chalkboard like it was a museum piece.

"I wish I could Instagram this," she told me, not turning.

I stood there, trying to see what she saw.

"What filter would you use?"

"I don't know," she squinted her eyes. "That's what I'm trying to figure out."

We stood there, brains scrolling through imagined Instagram filters, as zombie patients shuffled past us. No one said hello except a crooked vanilla-bean of a guy named Dijon who'd earlier announced in Group that he'd been in so many rehabs, he couldn't remember what his kids looked like.

"They moved Serenity," Aubrey told me.

"They did?"

"It was at 9 yesterday. Now it's at 10:30."

"Oh."

"I wonder why."

"I don't know."

"I don't like it when they move things."

Then she wandered off down the hall.

IT WAS IN the third day when things began to lock into place in my brain. I was starting to get the hang of it. Even with the revolving door of faces—the quiet vanishings of some, the seamless arrivals of others—I started to feel the glow of something.

"Maybe you're finding serenity," a counselor offered, chewing on an unsharpened pencil.

In the cramped office, I felt myself teed up to lie. The more lies I told, the faster I could get out of Parkside. And still, I sort of felt at peace.

"Maybe that's what it is."

"What does it feel like?"

The counselor, Rikki, was young with sharp, beautifully hawkish features and J.J. Abrams spectacles. She was eager to see people get better. You could tell she wasn't burned out yet— her senses hadn't yet been dulled by the parade of nonsense, so I was thankful to have one person at Parkside who could keep me sane. When she laughed, it was almost gorgeous, coming open like a flower. She had layers—ones that were worth spending time discovering. She closed her eyes and let the laughter come out. It was also good to remember what laughter sounded like, given the constant background noise of people detoxing all around me. She had also clearly heard everything before, so that helped, too.

"I'm not as angry."

"About being here?"

I nodded.

"Are you happy?"

"No."

"Are you angry that your roommate moved?"

I leaned back in my chair. *Yes,* my body language said.

"I'm not sure why Josh got to move upstairs so quickly and I didn't."

I felt like a nine-year-old saying it.

"Alcohol detox takes seven days. His detox took three."

"But I have a new roommate."

"Have you talked to him yet?" she tapped the pencil against her teeth.

"No." The only sign of life I'd seen were wet bathroom towels on the floor.

"Unfortunate."

"It's okay."

Rikki adjusted her glasses and offered me a smile.

"I think you're making real progress."

"I don't know about that."

"You're accepting things. You aren't giving up on things anymore."

"Was I giving up on things?"

"You certainly didn't want to be here. That's for sure."

"I still don't."

"No one does," she smiled, "but you're getting it. That's the first step."

"I WONDER WHAT the creek actually looks like when it's running," Josh asked Mike and me. It was twilight on the patio. The leaves rustled in the light breeze, and the creek was a gash in the earth, hinted at by the lights lining the walkways. I could hear murmured conversations all around us, seeing the cherry glows of cigarette tips in the gathering dark.

"It'd be nice just to hear it."

"It's not that nice," Mike intoned with a smirk. "Trust me."

"How's your new roommate?"

"He could be any one of these people. I have no idea. I never see him come or go."

Josh bummed a cigarette from a quiet man in his fifties, a truck driver who'd left his six-year-old granddaughter waiting in the car at an airport parking garage while he drank inside. He liked the airport because the bars opened before eight in the morning, the man shrugged.

"I'm already out of smokes," Josh winced. "Smoked so much I've got yellow between my fingers. Look."

"You know, you don't have to stand here with me," I told him. "I know you're allowed to hit the paths now. You're out of detox."

"You're not, though."

"I will be in a few days."

"Yeah, but..."

"Yeah, but nothing," Josh smiled in the dark. "I'm your boy. Not going to leave you hanging."

Some part of me was relieved. We stood in comfortable

silence for a while.

"They moved Serenity," I offered.

"Did they?"

"Aubrey told me."

More silence.

Then, finally, from Josh: "I drive a forklift."

I turned.

"You do?"

"Yeah," he blew smoke toward the purple sky.

"No kidding."

I found myself caring about Josh's job. It was a foreign concept, a strange feeling to think about someone else. I hadn't felt it in a long time.

"All I gotta do is get through this," he nodded. "Get back to that job."

I stared at the thin clouds sketchmarking the sky instead of responding.

"I'm going to get there."

I believed him.

A distant part of me wanted to help him get there.

"YOUR ADDICTION IS just doing push-ups out there in the parking lot, waiting for you," the red-faced speaker warned us, pacing the stage of the auditorium, like he was jacked up on something himself. "All it's doing is getting stronger. And it always has a way of coming in sideways. Addiction's a motherfucker, man."

Under normal circumstances, I would have laughed at

the cartoon character up there, as he stabbed fingers at all the patients. The auditorium was filled with bobbing heads. Some were tilted to the side, drifting asleep. There was a swell of phlegmy coughs through our sessions, too: kennel cough, they call it.

The speaker blustered right through it.

"Alcohol is cunning, baffling, and powerful," he said. "And worst of all, it's patient."

Josh leaned over to Mike.

"Isn't this guy supposed to be inspirational?"

"He's just being realistic," Mike whispered back.

I started to scribble down everything the man said. I channeled it like a madman. I looked up to see that Aubrey was doing the same exact thing.

IT WAS A sad state of affairs when the arrival of Uncrustable sandwiches at ten o'clock became a reason to rejoice, but I couldn't believe my luck. I took one, savoring it. Most everyone else tore into the wrappers and housed them in record time. The schedule had caught me in its own momentum. I'd taken to stealing little cups of peanut butter from the pantry. If I couldn't be part of the underground cigarette network, I decided I could stash cups of Jif from the pantry for that not-so-inevitable moment when demand in peanut butter shot through the roof and I'd be the king.

"There's a rumor going around," Josh said between mouthfuls of Uncrustable.

"Dare I ask?"

"I think they're going to make popcorn tomorrow," he smiled darkly. "Movie night."

I looked over at the depressing collection of VHS tapes lining both sides of the TV. It was the graveyard where movies go to die. Several patients were lumped together on a couch, washed over in the blue glow of it. Still, like everything else, I felt the first twinges of looking forward to a movie night in rehab.

I WOKE UP early. I had just two days left of detox but I was already riding the pink cloud. It was six in the morning, and I ambled down to the drug counter.

"You're up early today," the counter person nodded.

"Thanks."

I was given one fewer pill than the day before and a cup of water. Good sign.

"Almost out of the woods."

"I know," I swallowed it down. It tasted good.

He turned to the schedule, notepad tucked under his arm, and looked to see what's changed, if anything.

Nothing.

I decided it was going to be a perfect day.

SHARING WITH THE group used to be the hardest part. Suddenly, I couldn't shut up. I was a broken fire valve, torrenting sentences and sentences of regret and apologies and remorse and everything in between. I wasn't really talking about anything specific. I never shared absolutes or cases in point or examples from my past so much as my feelings about where I was. I told the group that I wanted to be there, that I was grateful to be an alcoholic, that I was thankful for meeting everyone—even when they were falling asleep right next to me.

I volunteered to help unload boxes at the delivery dock. I folded the laundry of others because they couldn't. I straightened the shelves of forgotten videotapes, alphabetizing them. I even rewound most of them.

"Who are you trying to impress?" Josh asked.

"I have no fucking idea."

DURING GROUP, RIKKI posed the question: "What If?"

It was an exercise, and everyone was supposed to finish the sentence off.

What if my dad hadn't left my mom when I was seven?

What if I "go back out" again when I'm out there?

What if my husband knew about that business trip in Manchester?

I was feeling so good about life, I joked that I wondered what if dinosaurs still ruled the earth.

My fellow patients just blinked.

The answers came fast and furious as the question cycled around the room. The nineteen-year-old heroin addict with daddy issues. The too-smart grad student who was less impressed with studying than he was with meth. Moochy, who'd been in and out of the rooms for ages, recalled the time he lost his daughter at a state fair and was too fucked up to figure out how to find her, so he bought more drink tickets.

Their answers sometimes made me wince, but I get it. I understand how their lives went from Point A to Holy Shit. But someone was missing in the room. Afterward, I found Mike in the hallway, waiting in line for the phone.

"I have to talk to you," I said.

"Yeah, man," he nodded, stepping out of line. I was a math problem he needed to figure out.

"You don't have to do that."

"What?"

"Step out of the phone line."

"You've gotta talk to me. I've gotta listen," he shrugged. "Let's go."

We stepped outside.

"Can you call my wife?"

He blinked.

"About?"

"Just to let her know I'm alive."

"But you're alive. And if she calls here, they're going to tell her you're alive."

"I just want her to know."

Mike could get in a lot of trouble for calling someone else—especially someone on another patient's behalf. Still, he did it. I scribbled a few notes down on a slip of paper for her and he translated them for her. I felt like I was smuggling information out of the country, Cold War-style.

Later, I felt like something was missing. I couldn't put my finger on it at first, but then it hit me. I went up to Mike again.

"I have to ask you something."

"You need me to call your wife again? She just said..."

"No. It's about Aubrey."

"Who?"

"The girl with the short black hair," I said. "You know her. She's always writing in that notebook of hers. Do you know if she's gotten moved to another group?"

Mike bit his lip. He could tell by the timbre of my voice that this was serious business. He absently did something with his fingers—a memory reflex of some sort.

"I don't know an Aubrey. And I know all the girls in here, brother."

Something inside me took an elevator shaft-plummet.

"You sure?"

"Yeah. When did you last see her?"

"Yesterday. Last night, I think, during dinner."

"If I have, I haven't seen her in a minute," he admitted. "I'll ask around for you, though. What does she look like again?"

"She's short. Maybe this high," I held out my hand. "Black hair. Always wears a guy's oversized sweatshirt. Always writing."

The description wasn't doing it for Mike, even though I could've spit out eighteen charcoal sketches of her.

"Doesn't ring a bell. You sure you're not thinking of that Rachel chick? The one with the...?"

"Nose ring? Uses country-music lyrics in her shares? No. Definitely not her."

"What about Irene? She's got black hair..."

"No. Look, it's not a big deal. I'm just—"

Mike shook his head, cutting me off.

"It *is* a big deal because it's a big deal to you. I'm going to find her."

I felt like my mast was broken or that my compass was next to a magnet. Mike did some asking around, and Josh did the same. Some other guys, too. No one matching Aubrey's description came back. Most of the time they keep coming back with names I'd never heard of, or pointing out someone who didn't remotely look like the girl I knew.

"What if she got discharged?"

"We would've heard."

"No one said anything?"

"Not that I've heard."

"She kinda keeps to herself," I said. "I'll ask around some more."

I could feel the panic rising. I was a sinking ship—salt water flooding the bulkheads. Moochy was at the stairs again as I wiped tears. He was greeting some new arrival alongside the girl with the faded snake tattoo on her neck.

THE NOT-KNOWING part made the walls of Parkside start to swallow me slowly, like a Venus flytrap. The place had never felt smaller or more designed to make a man go mad. I felt like a submariner who'd suddenly grown five sizes too large, bounding past the smudged walls and weathered wood of the place, pacing back and forth. I crossed from one side to the other in record time, then went back again. I wanted to scream when I saw workers still scrubbing out the fake creek with big long brooms.

I skipped lunch. I couldn't eat. One of the nameless doctors said that wasn't a good sign. The body, after all, doesn't lie. He tacked on another day for observation. *Just as a precaution,* he said. Then, I was released back into rehab like a wounded fish having to re-learn how to swim against currents that used to calm me.

I couldn't focus on my writing. While a speaker prattled on, I flipped through note page after note page of elegantly scribbled thoughts—all of them commenting on something Aubrey said in a meeting, or something Aubrey might like to read once she was out in the world. My latest effort was nearly five pages, intended to find its way to her while she'd be in her first month of a new job, maybe. She'd been looking for one after all, and that time, she'd be successful at finding one because she'd be on the straight and narrow, locked and committed, clear-eyed.

I asked her questions she hadn't been asked in Group. Things too private, too intimate to air out in public. I soon realized half a notebook was devoted to her. I'd need another one to start fresh. My thoughts came in sour jolts. I looked to the doorway of my room every ten seconds, hoping to see Mike there with good news. A knock came, catching me off-guard. Instead, it was one of the orderlies.

"Counseling," he intoned. "Time to go."

"I'm not feeling well," I lied.

I didn't look up. I needed to write. I had the fever of needing to messily scribble my thoughts on a notepad, the back of a flyer or the inside cover of a Big Book.

"Too bad," the heavyset man said. "You're here to go to counseling, not to write a novel."

I stared through the orderly.

"Tell you what," he licked his lips. "You take your new

roommate to the next session, we're even. Sound good?"

So far, my roommate was just Wet Towels On The Bathroom Floor. Now I'd have to get to know his name, I thought. The orderly pointed at my room and then the other guy's. Zero sounds came from the room.

"When that door opens," the orderly points, "he's your responsibility. Get him to the med counter, then get him to the first session."

"Fine."

I got back to scribbling.

WITHOUT CLOCKS, YOU can't say "like clockwork" and mean it. But my body was in tune with the schedule of Parkside. I realized that I'd been operating on an internal clock to get through every day. It'd gotten more pronounced by the moment. It woke me up at six o'clock—the visceral urge to get out of bed and hit the common area. I'd take inventory of the patients as they wandered in for Morning Spirituality.

According to my internal clock, it was almost ten in the morning.

There had been no knocks on my door, which was just as good. I'd hit a stride with my writing. I'd gone past the point of writing with the hopes of Aubrey accidentally finding the notebook lying around the place and then, like a fairy tale, picks it up, finds herself among the words, and all the walls come tumbling down. I was at Warp Nine, going through pencils one after the other. I quietly hoped there wasn't a pencil shortage on the horizon.

Then, the spare bedroom door creaked open.

I turned from the table to the doorway, where it was half-cracked. It was bright inside, harsh light slanting across the walls and floor. Impossible-to-sleep kind of light.

A gaunt man, six-foot-five, emerged into the shared room. I set down the pencil. I didn't even know what to do with the sight of him. The man's face was sallow and cragged. He was older with locks of white hair framing his yellow eyes. He resembled the brother of a rock star from the sixties—the sibling who didn't grace the teen magazines but did twice as many drugs as everyone else on tour. He moved tentatively, shakily. His lips were a different pigment than the rest of his body. He looked like a Photoshop project gone wrong.

"I'm going to be sick," he announced with no emotion and a vague accent.

"Like, now?"

"I might have already gotten sick," he stared at me. "I'm not sure. I don't remember."

I opened my mouth to say something. I watched the man as he moved in slow motion.

"I don't know if I'm remembering something or if I'm forgetting something that's about to happen."

"Well, the bathroom's right there."

"Don't need the bathroom."

"But you said you were sick."

"Didn't say I was going to chuck in the bathroom."

I wondered what atrocities washed this man up on my beach.

Then I promptly didn't care.

There will be another one right behind him.

I went back to writing. *I have to write,* I told myself.

WHEN YOU LOSE something you never really had in the first place, you lose it twice as much. You miss its presence without knowing the full weight of it—the heft of it in your hands, the feel of it against your body. To mourn the lack of a memory, to experience the sheer vastness of absence, to understand the gorgeously sweeping sense of grief that comes from losing whatever you expected to have in your life, is somehow more crushing than never having it in the first place.

For the second time in two weeks, everything around me goes quiet.

I felt nothing.

Absolutely nothing.

When I heard the news from Mike—that no one named Aubrey had been through Parkside in the last few months—I start questioning everything about how my brain worked. Or doesn't. She was real. At least to me. I'd been worried that she'd been discharged and killed herself, doing it without writing a note. Maybe she did it with pills and Grey Goose, having done it alone in her parents' house while they were on vacation.

I continued to write a backstory for her even when I don't have to. My brain wouldn't let me.

I walked over to Aubrey's preferred table on the veranda and it was empty. I touched it absently, but I didn't dare sit down. It was a museum piece now. Her molecules were somehow still wrapped up on it, I thought, circling and swirling there. She hadn't been gone that long, for my fingers to not brush against her atoms.

I wept quietly and prayed that it was the chemicals in my brain conspiring against me.

I STARTED RACKING up bonus days at Parkside. I was like a character actor who'd arrived on a sitcom six seasons too late and was now surviving the original cast, who were all moving off to bigger and better things. Pretty soon, maybe I'd earn my own ratings-starved spin-off?

I was deemed fragile. I was now officially "Pending" in the system, meaning that there was no set day when I'd be released from detox. Doses were slightly increased. Seeing my children got further away.

Josh frowned a lot more—especially since his own exit was scheduled for just two days away. He didn't know what he was going to do. Mike was constantly talking to all the new arrivals, letting them know they'd be okay—just like he'd done with me. A huge man, someone new, sashayed into the common room in a giant bathrobe. It was almost like a regal cloak against his imperious frame, tightly knotted at the waist.

"How do you do?" he asked me, eyes wide and crazy.

I almost wanted to answer him in Old English.

I still had a few days before I'd be released, and I couldn't take much more of the vise-grip of Parkside. At some point in the middle of the night, I wandered down to the front desk and tried to check myself out. I assured the front-desk clerk that I didn't have a drinking problem anymore. She smirked and said that's because the drugs were working the way they should.

"Maybe you should just go back to your room," she suggested. I agreed that this made sense, even though it didn't. My room was the last fucking place I wanted to be.

The next day, in between free time and group sessions, I decided to really make a break for it. I'd noticed that no one paid attention when there were shift changes. There was a real fifteen-minute gap where everyone was looking the other way. I felt so smart, like I'd been doing reconnaissance ahead of a bank heist. I shuffled down the rolling hillside and across the double-lane road to a golf course. Before Parkside, for me, golf courses were cues to drink, so just the sight of the links pissed me off. I found two kids, maybe high schoolers, on the green. I hopped the fence and, still wearing a hospital wristband, I asked them if they had a cell phone I could use.

The one kid reluctantly turned over his smartphone to me. I frantically typed Carrie's number into it, heartbeat in my throat. After two rings, she picked up with a cautious "Hello?"

I hung up almost immediately.

I needed to follow the rules to get out.

This wasn't going to help anyone or anything, I knew.

I apologized to the kids and ran back up the hill to rehab.

SOME FRESH ZOMBIES stared at me in the hallway as I was being processed out. It was a litany of paperwork, but I'm an English major, goddammit. Paperwork was my life. The dour-faced director who threw "anhedonia" at me floated by, in the middle of something else, and noticed what was going on.

"You all set?" he looked over his spectacles.

"With getting checked out? Yeah."

"No. With treatment. After this."

I got it. I knew what I was supposed to say. Just like Moochy said, I had to lie. Parkside had just planted a seed. It's supposed to grow and blossom, *blah, blah, blah*. Instead, it'd brought me nothing but anxiety, sadness, and a full-scale hallucination.

"Yep," I lied.

There it was. The lying. It was back. Hell, it hadn't gone anywhere. It warmed me like a comfortable blanket.

The woman got to the last piece of paper and handed me a pen.

"Just sign here," she said, "and you're out."

I scrolled through everything I needed—all the phone numbers I'd collected—and wondered if I'll ever need any of them again. A three-ring binder of my experience was tucked under my arm, too. I suspected it'd be in the trash before long.

I was smarter than sobriety, I knew.

That's what rehab taught me.

"Are you ready to start your new life?" she asked.

I nodded and signed.

24

I SAT IN a parking lot two weeks later, chugging a wide-mouthed Miller Lite in our Jeep Liberty. I slammed it down so fast and hard that the cold burned my throat and seized my chest. Punishment. The guilt tasted like aluminum or the aluminum tasted like guilt. I couldn't tell the difference. It didn't matter. It'd only been a matter of days but I'd forgotten how sweet beer was. In unemployment, I was hosting bar trivia on Wednesdays. That's what I'd been reduced to. Not an actual job. Just entertaining drunk people with trivia questions from the corner of a sports bar.

Trouble is: I was pretty good at it. It's not a job for people who are fresh out of rehab, though.

I sucked air through my teeth, feeling the bright burn of the alcohol, and immediately felt my self-worth plummet. It'd been an alien hand that had driven me to the beer section of the gas station in the first place. I just thought: *What the hell. What can one beer hurt?* And now I was about to enter a bar. I lugged all the equipment—my sack full of answer slips and golf pencils, speaker, tripod, MacBook. I set everything up, furtively downing another beer on the side, hoping no one saw me. Afterward, it sort of hit me—something dark told me that I could handle this. Rehab hammered out the kink in my life. It'd solved it. Since I'd gone to rehab, I was cured.

I could be a responsible drinker.

That's all I'd wanted anyway.

I immediately ordered two shots of whiskey at the sports bar, with a beer back, and went on trying to host trivia.

Now I had yet another secret to carry: I wasn't sober.

WEEKS AFTER REHAB and picking up some extra trivia shifts, I got a call for a high-level communications position with a local insurance firm. It was a late-afternoon interview and I struggled with that, knowing that my drinking hadn't vanished. It was just bubbling beneath the surface. It'd need to be tempered— fed like an animal in the dark. I got ready two hours early[30] and found myself in their parking garage, sitting there, tortured by

---

[30] My mother doesn't subscribe to the "if you're not early you're late" philosophy so much as she subscribes to the "if you're not two hours early and hating life, you're not doing it right" one.

my thoughts. I looked at the car clock.

This is stupid, I told myself.

I exited the parking garage and drove to the nearest liquor store I knew downtown, where they bagged up a pint of Popov just for me. I put it on the floor of the Bonneville and returned to my spot in the parking garage. It'd be the carrot on the end of the stick. Just knowing it was in the car would give me strength. If things got dicey in the interview, I could envision it, paper-bagged on the passenger-side floor. Then I'd spew something brilliant. Maybe I'd call on the pint like a spirit animal.

Ten more minutes passed. I stared at the bag as intently as the doubts began flooding in.

Certainly, they didn't want to interview me.

No one would ever want to give me *a job.*

They must have made a mistake.

I deserved to be unemployed.

I thought of everyone at home who was depending on me to get this fucking job. I couldn't handle that sort of pressure. I wasn't the right guy for that. This was high-stakes shit.

So I unscrewed the cap.

Smash cut to the interview.

It started off normal. Very corporate. I was led around, ushered between rooms named after Caribbean islands. The first interview was introductory and as easy as they come— *Hello, do you have a heartbeat?* I can do those in my sleep. They rely on charm and I can dial that up if I need to.

Then, the vodka kicked in.

I felt it unspring in my belly while I sat there in "Little Cayman" or "Cozumel" or whatever it was called. My face flushed warm, and sweat prickled the back of my neck. During the interview in front of the hiring manager and two of her directs, I jumped up and playacted things out; I told long and involved stories with great punch lines; I paced the room and did voices. At one point, I even high-fived one of the interviewers. No matter which way you slice it, I absolutely killed that interview. No one saw *that* coming. Hell, people are probably still talking about it. Still, I killed that interview in the same way I killed my chances at putting food in my kids' mouths.

WHEN YOU'RE A recovering alcoholic and everyone around you knows it, you're suddenly exposed. People know what to expect. You don't have to hide much. But when you're an alcoholic who's suddenly a recovering alcoholic who's trumpeting it on Facebook and showing off your 30-day sober coin while you're secretly drinking again, it becomes ten times harder to achieve the escape velocity your brain so desperately needs from reality. You can't just make quick, random trips to the store without getting asked a dozen questions. You can't excuse all your stumbling, mumbling, stuttering, and confusion and sweating and puffy-faced mood swings. (Well, you can, but it's not easy.)

Because I'm an alcoholic, I cut every corner imaginable. If there was a shortcut, you could sure as shit find me taking it. If I could make people *think* I was sober and still reach alcoholic bliss, that wasn't cheating. That just meant I was smarter than everyone else around me. Of course, you can't sustain that sort of charade for long—especially when you're dealing with booze. Drunks aren't the most meticulous people on the planet. Details get fuzzy and things get overlooked. Very often, I'd forget where I'd hidden my half-drunk pints of vodka, which simply turned my house into the world's saddest version of *The Hunt for Red October*: my wife and I silently circling the house, not speaking, but both keenly aware that there was something lurking in the dark. In the end, it was just a matter of who'd find the bottle first.

Carrie found three empty Smirnoff bottles tucked under a pillow in the spare bedroom, a particularly lazy hiding spot. I didn't even know what to say other than, "Oh well. You got me." Her face was pinched with disappointment. She was more upset that I was talking about sobriety with other people who were actively trying to find it. I'd scored the cartoon version of sobriety—the one that gets played in late-night syndication.

AT THE HEIGHT of my secret drinking, I apparently texted my sister at 2:30 am. All it said was "Help me" or something to that effect. I heard about this much later from my mom, when I'd finally gotten sober. I don't remember sending the message, but it sounded like something I'd do—especially after putting away a pint of cheap, bright-smelling vodka. But it was a far cry from the messages I normally sent out into the world at two in the morning: garbled Facebook status updates, random messages to long-out-of-touch friends, the occasional phone call and slurred voicemail. Near the end of my drinking career, I dimly knew I was in trouble, but it was only in my darkest, blurriest moments that I tapped into truth. Turns out, drunk text messages were some of my first, most important steps into recovery.

When my alcoholism was finally clear to me after seeing some of what I wrote, I no longer had just a drinking problem— I'd hurtled way past the point of no return. My texts and Facebook messages pointed to my troubles. No one needed the Rosetta Stone to translate those; it was pretty clear. But the nature of my messages started to change. They started to get more precise, like smart bombs surgically finding a house instead of flattening an entire city block. Some part of me knew I needed help, and it started to reach out even when the rest of me didn't want to get sober yet.

With my wife and kids asleep, I zoned out and started aggressively posting music videos, movie clips, and funny cat videos on people's Facebook walls. But something that night was different. I was lying there on my couch, wondering why alcoholism had happened to *me*. Bad news is always supposed to happen to other people, not you. So I searched my phone, closing one eye as I scrolled through my contacts, and found the number for Mike from Parkside. I sent him a quick hello.

I was horrified to see, immediately, the ellipsis appear on my iPhone. Those three dots told me this guy was texting me back in the middle of the night.

"How are you?" it asked.

The question stabbed back at me there in the dark. It was just too real. More than that, I didn't know the answer to his question. So I did what I always did when I was drinking—I hid. I didn't reply. I went back to Facebook and eventually passed out. The next morning, I went through my normal routine of surveying what public damage I'd caused just hours before. I assessed the nonsense I'd put out into the universe. When I saw the text to "AAMike," I winced. His reply just sort of hung there against a white space, orphaned. I ignored it for a couple of days. Then, when I drank myself into watching old *Twilight Zone* episodes online, I summoned up the courage to text him back. It was well after midnight and right around the time William Shatner thought he saw a creature on the wing of that 747.

"Sorry, man," I wrote back. "Got busy."

This was a bald-faced lie, since I was unemployed and both of us knew it. There was no excuse. Either way, once again, the three dots popped up almost immediately.

"Hey, no worries," he replied. "How are you?"

Again, I had no idea how to reply, so I went for broke: "Will you be my sponsor?"

It was like asking a stranger if I could accompany him on his Caribbean cruise.

There was a pause, then the dots came.

"No."

I was taken aback. I watched as that sky-monster lumbered across the 747's wing in black-and-white, with Shatner not believing his eyes. I felt the exact same way. Then again, it's not like I even knew what the hell a sponsor was. It just sounded like something I needed to ask, and I'd been rejected. I had to face the *Twilight Zone* monster that was my alcoholism, which still lurked just beyond the window.

I HAD ONE real job: find a job.

Beyond that, I had the responsibilities of taking Oliver to his daycare and Elliott to school. Those, I did without fail. But there was a lot of preamble to that. There was a basement where I'd hidden all my morning beer and my completely fucked-up sleep schedule. I'd pass out around 8:30 p.m. and then wake up around 3 a.m. An afternoon-nap was guaranteed. I'd crawl down into the dark, crumbled-floor basement where there were two cases of Bud Light cans waiting under a table of Carrie's scrapbooking stuff. I opened two at a time and slammed them down. I did that under a solitary lightbulb, staring at all the cobwebs and concrete.

I'd then beach myself on my couch for another ninety minutes, writing epic Facebook messages to people I wouldn't ever seek out on my own outside Facebook. But that was my life: extending artificiality as far as it could go. I'm a master of acquaintances. It's like I'm a film director who stacks his ensemble casts with nothing but character actors.

The schedule actually worked pretty well—until the one afternoon where I slept straight through my afternoon-nap alarm and my neighbor was banging on my door, having been called by Carrie. My own phone had eight missed calls and frantic messages from my wife. I'd missed picking up Elliott from elementary school—by a full half hour.

I rose from the couch with the sort of jolt reserved for cattle prods or Tasers. I scattered two bottles in several directions. Our neighbor Sherry came in, confirmed with Carrie (who she was still on the phone with) that I was alive, and thankfully cut out the part where there were dozens of beer bottles everywhere. I was supposed to be sober. I'd told everyone on Facebook, remember?

The look on Sherry's face wasn't something you forget. It should be distilled down into a liquid—bitter, sad, brokenhearted, understanding. Seconds after waking up, I raced into my car and found Elliott sitting in the principal's office. I mumbled something about there being a mix-up between his mom and me about picking up Elliott, but it was clear to anyone with a heartbeat that I was an out-of-control drunk with pillow creases on his face who'd forgotten to pick up his son at school.

That was it.

That was the moment.

That was the bottom.

I may have had other bottoms along the way, I told myself, but that was the bottom that actually mattered.

25

THE IDEA OF suicide didn't just arrive in my head out of the blue. It didn't announce itself one day like the Kool-Aid Man suddenly crashing through a wall, going *"Oh yeahhhhhh."* The idea visited me like a storm migrating across the plains, building and growing until the thunderhead just couldn't hold any more weight. I knew it was coming. With laser precision, I knew all the precipitation it was going to bring. But you sort of assume it'll evaporate before it actually comes. Maybe it'll just dissipate. Slow-rolling convection from other storm fronts colliding. A dying of molecules. Dry walls and occluded fronts.

Storms do that. They fizzle out without warning.

But suicide started coming to me more and more as an idea. When it wasn't blustering through my brain, it was throbbing in the background. Unemployment started to eat away at more than just our bank account—it was eating away at my self-worth. Other people were getting up and going to work. Our neighbors on one side were teachers; on the other side, there was corporate-office-park folk. I heard their cars leave in the morning, followed by the eerie quiet after. All I could hear was the deafening silence of feeling worthless.

I was miles past pitying myself. I wasn't doing anyone any good. The longer I was around, the more I was holding everyone down, like a sci-fi gravity well pulling starships out of orbit. Everyone needed to move on. The kids were young enough that I'd be that person they'd recognize only in photographs and Facebook posts years later. I couldn't do any more damage if I was gone. The details of my life would be limited to my kids' mumbled, shared memories—never quite getting it right. Their new father would be put-together. A doctor, maybe. Someone sure of himself, comfortable in his skin, unafraid of the world.

The kids were winding down their last week of daycare (which we couldn't afford, either) and I was sitting at the kitchen table, knowing we wouldn't have enough to pay the mortgage. But I still had money for booze. Always. I didn't know how, but I did.

That morning, I imagined how it'd actually be. It was tomb-quiet in the house as I wandered it, taking charged hits off my plastic pint of vodka. I'd seen suicide in enough movies to know it could be quick and painless. My buddy Shawn was a Marine and, one time, matter-of-factly told me how to put the gun right under your chin, angling back a little bit. He told me this in passing. Guaranteed success. The subject wasn't even suicide. But my brain sopped it up. I kept that fact in a steel box for safekeeping. Now, it was useful information.

Things would be better for everyone if I simply wasn't here anymore.

But I couldn't use a weapon. Hell, I didn't even know where to find one.[31] Maybe I could steal someone's hunting .22. Then I considered that I didn't want to leave a gruesome body for someone else to find. I had to figure out the best thing for everyone. You know: a win-win suicide. My brain spun through possibilities. I didn't want to shoot myself outside—I figured that the bugs and animals and humidity would have their way with me before someone would stumble across my body. I considered running a bath and slitting my wrists, but I'd have to do this when I wasn't looking. I'd have to get good and drunk, then seconds after taking a bracing belt of whiskey, maybe I'd drag a utility knife across my wrists. I honestly Googled "Warm or freezing water for bathtub suicide?" I also considered that running headlong into a semitruck ran the risk of hurting other people.

Pills.

The idea came to me while I was drifting to sleep, thanks to the Ambien my doctor was prescribing me.

It's going to be pills.

That's where my story would end, I decided.

---

[31] Ironically, I didn't know where to find drugs or booze in high school, either. It wasn't until much later that I realized debauchery was everywhere.

ONE WEEKEND, not long after the school incident, Carrie decided to visit her family. She left on a Friday and said she wouldn't be back until late Sunday. *Fine,* I shrugged. Black depression was knotted around my every thought, and I was feeling pretty sorry for myself on the couch. She knew that it was probably best to leave me alone for a weekend. My brain was still repairing itself. That's what everyone in recovery told me, at least. I had months, if not years of rewiring to go through yet.

It wasn't unusual for her to visit her family alone. After all, I was the ghost-husband. Sort of there, sort of not. Carrie was used to showing up to events and gatherings and school meetings alone. People stopped asking where I was, or if I'd be coming later. I was a bonus if and when I showed up. An ancillary character in the script.

No one knew how miserable it was being me, I lamented. I was convinced I was the only human on the face of the planet to ever feel this horrible and this darkly unique. It was only a few days after I'd forgotten to get Elliott at school, and I was still mortified with myself. I couldn't imagine showing my face to anyone. I even seriously considered how I could avoid ever seeing my next-door neighbor Sherry again. I just needed to hide.

"You sure you're going to be okay?" Carrie asked wearily, for real, in the doorway.

I nodded, staring at my boys for the last time. I wouldn't hug them long. If I did, that'd give away my plan. She might start to get worried and stick around. I didn't need that. So I hugged them each, breathing their smells in deeply, kissing their hair.

"Yep. I'll be fine," I lied.

She hesitated for a second, but left. We didn't kiss or hug goodbye anymore, anyway. We weren't that married couple.

"Drive safe," I said. "Text me when you get there."

"Will do."

I wouldn't be alive to get that text message.

When they were twenty minutes outside Columbus, I started plotting it all out. Kroger had started selling these tiny little wine bottles—the kind you'd get on an airplane or at a hotel minibar—and they had them in these oversized bins right in the beer aisle. Tiny little reds and yellows. They looked kind of cute to me, like those old novelty wax root beers from my childhood. I'd grab three or four of them at a time and jam them between my knuckles, tossing them into my shopping cart like party favors.

They were screw-top twist-offs, too. The best.

I twisted one off in the parking lot and chugged it down. That's when I discovered I sort of loved the gym-sock smell of warm chardonnay. I could feel it rising in my blood—the instant promise and false hope of maybe finding a job, the urge to listen to Radiohead, the absolute need to text friends, the dull electricity of fake confidence. I'd twist the cap off another one while no one was around and chug it. For some reason, I decided these things were like little, bottled shots.

I pulled up to the intersection, sick. I'd gagged down the chardonnay wrong and got so queasy that I couldn't hold it anymore. I tried catching the vomit with my hands, but it simply exploded between my fingers. I aimed my head for the cup holders and got most of it there.

I brought the rest of the bottles home and lined them up on

the dining room table. Seven little soldiers. I absently scrolled through Indeed.com for the billionth time and cursed the fact that my parents encouraged me to be a writer. (Seriously, there is nothing more humbling than searching for "editor" and "writer" as a job keyword.) It was a bleak landscape online. I needed to be sure I was right: that nothing was waiting for me, job-wise. I took some searing shots of vodka. I was getting some bedrock in my belly for what was coming later. I blindly sent my resume into dozens of black holes, took their soulless questionnaires, and registered myself on countless websites. I didn't do it to get a job; I did it to remind myself that I'd been applying for jobs for a year now and it was time to shut down my life.

I felt like less than zero.

I started writing farewell letters to everyone I knew. Reams and reams of pages aimed at all the people I'd wronged over the years, starting with my parents. They hadn't raised a bad kid—they'd just raised a son who hadn't developed a second skin. Someone who let everything in. I couldn't interact with the world unless it was with a pen. I just couldn't seem to get anything right, ever. After all, disappointments are worse than flat-out failures—and that's what I was: one giant disappointment. I wrote one to my uncle (and the best man at my wedding), apologizing for coming up short in life and letting life cause a quiet rift between us. I owed him money, a fact that absolutely ate me alive, so I would make sure whatever trust was left would pay the balance. I put my wife and kids off to last. There was just too much to say. So I zeroed in on the middle. I wrote to Crow; I wrote to Big Neal; I wrote to Mark; I wrote to Leslie; I wrote to Matt. Even Cole got a letter. Then, I eventually discovered I had too many people to write letters to.

I figured that when I died, they'd just have to infer their own meaning as to why I killed myself—and how I was sorry.

I was a writer who was simply out of words.

I HAD EIGHT peach tabs of Ambien left, plus two random Percocet pills. I lined them up on the dining room counter next to the wine bottles. I started getting anxiety that it wouldn't be enough, but 80 milligrams of Ambien sounded heavy-duty. It should do the trick. I just wanted it to be fast, dreamy, like when I'm pulled under by the black drape of Ambien at night. I also started lining up my reasons:

I didn't belong anywhere.

I was unemployable.

I couldn't face a sad, colorless life without booze.

I was an absentee parent and husband.

I had a wife who was done with me.

I had in-laws who couldn't look me in the eyes.

I had parents who didn't know where their son had gone.

No one loved me like they did when I was younger. That sort of love wears off the older, and drunker, you get.

These weren't problems with other people. They were problems with *me*. I was the common denominator.

I looked at the pills and the wine.

Cause and effect. Problem and solution.

So, I lined up the apology letters I'd actually made it through, stuffing them neatly into envelopes. There were six in all. Then I considered that I was hurrying to the main event too quickly. Maybe I should try a second round of amends notes. Maybe I should write to people who'd died, long gone. My grandfather, maybe—who I wanted to thank for letting me stay in his house and teaching me about manhood, even though I could never ever rise to that occasion; my grandmother, who probably had such a horrifically cold Catholic upbringing that all her cold, barbed interactions with me had less to do with me than her childhood; my friend Matt Heid, who died in a horrible car crash (a crash his dad survived) right after high school graduation. I was crying by this point, realizing that it was no use. None of it mattered. There were too many people to address in the universe, and I didn't have the attention span.

I shut my phone off, and I stared at its black screen for a while.

That's the last time I'll see this iPhone, I thought.

Just think of all the photos and videos inside that device, I considered. *An entire life lived.*

I kept it shut off, turned around and thumbed through my record collection. *This is the last time I'll see any of these records,* I thought. I flipped on a Bruce Hornsby album from the late 1980s: *Scenes from the Southside.* Of all the fucking albums: a second-rate Hornsby. When people find me dead, I thought, I should have been listening to something meaningful. But I wasn't going to leave an elaborate code for my friends to untangle. I was hurting too much to put one together. I played the record and about two songs in, I decided I couldn't die that way. No one should die listening to Bruce Hornsby and the Range.

I put on a Bond movie playlist. Four of five of them, all lined up in a row. Fitting.

I twisted off all the wine bottle caps, one by one. The bright smell of cheap chardonnay filled the dining room as I watched an impossibly young Roger Moore wander around Harlem. Morning light came through the dining room, slanting across the table where I'd laid everything out.

I palmed the pills, rattled them around a bit in my fist. I walked around the living room, feeling my heart in my throat. *I'm really going to do this.*

I toured the house, looking at every detail of it as if it was the last time I'd see it. I soaked up every contour, every seam, every nail. I walked up and down the stairs. I went into the basement where Cole and I used to blast shoegaze music at one-thirty in the morning. I wandered into the kids' room where our boys had slept in their cribs, where Elliott had learned the alphabet, where Carrie had rocked them to sleep as infants. I sat in my office, scrolling through all the hiding places I'd created there: under the spare bed, in my filing cabinet, in the closet. They were clean.

I went back downstairs, drew in a breath, and knew this was it. If I think about anything too long, I won't do it. I had butterflies like I was about to jump onstage.

So I crammed the pills into my mouth and swallowed them with not one, but two tiny bottles of warm wine. I choked down the pills and took a breath. I could feel that neon-glow of the wine rise inside me again, but at a much higher level. I was surprised, as if I should have suddenly felt the effect of my body immediately shutting down, one system at a time. Nothing. I scooped the remaining Percocets off the table and grabbed another bottle of wine.

I shuffled into the living room and watched Bond shoot his

way through a giant submarine-swallowing ship. I unscrewed the wine and swallowed down the other pills. I stood there, watching the movie and starting to feel the first twinges of something. I could feel a few of the mooring ropes in my brain loosening up—I was coming free.

I drew in even breaths.

It's not time to panic, I thought. *This is it. Let it come. Just let it happen.*

It honestly felt good: the hazy glow of the wine and chemicals alight in my body, drawing down the curtain on my mind. I couldn't keep my eyes open, but I could hear the soundtrack. I'd seen the movie enough to know all the beats. I could recite it. I drifted, sort of feeling as if I was tumbling backward. But I was still standing there. I wasn't there, yet I was.

Bond was now getting chastised by M.

This is it.

Let it come.

I sort of knelt down on the hardwood floor, which gave way under my knee like a hammock. Nothing had any solidity. I crawled up into the couch, which was gummy and warm. My eyes were closed the whole time. I felt the black veil of Ambien wrapping itself around me, binding me, preparing to take me to the other side.

Just let it happen.

Goodbye.

I'm sorry I wasn't better.

I REMEMBERED HEARING voices. Dreamlike. They came to me from a great distance. *Casino Royale* was on. It was one of the those scenes I'd overlooked—the one where they're sitting and having dinner after Vesper's rescued Bond from a heart attack, and they're having dinner and naming martinis.

My eyes opened and struggled to draw focus. It was like looking through the wrong end of a telescope. I realized I was lying on the floor of the living room, sprawled out. The seams of the hardwood floor looked like vast roadways that close up. I studied them, pretending I was traveling their lengths, getting lost in the vast canyons of the grain.

Every single muscle was sore, tight. It felt like someone had punched me square at the base of my skull. When I moved, my head seemed to follow three seconds later, delayed. Underwater. I was queasy and struggled to upright myself. When I finally did, many minutes later, I saw a clear slick of vomit and pills, half-dissolved, just to my left on the floor. I stared at it, trying to understand what I was seeing.

I'd wanted to die but, apparently, my body didn't agree with that plan. Not long after, Bond was hunched over Vesper's body—his blue eyes filled with tears and rage and grief, not sure what was coming next.

I knew exactly how he felt.

FOUR

Call it any name you need.
Call it your 2.0, your rebirth, whatever.
So long as you can feel it all,
So long as all your doors are flung wide,
Call it your Day #1 in the rest of forever.

If you are afraid, give more.
If you are alive, give more now.
Everybody here has seams and scars.
So what? Level up.

—Vienna Teng

26

HONEST-TO-GOD SOBRIETY happened the second week of January. I ignored the wound that was my second-by-second need to get alcohol: the sort of fresh, throbbing scrape that still needs days to scab over. I felt exactly like Ohio in winter: gray, snowy, wide open. I didn't identify with people; I identified with long country roads scorched with salt. And while sobriety was so new as to be cloudy and exhilarating at the same time, I sensed something very familiar about it all.

I'd felt this before.

Four days after my final drink, I nervously paced our house. My brain was on fire—a rat's nest of frayed wires and jangled nerves—and I wasn't sure where I was supposed to be. For years, my mind had been a beachball held underwater. Now, all at once, every single emotion, thought, and impulse was rushing forward. I wanted to simultaneously listen to Spotify, enjoy complete silence, cook every ingredient in the kitchen, never eat again, call my parents, hide from the phone, jog around the block, lie on the couch, Facebook all my feelings, and chuck my MacBook across the room. I wandered from room to room to room, unemployed and untethered.

I had the single worst thing an alcoholic can have in their first sober days: time to think.

I wandered into the living room where Elliott was parked in front of PBS Kids. Becoming sober isn't unlike one of the cartoon characters who's running so fast that they zoom off a cliff and keep going in a straight line. They get fifteen steps out into the sky and stop, legs still pedaling, suddenly realizing they're in midair. I felt seconds away from free fall. Something inside me cracked when I saw my son sitting there. Before I knew it, I was geysering apologies. "I'm sorry," I heard myself telling him, as if a five-year-old kid can actually process his father crying, let alone a freak apology out of nowhere. To him, I was a thunderbolt on a cloudless day.

I'd sincerely never felt so ashamed—ashamed of my drinking, ashamed that we'd have to sell our house, ashamed that I was apologizing. To this day, I don't know how much my son understood about where I'd gone when I went to treatment, but all that mattered to him was that I wasn't there for his kindergarten Halloween party.

He just blinked while I stood there, crying. He didn't even say, "It's okay, Daddy," which is all I was selfishly seeking. That's right: I actually wanted validation from a five-year-old. I wanted to hear that all my bottle-hiding and endless happy hours and constantly telling him "Not now," was okay. He didn't understand why a realtor was hammering a "For Sale" sign into our front yard and yet, for entirely different reasons, neither did I.

This can't be my fault.

This stuff happens all the time to people, right?

This is what other people have to deal with.

Alcoholism didn't suddenly come sweeping in and change things. It was corrosive and patient, working its way through the walls of my life like water damage. Drinking slowly ate away at my ability to function as an adult. Maybe we're all just pretending to be adults, but if you slam a tall boy of Labatt Blue at 8 a.m. before taking your son to kindergarten, you're not even trying.

There's a lot to be said about waking up in the middle of your life, wondering how you've arrived there. I wasn't willing to let another Monday morning come where I'd wince, hungover, as the recycling crew loudly emptied out my bins in front of my house—the previous week's damage echoing through the neighborhood.

It was time to grow up.

It was time to be present.

It was time to be a human being.

IN MY VERY first AA meetings, I was shell-shocked. I couldn't process what I was feeling or, for that matter, the realization that I was feeling anything at all. My drinking had erased several years of my life from the map like a WWII carpet bombing. There wasn't much left to show for it all. Many of the things that were precious to me—a job, friendships, financial security—were gone. I sat in those rooms, only half-listening to the people around me when I wasn't counting floor tiles. I knew I probably belonged in AA years before I finally found myself there. Those first church basements and VFW meeting halls were windows into a completely different world, but one that was as welcoming as it was strangely familiar. Still, surrounded by all those people, I couldn't help but feel alone and disconnected. Turns out, I was experiencing something I hadn't had since my grandfather passed away.

Full-on, hurricane-strength grief. All five stages. Every goddamn one of them.

I'd trusted alcohol. I'd assumed it'd always be there. It'd gotten me through a lot of family gatherings and, thanks to hangovers, out of a lot of obligations. Alcohol was torn from my life as if we'd had a bad, slow breakup. I'd convinced myself I could have a different relationship with alcohol. It wouldn't be as intense or irresponsible. I could start dating it again or, worst-case scenario, just occasionally flirt with it.

I sat in AA meeting after AA meeting, stunned and genuinely wondered where it'd all gone wrong. After all, alcohol and I had an understanding. We had a long-term relationship that, sure, had its ups and downs, but it was more permanent than any other relationship in my life. If everyone else in my life pulled up stakes and moved away, I'd still have booze. That was the deal. Alcohol promised me things along the way, including the fact that it'd never leave me.

Yet there I was, having survived alcohol's death in my life. To add salt to the wound, I also saw my friends evaporate, one by one. I couldn't process the immensity of those losses. Straight-up denial. Surely, this wasn't my life. I'd refused to imagine a life without wine at the holidays or beer on my birthday. That wasn't a life worth living.

Then, as if on cue, I got pissed. I wasn't numb anymore. Instead, I started attending AA meetings with the sort of arms-crossed, *prove-it-to-me* anger typically reserved for teenagers who have life all figured out. I listened to people in those meetings and silently scoffed. They didn't understand alcohol like I did. We'd had a good thing going. *Those* people had drinking problems. They were fooling themselves into thinking they were happy, being sober, or that their lives were now suddenly more fulfilling than before. I honestly felt sorry for all of them. They just didn't get it. I knew that alcohol hadn't meant to hurt me. In fact, if I could figure out how, I'd welcome it back into my life with open arms. In those first few weeks, I'd have given anything to have alcohol back. I was sure the people in those AA rooms didn't know the midnight charge vodka gave me or any of the lusty, loving things cabernets whispered in my ear. And yet, against my better judgment, I kept going back to those meetings and listened.

Through it all, I kept bargaining with my brain. Certainly,

there had to be some solution that didn't involve step work or, worse, sharing coffee in a church annex. I seriously gave it thought. I obsessively read about moderation, tapering down, and trying to unlock the secrets of how people successfully drink. All the while, I attended AA meetings, met with a counselor, and started to see the first glimmers that my life was improving (who knew that quitting drinking would result in weight loss?). I went through endless attempts at the sad math of "What if?" or "If only…" I simply couldn't find the right angle; I couldn't figure out the physics that would help me avoid the misery that awaited me if I drank again. Some people could leave a quarter-glass of wine behind on their restaurant table. That never computed with me, but I was envious.

It started to dawn on me that, maybe, I just wasn't programmed to handle booze. I wasn't wired that way. And that's when the bottom fell out of my hopes. There wasn't any safe way for me to get back into alcohol's orbit. No amount of NASA-calculating was going to get me back to Earth, like Apollo 13. Pitch-black depression washed over me. I sullenly went to my therapist and said very little. I slumped in my seat at AA meetings, passed when it was my turn to talk, and didn't reply to texts from friends I'd met in recovery. I actually started to plot how I'd eventually stop going to meetings altogether, imagining I'd tell my wife "AA just isn't for me." My life wasn't supposed to turn out like that.

Then, one night at a meeting, when it was my turn to share, I said it all out loud. It just torrented out. I told a big circle of sort-of strangers that I felt like I was in mourning, like my best friend had just died in a horrible car crash or something. I saw nods of understanding that night. I connected.

I didn't accept my reality right away. In fact, some days, I'll catch someone wandering one of those gas-station "beer caves" or see a perfect-looking cocktail on Instagram and I'll feel a cold stab of longing for what used to be. For me, acceptance isn't about suddenly saying everything is okay. Far from it. It's been about accepting life for what it is—and mine doesn't involve alcohol. It's just not an option. That's what recovery is all about: learning to live with reality. I don't feel like I've moved on from alcohol so much as I'm now keenly aware of the toxic relationship we had. From time to time, the loss still haunts me, but that's simply part of what makes my grief very real. Time has taught me that I wasn't mourning drinking—I was mourning the life I'd never actually lived in the first place.

FOR ME, PART of the quiet "fun" of attending an AA meeting is finding it. There's a real speakeasy quality to them that appeals to the secret-keeping alcoholic in me. No signs, flashing lights, or cartoon arrows. They're as hidden as they are meaningful to me. But as much as I enjoy discovering where AA meetings actually are, I've learned to be careful about discovering too much about my fellow alcoholics' lives. I wrestle with whether to keep my comrades at arm's-length or let them in. It's a genuinely slippery slope, especially when the very reason you're sitting in that room is to help the people around you as much as you're trying to help yourself.

In my very first few AA meetings, I had a hard time wrapping my brain around it all: the routines, the lingo, and the subtle differences between meetings. Even the cheerfulness of everyone baffled me. I just didn't get it. I mean, wasn't everyone supposed to be as goddamn miserable and shaky as I was? Turns out, most people in recovery aren't. They're not Patch Adams, but they're not all swirling half-empty coffee cups in despair, either. I discovered that my alcoholism was a lot like the Upside Down from *Stranger Things*—a shadow version of the real world. The real world was brighter and way harsher. Still, sitting down in room after room after room, I'd nod "hello" and maybe shake the occasional hand. I'd then check my phone and nervously glance at the clock. *Let's get on with it,* I'd think, like I was waiting for a movie to start.

In those first meetings, though, all I was really trying to do was figure out how to be a smarter drinker or how not to be like These People. This was where the misfit toys ended up. Whenever someone sitting close to me would start talking, I'd actually shrink back a little bit, like I was afraid of catching whatever sober germs they had. I wasn't even sure I was an alcoholic. I was just a tourist, trying to get a brief lay of the land and make a good show to my family like I was trying to not be a complete fucking disaster anymore.

But I kept coming back. I knew the beats of everyone's stories a little too well—I knew exactly where their dark narratives were headed. I understood the guy in the trucker cap who talked about being nothing more than a 45-degree angle for his daughter to sleep against. I got the bookish woman who said she would throw her grocery store receipt out before her husband could see just how much extra beer she had bought. I even related to the spindly line cook who used to tuck a pint of whiskey in his pants as he worked the grill.

It didn't take me long to get hooked on the stories in the rooms. I also zeroed in on attending the good meetings. The best ones have a lived-in warmth to them: easy smiles and a shorthand between the old-timers who've known one another for years. Still, I wasn't comfortable. I'm an anxious person to begin with (enter alcohol, stage right), and I'm not exactly the world's best small-talk artist. So, for me, showing up 13 seconds before a meeting starts and leaving two seconds after one ends is just about perfect.

For a while, I tried to casually 007 my way into the rooms: arrive without incident, remain invisible for the hour, then vanish without a trace. I stole whatever sober secrets I needed and no one was the wiser. Unfortunately, I couldn't keep that up. After a while—especially when you start attending the same meeting over and over again for several months—you can't help but get to know the people around you. It's like sort of half-watching a TV show for an entire season—you're going to learn about the characters and their backstories without trying, even if you're reading a magazine the whole time. Same with AA meetings. I discovered that Trucker Cap, Bookish Library Lady, and Line Cook all had names. What's more is that they eventually learned *mine* when I finally started opening up.

I stopped racing in and out of the rooms. I began showing up early, and I lingered a bit afterward. I volunteered to scrub the coffee pot. I congratulated people on their anniversaries. I shook hands and I gave hugs. I even drove strangers home from meetings when they needed a ride. Then, thanks to Facebook, I started to get friend request after friend request from people in the rooms. And that's when I suddenly realized their lives, like mine, existed well beyond the walls of the rooms we share. It was like invisible ink emerging under a black light.

Still, I accepted every single one of them. And every time, I went down the rabbit hole of their lives, spinning through their photo galleries and status updates. I got a weird jolt discovering that they had families, friends, favorite movies, and opinions unrelated to alcohol. (Chillingly, some of the people I identified with most in the rooms turned out to be Jimmy Buffett followers, which, to this Radiohead fan, was a bridge too far.) Eventually, I stopped accepting every one that came along. I couldn't let everyone in. Whatever visceral thrill I got from learning people's last names or seeing them in real-world situations evaporated pretty damn quickly. I had to start giving friend requests serious thought, like I was cosigning a loan or something.

When you connect with people outside of the AA rooms, you're opening yourself up in a far different way than simply sharing your stories. You're opening yourself up to hurt and disappointment as much as you are love and belonging. And that's terrifying—especially to people like me who've spent the better part of their adult lives hiding from anything that resembles an actual connection. For me, I have to be careful about who I share my life with. Just because we have addiction in common, doesn't mean we're perfectly matched puzzle pieces.

I've experienced both sides of the coin. I've forged deep, lasting friendships where we both shake our heads in "I'm so happy we met" awe, and I've also found myself in situations where I'm like a cat tossed into a bathtub. I can't get out fast enough. For all the times I wondered how the hell I'd ended up where I was, I've also had plenty of other occasions where

I've been happy to lend a hand, say, when someone from the rooms needs help moving from one apartment to another. Sometimes, there's no greater reward than coming through for someone who understands how difficult it is for people like us to come through for other people.

Still, I tend to prefer the vellum of anonymity—the fogged glass that shows movement and life, but no actual details. Maybe it's because the details of my own life remain unclear and are, after all this time, still coming into focus. More often than not, I realize I'm as much a stranger to myself as the people sitting around me. Perhaps the person I need to connect most with is me.

As an active alcoholic, I was a husk of a human being, with an insecure, wounded person slithering around inside. In sobriety, those parts of myself have hardened. I'm now solid, assured and confident in who I am. All the insanity and chaos in my life has started to vanish. I'm not spinning my wheels and acting at virtually every turn. I still don't necessarily love appointments and routines, but I lean into them now. I appreciate structure as much as I need the normalcy. I need walls and borders. The part of me that misses chaos is simply the part of me that enjoys missing out on anything that matters. Now, I'll happily trade an hour of my past craziness for an extra hour of rush-hour traffic, because I know exactly where I'll be and where I'll end up.

Not long ago, I got a text message from Josh, my roommate from treatment. He was reaching out because he needed my help. (I was apparently the only sober cat he knew.) Josh had gotten himself into some legal trouble—kids, ex-wife, drugs, the whole nine yards. He lobbed desperate messages at me for a while, but it became clear that I couldn't help him. He'd given up the pills but not the bottle. It was kind of like one of those World War II movies where two crewmen are in the bowels of a sinking ship, water rising, and they have to close a hatch between them. One person's going to survive and one's not. But they're staring at each other through the hatch glass. It kills me, but the truth is that I can't get anyone else sober. No one could do that trick for me, either. I just have to remind myself that I can't fix everyone I meet. I've driven hours to drag someone to an AA meeting and all that did was put miles on my vehicle, not that person's sobriety.

Saying you want to visit Australia isn't the same as budgeting, planning, and saving for that trip. When you're an alcoholic, words come easy. That's pretty much all you have. But when you genuinely find sobriety, you also find that you don't need many words at all. At that point, there's not much left to say.

It's when you stop talking that sobriety actually starts speaking to you.

27

LIVING IN A major city, I'm pretty spoiled when it comes to the sheer number of AA meetings around me. I've visited church basements, detox centers, VFW meeting halls, a bank, a grocery store conference room, and, one time, a swanky hotel suite. I even attended a meeting at an old neighborhood bar that a local recovery community had reclaimed. It was as surreal as it was disquieting: all the original stools and tables were there, along with the burned-in reek of cigarette smoke. A dead TV set stared down from a high corner while people stood behind the bar listening to the lead. Shadowed into the linoleum were the ghosts of the pool tables. It was such a meta, big-city experience; I was bothered by how much I enjoyed being there.

It's almost to the point where the harder a meeting is to find, the better. Maybe it appeals to my love of James Bond movies or something, like when Q hides his gadget labs in half-sunken freighters or exotic bazaars. All that's missing are secret handshakes. Just *knowing* there's always a meeting within 10 miles is sometimes enough to keep me sober. Two years ago, I'd imagined AA meetings where a half-dozen people crammed into a closet-sized space with cold coffee.

Unfortunately, when I drive outside central Ohio, I'm not really wrong about that. The meetings grow thinner and painfully old school. It's kind of like comparing the infinite number of TV channels today, to how many networks there were in 1980. If you're the only game in town, you don't really have to worry about what you broadcast. You can get away with airing *Mama's Family*.

The town I'm from is the size of a postage stamp. Once, while visiting some relatives, I went to the sole, once-a-week AA meeting. There about 10 people sitting on folding chairs in the town hall basement. Most of them were in their 60s or 70s, arms crossed. They were fixtures. Everyone clearly knew everyone in town anyway, so the notion of anonymity was kind of a joke.

We listened to a young woman recount a teary, heartfelt story about her pill addiction and having to come clean to her mom. It was her first AA meeting ever, and it was pretty brutal to sit through. I understood every beat of her story. She talked about how she'd had a sports injury, how she'd always been "the good girl", and how feeding her addiction was like an out-of-body experience. She'd been prescribed Vicodin and discovered it went really well with wine coolers she bought at the gas station. Even as the wheels came off, she loved the feeling of having "a blizzard in the brain," as she called it. She'd quickly found herself ransacking every medicine cabinet she could find. I remember the desperate look on her face as she hoped to connect with someone. Her life was unmanageable, and this meeting was clearly her port in the storm.

When it was her neighbor's turn to speak, he let out a giant sigh.

"I remember when all of *this*," he twirled his finger around the meeting room, "used to be about alcohol."

I cringed. Until then, I'd never seen lines drawn in the sobriety sand like that. I immediately felt defensive—not only for her, but for myself. I'd gotten something out of her story even though I wasn't leaving a wake of stolen pills behind me. And then the person next to him chimed in, echoing the exact same sentiment about the AA good old days. By the end of the meeting, almost everyone in the semicircle had made the girl walk the plank for bringing her painkiller problem into their room. I couldn't believe how cold and territorial they were. I wasn't surprised, weeks later, to see she hadn't returned. Her first AA meeting had been her very last. She'd been playing different songs on the AA radio, and they hadn't liked what they were hearing.

The smaller the room you're in, the more you are at the mercy of old-timers and their hurricane-strength opinions. The fewer the voices, the louder the words. For an AA newcomer, I think small rooms can be downright dangerous. Your role is clear: *Be quiet.* I remember a meeting where someone talked about struggling with a switch between his Lexapro and Cymbalta prescriptions. "This is really a conversation for you and your doctor," an old woman yawned, kicking off a 10-minute lecture on the way things "used to be" in AA. (I can't imagine that the old AA rooms were actually real in the same way that I can't imagine that the world wasn't actually black-and-white in the past.)

For many old-timers, there's no space in the AA margins for painkillers or needles or 8-balls of coke. It's like there's an undercurrent of "I'm an alcoholic, but at least I'm not a drug addict," which really makes me sad. The best meetings I attend rarely ever mention alcohol, let alone any other substances. They're about how we keep the mind and spirit clear. I don't go to meetings to hear if anyone else was as talented as me at hiding red wine bottles under bathroom sinks; I go to hear other people talk about how they're finding strength in their vulnerability. I don't know how many times I've heard myself in someone else's story, no matter how far-flung their experience is from mine. I haven't found myself shooting heroin in a McDonald's bathroom stall four hours after getting out of rehab, but I can totally follow the dark, ugly logic that got them there.

In the smallest rooms, maybe it's easy for old-timers to forget why they're there. I don't ever want to become the person who only wants to hear alcohol-only stories. Those people have the power to singlehandedly kill a newcomer's sobriety. Show me someone who thinks they're protecting the spirit of AA, and I'll show you an old-timer who's terrified that the program they know is vanishing. To me, there's no difference in any of our stories—alcohol or none at all. Maybe we're all just orphaned puzzle pieces, scattered together. We don't neatly fit together into some pretty-perfect mosaic, but we can take some comfort in the fact that we're all in search of the boxes from where we came.

EVEN NOW, AFTER everything, if you put a gun to my head and ten seconds on the clock, I'm not sure I could tell you what Step 11 is.[32] Not right off the bat, anyway. It's a maintenance step, I know that much. I'm not good at memorizing things. (Aside from being a terrible actor, it's one of the reasons I was a human grease fire in high school plays: I can't memorize stuff.) Step 7? No fucking clue. Ask me to tell it to you, word for word, and that gun to my head would go off. Sit me in an AA room when someone reads out all the steps, though, and I can recite them verbatim. It's weird how disconnected I can be from the very things that saved my life. It's kind of like when you hear a song you haven't heard in at least a decade, and you instantly remember all the lyrics.

That's where David came in.

When I first met him, he was something of a sage in my rooms: always leaning back at a ninety-degree angle in his chair, hands clasped at his belt, long scraggly hair to his shoulders, pirate-hoop earrings, bookish glasses. He always had something thoughtful and insightful to say. He chose his words carefully, which meant I liked him immediately. When I

---

[32] "Sought through prayer and meditation to improve our conscious contact with God as we understood Him, praying only for knowledge of His will for us and the power to carry that out."

told the room that I felt like alcohol, my best friend, had died—
he's the one who came up afterward with a look on his face that
was just as pained and hurt as my own. Seriously, it looked like
he just wanted to give me a hug. That meeting, I was thinking
about how I'd probably come back to try one more meeting and
never return. Maybe he sensed that—I have no idea. Maybe I
was giving off that last gasp of desperation before turning back
to the bottle.

"I hadn't thought of that in a long time," he said.

"What's that?"

"What you said about mourning alcohol," he nodded. "Like
your best friend let you down."

"Ah, well, yeah. That's what it feels like right now. It's brutal."
He nodded again. "I know."

He asked me a few questions—how long I'd been sober,
whether I had a sponsor yet, was I working the steps, how many
meetings I was going to. Stuff like that. We exchanged numbers
and next thing I knew, I had myself a sponsor. I met with him
the first time simply to make a show of going to see someone.
I fully planned on telling my wife that "he just wasn't for me."

But David ended up being exactly who and what I needed.
Seriously: if God exists, that proof isn't in my sobriety—it's
in David being ushered into my life. David shares a similar
worldview: we'd both thought we had life figured out when
we were drinking but had become humbled by the truth
that we had no fucking clue. We also had thought, while we
were drinking, that no one was taking us seriously in life. We
deserved more attention; we deserved…well, more. We felt we
were super-talented even when we were drunk, and that made
us gloriously arrogant. He talked about how he could teach

grad seminars while taking sips of whiskey from an oversized plastic Pepsi bottle. Even blotto, this guy was a genius. He was a former academic who was now something of a celebrity in the bookselling world, if you can be that. He owned a solid business selling books to serious collectors around the globe, so his office was filled with leatherbounds from the 16th century—great tomes that had once belonged on the shelves of aristocratic families and kings and queens. I felt at home in his office, where we started meeting.

He was unassuming in all the ways I looked forward to visiting him on Saturday mornings, surrounded by his shelves and shelves of antique paper.

We talked about life. I scribbled notes. I just wanted to get ahead to the part where I was apologizing to people, telling them how sorry I was. He told me that wasn't for a long ways down the way. In the meantime, I needed to focus on me—my faults, my resentments, my problems. I had to make a fearless moral inventory.

I still have the list I sent to David, which I'll share here:

Am I a fraud?

Fear of failure

Fear of success

Am I a good person who does bad things, or a bad person who does good things?

Having already let my life pass me by?

Not taking advantage of opportunities

"Is this it?"

Not living up to my potential

Not being liked

Why do I think I'm so goddamn special all the time?

Being perceived the wrong way

Not loving someone fully

Am I even capable of love?

I had a lot to build on, a lot of resentments that were clearly festering like untended wounds. And over the course of several Saturdays, David and I unpacked them. (I'll spare you the dark magic of a sponsor-sponsee relationship, which is almost sacred territory. At least *mine* is.) But the best part is that David told me to take my list and focus on positives. Don't write a list of all the things I'm awful at. We had to see what we had to work with.

I wasn't sure I had anything left to give.

A FRIEND LAUGHED that we alcoholics should be given a medal for surviving wedding receptions with our sobriety intact. I absolutely agree with her. Nothing gets under my skin as much as the pomp and circumstance of a wedding reception—which is a total 180-degree turn for me. Weddings used to be less celebrations than alcoholic calls to action. My wedding reception game used to be crazy-strong, too. I knew the art of how to pinball between multiple bars without getting weird looks from the bartender for returning mere minutes later, not to mention having someone else order you a drink when there's just one bar. I had all the angles figured out.

Now, weddings are capable of bringing me all the panic and anxiety I had at social events when I was in very early sobriety. I'm not exaggerating. Amazingly, I don't have a lot of triggers as a recovering alcoholic. I can walk down grocery-store wine aisles and survive bachelor parties just fine, but put me in a reception hall with white tablecloths, a DJ, and a dance floor, and I'm a goddamned mess. The first time I went to a reception sober, I lasted maybe five minutes at our table before I had to excuse myself to go to the bathroom and breathe. There's something about receptions that I lock into—too many good memories, maybe, soaked with free gin and tonics. (Play the "Electric Slide" and the spell is broken.) It's hard being the guy who used to get smashed at receptions because, well, that's what I thought you were supposed to do.

When my friend Shawn announced he was getting married, I was thrilled. We'd known each other since third grade, and he'd never seemed happier—full of live-wire energy, excitement, and not an ounce of nervousness. He was all-in. Then, he asked me to be his Best Man. Again, I was thrilled. Honored. All that jazz. Then it dawned on me: I'm going to have to give a speech. In front of people. At a wedding reception. And not just a speech: a goddamn toast. I could already feel the reception closing in on me like a Venus flytrap, slowly swallowing me whole.

I suddenly wasn't looking forward to the reception anymore so much as I was wondering how I could fuck it all up for

Shawn. I weighed the option of using a glass of real champagne, then I stupidly thought: "What if I forget it's real champagne and drink it on accident?" Then, I worried for weeks about whether the bartender could hook me up with a stunt glass filled with grape juice. I even Googled "Is it bad luck to give a toast with water?" (Spoiler alert: it is!) I shifted my alcohol brain cycle down from its typically high RPM and thought it through. I'd just use an empty glass and be done with it. End of story. It wasn't going to be that big of a wedding, anyway. It was going to be in our hometown village's town hall: modest, quaint, reserved.

And that's when Shawn told me there was a slight change in venue. He was now getting married at the Cleveland Rock and Roll Hall of Fame. You probably know the one. You don't have to be from Ohio to have seen the seven-level, 55,000-square foot museum dedicated to music history, as designed by I.M. Pei. Oh, and it was also going to be housing 200 guests—all of them staring at me while I tried not to ruin Shawn's special night. The older I get, the more I hate public speaking. I can give presentations at work, no problem, but sharing heartfelt words? Sober? No way. I'm not the first person in the history of the world to say they hate getting up in front of people and saying some words, but it gives me the same nausea as thinking about what an astronaut must feel like seconds before launch, realizing they're strapped to a rocket and about to hurtle into the atmosphere.

Drinking was my crutch through that stuff. One time, I was asked to give a quick speech for my sister's engagement party, and I remember thinking how clever and funny I felt. I'd gone completely off-script, beer and vodka flushing me with confidence. I later saw the speech on video and was blown away by how terrible it was. I was a sweaty mess, staggering a little and putting way too many spaces between my sentences. Without drinking, though, I wasn't sure how I'd dull my senses to the fact that hundreds of sets of eyes would be on me. I enjoy attention as much as the next person, but not *that* kind of blue-flame intensity. So, I freaked out all over again, just like a good recovering alcoholic does.

The nights leading up to that reception, I worked on several different drafts of my speech, but I didn't prepare for it. I couldn't practice because it made the experience real. I know that practicing in private ensures you won't fail in public, but I didn't care. So long as it was well-written, I didn't care how it was delivered. When we arrived at the Rock Hall and I saw the layout of the place—the epic openness of it, the countless tables, the giant stage—I almost threw up. I went to the bathroom and gripped both sides of the sink. As the night wore on and it got closer to my speech, I could feel my heart beating at my temples. But when I stood on the stage with Shawn and Tara sitting there, I just went for it—all exposed nerves, raw. I'm pretty sure I looked like a clenched fist up there. If you can have a full-body cringe, that'd be me giving that toast. I got through it, though, unsmiling even when I told jokes, and held up an empty glass (bad luck be damned!) to the bride and my friend since third grade.

As I sat back down, I remembered how Shawn had been texting me the morning I went to rehab, assuring me over and over again that I'd come out on the other side of it a better person. He was right, but I had no idea how he'd also be talking about the night of his reception. I may not win any awards for that speech and I'm not exactly going to go down in the annals of the Rock Hall, but I was sober for it. I wasn't just clear-headed. That night, I was present for Shawn in all the same ways he was part of ushering in my future.

DAVID CLEARED AN entire day to do our Fifth Step.[33] Weeks ahead of it, Carrie was going: "Wait, all day? You need all *day* to do this step?" And I'd just shrug. David knew best. If he said it was going to take all day, it was going to take all day. It's not like he was looking forward to forfeiting an entire day to learn every last detail of my drunken destruction and the vast depths of my secrets. But as I sat in the parking lot, ready to go, I told myself that I'd tell him every ounce of truth. I wouldn't ignore the seven or eight extra truths I had hidden in the floorboards. What he didn't know wouldn't hurt him after all, right? No, I was going Full Honest. For the first time ever. I wasn't going to lie by omission; I wasn't going to emphasize one part or switch whose role I was in the story so I looked better or smarter or oblivious. Whatever suited me best.

I was going to tell another human being the exact nature of my wrongs.

So one Saturday, we set up shop in his office, planning to order pizza for lunch. He told me to get comfortable. There was no preamble. We started working through every beat of my alcoholic story—every sagging milepost, every crooked beam along the way. He teased out details I'd forgotten, things I skipped, tricks my brain had played on me, rewriting the past.

---

[33] "Admitted to God, to ourselves, and to another human being the exact nature of our wrongs."

Main characters would appear and then vanish without a trace. Inconsistencies revealed themselves. Plots were jumbled. It was remarkable how I couldn't keep the threads together. People just vanished, never to return. They caused no end of drama in my life and then disappeared. All my drinking buddies whispered off, too.

But I was honest with all of his questions. Every single one, I answered like I was testifying in front of a courtroom. And with each question, the answer just sort of shuddered out of me, cold and unprepared to be kicked to the curbside. But I did. I had a hard time making eye contact with him as the secrets spilled out. At a certain point, he had to take breaks—it was too much information to absorb. He'd stand up and pace, stretch.

"Jesus," he shook his head at one point, walking into the other room to get coffee.

And I'd sit there alone, checking myself to make sure I wasn't embellishing or anything. No, I realized. I was telling the 100% truth, which just sounds different coming out of my mouth—even today.

About five hours later—my notes say four, but I think it was five—David felt we'd completed the step. He learned more about me than he bargained for. But now, he was bound to me for life. He knew things that no one but some random security cameras and friends with loose lips had knowledge of. All the secrecy I would keep folded up inside myself, bundled for safekeeping, was now being passed around.

And I felt amazing.

Sincerely amazing.

When someone says they have a weight off their shoulders,

they sort of get how enlightened I felt after that conversation with David.

"Just remember, Paul," he said, "you're only at six months. This doesn't end. Some part of your brain is always going to be trying to kill you."

That gave me pause—but good pause. My life was now going to be a constant war within. I had to live with that. I had to understand that I couldn't weather another relapse and starting over. Part of me, unbelievably, didn't believe him—that my brain was constantly working out how to ruin my life.

I thanked him and went to a used book store on auto-pilot, looking for old James Bond paperbacks. I was in a complete and utter daze. I didn't find any—or maybe I did, I don't remember—and I left.

WHEN I STOPPED drinking, I felt like I stopped being a man. I firmly and sincerely believed that. I'd suddenly abandoned a fundamental part of manhood. I'm not a "guy's guy" who's steeped in ESPN, motorcycles, UFC, or *Maxim*, but in my first months of sobriety, I heard a very clear voice cutting through all the static: *Men are supposed to drink. You're weak. You're a failure.*

I wasn't ever going to be a sober man. That's not who I was. I was the guy ordering another round of shots for everyone as soon as we finished the first one. As much as I loved being a Goodtime Charlie, I absolutely hated being a drag on the ticket. I dreaded telling people—especially my male friends—

that I was sober. I was so terrified of telling my buddies, that I practiced excuses in front of a mirror, almost to convince myself: *I'm on antibiotics. I'm driving later. I have a stomach bug.* I feared seeing a light dim in their eyes—flickers of disappointment, of pity, of farewell.

It still doesn't compute with a lot of my male friends. "You can't, like, *ever* drink again?" "What happens if you just have one?" "This is a Michelob Ultra, man. You can practically hydrate with this." Certainly, in their eyes, I should be able to handle one 12-ounce can of light beer. I used to agree with them. I've always been taken with the hard-drinking protagonists in novels and movies—all of them fueled by whiskey and riding into the night full of resolve. Seeing Clint Eastwood gun down a bunch of outlaws before sauntering up to the bar? He earned that shot of whiskey. That's how I felt about my drinking: I was entitled to it because I was a man, goddammit. It was part of our chromosomal makeup to hold our liquor. That's why there's nothing endearing about a dude staggering on the way home from the bar, puking into a snowdrift. No woman is ever five paces behind him, thinking: *Maybe there's still a chance he'll sleep with me.* It's always the other way around.

I don't want to know how many nights I've spent with the bar slowly kaleidoscoping away from me as I tried to keep up with others. "Trying to keep up" yielded me a DUI, broken relationships, job losses, financial problems, and more slurry-brained mornings than I knew what to do with. What I've come to realize is that no one expected anything of me or my drinking. I was the loneliest pace car hurtling around an empty track. Still, at my velocity, most normal people would've simply quit drinking. Instead, I simply trained harder. I was committed to awakening whatever drinking talent laid dormant in my cells. "Being a man" would magically kick in, and I would be able to handle what I was putting in my body. I was convinced if I just found the right alchemy of beer, red wine, and Jagermeister, I'd get it right. Hell, if I could harness it, maybe I'd level up and unlock a superpower. After all, none of my drinking buddies seemed to have a problem. They could drink like men and wake up the next day, just fine.

Truth be told, countless women have drunk me under the table, too. I can't tell you how many shots of Cuervo I've tossed back as a pissed-off reaction to some girl challenging my masculinity, only to regret the decision every single time. I didn't even like tequila, but I hated the idea of being someone's trophy even more. A lot of women I knew prided themselves on being "one of the boys," knocking back drink after drink, wiping their chins with their sleeves. Women who held their liquor were rare creatures to me. If I found one, I felt like I should immediately put her behind glass in a Ripley's Believe It or Not! Museum, like a cat who can bark. With every woman who could drink, I felt a challenge rise inside me. I had to prove I was a man. And still, I never understood why I was constantly losing a competitive sport I was programmed to win. If I couldn't keep up with the ladies, something was wrong with me. I've chased that ghost down—that specter of certainty that I would eventually triumph, win the night's drinking, and steal back that drinking crown.

In the end, I was a bobblehead with an encyclopedic knowledge of movie release dates, five-syllable words, and whatever else could get someone's attention. I drank because I felt like I had to. Alcohol is how I asserted myself, it's how I played my role, and it's how I protected my pride as a man. If they made action figures of drinkers (or should I say *inaction* figures), mine would come with accessories like Bottle and Sarcasm. It's laughable now to think I believed being a better man meant being hunched over a shot glass with shaky hands.

I still feel a sour pang whenever I see Instagrammed martinis or raised glasses of cabernet against a fireplace on Facebook. But it's fleeting—a quick stab of sadness like when you see postcards from an exotic locale you'll never visit. I realize now that it's all stylized, like food porn. I'm not less of a man for not being able to knock back a beer while I'm grilling outside with neighbors on a hot summer day. Now I find strength in my vulnerability, much like how bones grow stronger in the places they've broken. A lot of that strength happens on its own, too. Most of my drinking buddies have quietly fallen out of orbit with me. Happy hours have turned into nods and occasional text messages. But I've grown stronger in those places—I've found self-confidence, ambition, and determination.

Drinking hasn't ever been a competition about my manhood—it's been a struggle with who I am as a person. Now, it's more rewarding and somehow more life-affirming to tell people I don't drink. I don't fear it anymore. What I've learned in sobriety is that being a man, drinking or not, is about standing for something. I have to own *why* I'm sober. I'm not letting anyone else down by not drinking—I'm letting people down if I *do*. I can't feed the imagined two-second glimmer of sadness I *think* I'm seeing in someone else's eyes when I turn down their chardonnay. Asking for help is the bravest thing I can do as a sober guy. I guess I've decided to finally stop at the side of the road and, against every instinct, ask for directions. I'm not aimlessly wandering the countryside in circles just because that's what men do.

28

MOST EVERYONE KNEW that my sister's husband Michael was drinking all the time. A lot of people were even covering for him. They did a huge amount of maintenance, insulating him from the world. I don't even think they knew they were doing it. My parents are endlessly optimistic people who afford people they love, "slips" and "accidents" and "lapses in judgment"—

more than they would afford for most. And that's what they'd do with him. It made some sort of quiet, shriveled sense to me, even though I'd been beating my head for months about how everyone could be so blind.

Then I started getting texts from my sister:

> He admitted his drinking use. It's out of control.
> Looks like a liter of vodka per day.
> I cut off his source.
> Went to the store where he was going.
> Told them to not sell him anything there anymore.

I laughed out loud when I saw these. Not because I hate my sister, but because I felt so sorry for just how out of depth she and my parents were. This wasn't going to end anything. In the end, she was dealing with quarter-truths. When you're living with alcoholics like Michael and me, you're working with water—no details; facts slipping and spilling all over the place. We're good at giving you a piece of a larger, more terrible truth. You turn the little piece around in your hands, relieved and happy that you've been given something real, that you don't even care there's so much more where that came from. It's just like submarine countermeasures in wartime, though. Those truths just deflected you from the actual ones you needed to really worry about.

I told Laura he was still drinking. And he would continue drinking.

"He's going to stop. Cold turkey. We talked," she said defiantly.

It didn't break my heart to hear what she was going through—I wasn't feeling much in those first weeks of sobriety—but I knew for a fact that she was setting herself up for one of the worst possible seasons of a TV show ever. This was going to be the dark one where the Laura character has to endure her husband's alcoholic downfall. Once again, just as it'd happened to me, I could see his alcoholic life as gum stretched between two fingers—thin and sagging in the middle under its own weight.

"Well, that's good, I guess," I did my best impression of being supportive.

"Yeah, we'll see," she was smiling through the phone. I'm sure there were tears. "I think it's getting better. It'll get better. I know it will."

I decided to believe that Mike was going to own up to the fact that he hadn't yet processed the death of his father and he was going to stop using alcohol as the crutch. He could get past this.

I honestly believed he could.

I bought the lie.

I'D GET THESE random texts from Mike at three or four in the morning, then sometimes a missed call at seven. He'd stopped drinking with the sort of ease reserved for wizards and magicians. I couldn't believe how he'd done it. I was, quite honestly, pissed off that he'd been able to do it. I called him on the third day to check in on him and he shrugged everything off.

"I'm good," he said over the phone. "I'm honestly good."

Goddammit, I thought. *He even* sounds *good.*

"Yeah. It's not that big of a deal. I'm doing all right."

I instantly replayed all the hell I'd been through in rehab and outside of it. I wondered why I couldn't do the same thing. For many people, recovery was just a gear they could slip into. My buddy Eric from college had thoughtfully called me when I'd decided to get sober, talking me through it. There'd been no rehab or AA for him. Just recovery. Mike seemed to be no different. The bastard could just shut it all down with the click of a finger.

I wasn't mad. I was impressed.

Well, I was mad, too, but still.

For a split-second, I considered that he sounded put-together enough to be someone's sponsor.

LAURA STARTED FINDING BOTTLES. Mike insisted they weren't his and/or they were from "before." This is the same shit I pulled with Carrie. It's a reflex, the lying. The truth was that he'd never stopped drinking. That was his trick. He'd actually just started drinking *more,* keeping his foot on the accelerator, to appear like he was different. He'd fake the change of becoming sober by becoming even drunker. Come to think about it, it was kind of genius. She thought she'd beaten it back when it was really just flowing underneath the floorboards and pillows and in garage cabinets. It was everywhere around her, filling up all the spaces.

She's one of those strong-willed people who's so loving and open that it's almost a crime to take advantage of her kindness.

But he'd taken it to a new level. You can only hurt my sister so many times before that look of shocked pain turns into a hardened, skeptical scowl—a fixed expression of *I'm onto you,* which lives in the same locked-door neighborhood of *I'm done.* Everything becomes a question after that: *Why do you have to go to Kroger at nine o'clock? Why are you so awake?*

Laura is as no-bullshit as they come.

She's as loving as she can be brutal, which, as it turned out, Mike needed—and couldn't deal with.

MIKE STARTED NOT showing up to dinners and events, then started just cancelling things. I got whispers and the occasional text from my sister that they were really trying to keep him away from booze. When I did see him, he looked like he'd aged another twenty years. He'd lost a ton of weight, his skin seemed tight against the skull and the whites of eyes were purplish orange. Mike seemed like he was auditioning for a pumpkin-patch mascot who liked getting into fights. He was out of it—you'd ask him a question and all the classic Mike-isms weren't there anymore. None of the stuff I had groans ready for. Mike was just suddenly a reanimated corpse. His marionette strings had been cut. He was pleasant, picked at his food, nodded at my kids. But mostly, he was quiet and kept to himself. It haunted me.

I missed the Old Mike, I told myself, but that was the sort of thing alcoholics do. We mourn known quantities. We like counting on things being the way they are because we're usually the wild card. Watching Mike pick at his lunch, wordlessly rolling around peas on his plate, bothered me like nothing else. He'd stopped drinking—or was trying.

He was miserable.

I STARTED GETTING fast and furious texts from my sister not long after that, telling me that she—the brand-new nurse—was going to detox him at home. They'd found even more bottles in the house and their dance studio. It sounded like a recipe for disaster, but part of my morbid curiosity kept my opinions to myself. The texts that came in all hours of the night were horrifying, too. I saved some of them, if only to remind me how bad it can get. I shared some of them with my sponsor who nodded and said, "This is where it ends up. That's you if you didn't have me."

Without being around other sober people and minus the balm of Ativan and other drugs rushing through his bloodstream, Mike was facing his demons head-on for the first time in his life. He was sequestered to his bed—vomiting alcohol and when there was nothing left, bile. Then he retched blood. He started screaming in the middle of the night, taking wild swings at people who weren't there and called for people from his past. He growled, he nervously paced the house, kicking things, knocking over bookshelves. Full-on hallucinations. Still, Laura kept him there, firmly believing she was going to break him.

To me, it seemed alternately cruel and fascinating. I mean, if Mike made it through this, he'd be a goddamn hero in my eyes. A true man's man. It also reminded me that no one who drinks like us and then suddenly quits, doesn't suffer consequences. That's not how the universe worked. Everything was in balance. There were always consequences. In the history of the world, no one drank how we'd been drinking and suddenly, you, felt okay. Your body didn't decide to spare you the hummingbird-heartbeat hellish anxiety that follows. It doesn't happen.

Two days later, I checked in.

Mike was suddenly fine. My parents and sister circulate lots of group-chat messages with heavenly-prayer emojis. *He's eating things now. He has an appetite!* You could practically hear my sister weeping through the text message. They started posting Bible scriptures on Facebook after every little miracle related to Mike's recovery from hell. No, he wouldn't be a liver candidate, but his numbers were improving. (He'd destroyed his liver.) But something just didn't sit right with me about it. After my treatment program, I still felt my brain had been sucker-punched and the rest of my body followed: sore, aching, tentative, jumpy.

I called Mike and got a very laconic version of him, watching *SportsCenter* in the background.

I was calling to wish him well—to tell him just how rough these first few weeks of sobriety are. Misery loves company. I wanted to talk about how early sobriety can make you feel like your skin's translucent and everyone can see all the notes you passed between classes, all of your stolen *Playboys*, all the torn-up Valentines from grade school, all of your failures, and every bad decision you'd made. All of it blusters through on parade.

There was none of that with Mike.

I kept asking him how he was feeling.

"Getting a lot of sleep? But not that good sleep? That edgy

sleep where you feel like you're just falling to sleep, only it lasts hours?"

"Nah, not really. It's pretty much just over. I slept pretty good last night."

"Weird. Do you feel it heavy somewhere? Like in your shoulders?" I asked. "My counselor tells me my cravings rest in my chest area. Right through here."

"Nope. I feel fine."

I was getting nowhere. I promised him we'd reconnect some day.

He said he'd like that.

Later that night, Laura texted me to say that he'd been drinking on the sly again. He thought hiding vodka bottles in a boot would work.

IT EVENTUALLY HAPPENED: Mike called and asked me to be his sponsor. I told David, my sponsor, that I had a bad feeling about it, to which David had a number of even-tempered reasons why it was a horrible decision, too: I wasn't ready; I wasn't living where Mike did; I wasn't going to keep him sober; he's not prepared for a sponsor. Most of all, David argued, he doesn't really want to get sober. The people around him wanted him to be sober. "He hasn't hit his bottom yet," David shrugged. "It's sad, but true."

"That seems impossible," I said. "These are pretty bad bottoms."

"There's always a trapdoor at the bottom."

Sure enough, one night, my phone rang and a drunken Mike called me. Pots and pans were clanging in the background—I imagined Laura was angrily hurling them around, shattering ceramic cups.

"So, Paul," he said, speaking with the knowing voice of someone who got caught doing something wrong. He was only mad he got caught, now that was hiding more bottles around his house than ever. "I think I need a sponsor."

"That's a step in the right direction."

I'd already bought Mike a Big Book to mail, but since it's such an antiquated book, a bit of explanation needs to happen. You can't just mail someone a Bible and expect them to retreat to a corner of their house to absorb everything. You have to tell them what the deal's all about.

"Will you be my sponsor?"

Because I'm such a fucking people-pleaser, the word *Sure* spiraled into place but I swatted it back. I drew in a breath and tried doing the right thing—even though it felt like the wrong thing.

"No. But I can be your temporary sponsor," I said.

I explained all the limitations of our arrangement—how I was two hours away, how he needed to get to AA meetings, how he'd need to actually stop drinking. But all he heard was that I'd be his sponsor. He'd gotten that checkbox clicked.

We exchanged texts here and there, nothing like David and I did; they were more pulse-checks.

You alive, man?

Yep.

And so it went for a few weeks until my sister asked me to take him to an AA meeting. Mike's life was less dancing those days than it was occupied with going to doctor after doctor, trying to figure out what the hell was going on with his liver. His eyes seemed to glow yellow now, like Data's on *Star Trek*. I'd never seen anything like it.

One weekend, Laura's job required her to work three nights in a row, which, for me, would've meant three days of slipping into unchecked alcoholic bliss. She asked if I could take him to an AA meeting. I said sure. Two hours up, two hours back. It'd mean something. It'd bond us, maybe. I called him that morning and confirmed. He said he was just messing around with some stuff in the garage and that he'd be ready later.

I took the drive as an excuse to catch up on podcasts and decompress from my kids. Mini-vacation. I didn't mind the distraction. So I got there and Mike opened the door, shaking my hand three squeezes too hard. He flashed me his toothy grin but wouldn't spend more than two seconds looking at me. He was jumpy, bouncing from one place to the other in their house. I chalked it up to him being nervous about having his years-younger brother-in-law carting his ass to an AA meeting.

"You good?"

"I'm good, brother."

"How's married life?"

"Oh, you know your sister," he sneered, meaning it as a joke but just coming out mean. "She does nothing but eat chocolate and complain about eating chocolate."

I clenched my fists but drew in a breath. I was there, present and sober.

"You ready to go?"

"To where?" he seemed taken aback. "I thought we were staying here."

I thought this was another of his stupid jokes.

"To the meeting."

The words caused him physical harm. You could see the sentence strafe his brain, dragging deeply into his thoughts. He was being forced to do something he didn't want to do.

"You sure you want to go there? You just made a two-hour drive here," he said. "Huron is another twenty minutes. Sure you don't want to just watch football?"

"What's another twenty minutes?" I shrugged. "Besides, football. That's sports, right?"

He laughed, but only in a way that filled up the room with something other than awkwardness.

"Well, give me a few minutes. I need to get ready."

I looked him up and down. Dude was ready. Shoes were on, nice dress shirt, pressed pants. Whatever. Maybe he needed to douse his chest in Drakkar or something. He disappeared into the garage, where I heard some rumbling around and cursing. I opened the door, and he immediately laughed me off.

"Don't mind me," he said. "I'm just trying to finish a project from earlier."

The workbench was empty.

Minutes later, he emerged and clapped his hands. "Ready to go?"

"Sure thing."

We clambered into my vehicle and prepared to drive to the 7:00 meeting I'd never been to. Neither had he. We talked about how Laura had been killing herself at the hospital and the dance studio, covering for Mike since he'd been out in recent weeks, unable to teach. He winced and told me that she'd sort of let herself go, eating more than she should without working out, which made it impossible to keep a good dance studio afloat. He went on and on and on about how it was Laura's fault their clientele was suffering. She wasn't taking care of herself.

Finally, I hit the brakes and my Liberty came to a slow skid at the side of the country road. Through the trees just past Mike, I could see the vast railyards of the Wheeling and Lake Erie Railway company—all the switchbacks and engines and maintenance equipment glittering and moving around under hundreds of floodlights.

Mike was trying to figure out if I'd missed a deer he hadn't seen.

"Would you fucking knock it off about Laura?" I said.

"What?"

"What do you mean *what?* All you've done is crack on how terrible she is for the last few weeks."

"Well, she used to be tiny and petite. An actual dancer. But let me just say what we're both thinking: a diet of chocolate and Doritos doesn't look good on her."

I felt the anger rise inside me—the kind of easy venom that boils over when you feel right and entitled to be angry. But my recovery had taught me to shelf that. I narrowed my eyes instead.

"Have you been drinking?"

"Today?"

"Sure. Let's start with today."

"God, no. No way."

I sat there, letting three awkward beats elapse. It did the trick.

"All right, I had a beer."

"A beer."

"In the garage?"

He closed his eyes. "Yep."

"But you're…"

"Sick. I know. I'm not supposed to drink. That's what all the doctors tell me. I go from test to fucking test to test to test to test. And it's your mom who's driving me around all the time. You know how embarrassing that is? I need the beer."

"But they're telling you the beer is killing you."

"I fucking know," he said, not even mad.

More seconds, then I decided to push.

"It's not just one beer today, is it?"

Mike turned to me, his eyes completely gone, and I understood why he'd refused to make eye contact since I'd gotten there. I nodded and pulled off the curb. We drove the rest of the way in silence, even as it dawned on him that I was still taking him to the AA meeting.

AT THE METHODIST CHURCH, there was a small circle-and-triangle symbol emblazoned on a modest placard. That's all there was. The symbol and an arrow pointing to the basement stairs.

"I think that's a church club, man," Mike disagreed as I started to walk down the stairs.

"No. That's where the meeting is going to be."

"They don't announce meetings. They're AA meetings. They're private."

I sighed and insisted I was right: teaching him quickly how the triangle sides equaled unity, recovery, and service surrounded by the circle of wholeness.[34] As alcoholics, we like to pretend we know things we don't. I certainly didn't know what I was telling him, but I was lucky I was right. Hope was found in any AA meeting, so I didn't feel too bad.

Most of the lights were off downstairs, but in one of the corners, five people were huddled, laughing. One of them was a toothless old-timer; two other men were in their middle ages; the remaining two were women—one of whom had been court-ordered for the appearance and was barely aware of her surroundings. As we introduced ourselves and got into the discussion of the night, I paid close attention to Mike. He was quiet, he listened, he gave endearingly honest answers ("Yes, I drank today." "Yes, I could die.") because of the honesty in the room. No one was judging him. For an hour, he was 100% honest.

I felt proud of him for the first time ever.

Afterward, he gave hugs—real hugs—and exchanged genuine words, not zingers and gotchas and worn-out punchlines. He shook some hands and came away with the fifteen-second glow of someone who'd experienced hope and glimpsed at a life he *could* have. The whole car ride back, he was silent. Not angry-silent—just thoughtful. Every once in a while, he'd ask me how different that meeting was from the others I attend, then he'd nod and think, staring off in the distance.

HE STARTED CALLING me more regularly—probably once a day. He'd ask me questions about a reading or a spiritual

---

[34] Turns out, I was half-right: the arrow lines also correspond to the mental, emotional, and physical elements of the disease.

passage he'd come across. He seemed to be doing work that *I* wasn't fucking doing in my recovery. I started going to more meetings, feeling a weird competition in my veins. I couldn't let him be *more* sober than me. That wasn't how it was supposed to be.

Two weeks later, during Carrie's family's Christmas party, I'd missed a frantic voice message from my dad saying Mike was in the hospital and "it didn't look good." I did pick up when Laura called, crying, saying that Mike wasn't going to make it. The details were sketchy: broken ribs, vomited blood, CPR, low blood pressure. I couldn't tell between the sobs.

THE ICU ROOM telescoped away from me when I saw Mike, so small and frail in his hospital bed. He'd been intubated and his yellow eyes were lolling all over the place. He couldn't speak. Laura was on one side, tending to him and talking to the nurses flitting in and out of the room; my mom was on the other. My dad stood near the windows, hands in his pockets, stoic. The room was alive with medical equipment—not the kind in the backgrounds of movies and TV.

They watered his chalky lips with ice.

"What's going on, man?" I heard myself ask.

What a dumb thing to ask, I thought. I just didn't know how to process what I was seeing. He'd drank himself to this point.

There was nothing anyone could do.

After a few hours, when Laura and the doctors finally decided to let Mike go, a massive relief gave way in the room—and not a good one. My sister geysered tears. She thanked him for marrying her, for teaching her how to dance. His EKG hiccupped and sputtered. He was slipping away faster than I expected. It was happening with me in the room. I wanted nothing but to slip away into another room, to wait like an eight-year-old hiding until someone told me it was safe to come out. But I stood there, arms crossed tight against my chest, watching Mike die.

My mom sat by his side, holding his hand with one hand and caressing his head with her other. He shifted uncomfortably, unable to speak, eyes darting around, not understanding. She whispered to him, she told him everything was going to be okay. Every time she did, he'd relax a little, settling down—his brain believing what his body did not.

I remember his eyes locking with my mother's for three solid seconds. Thankful knowing. I know she saw it, too, but blinked it away. She soldiered forward with comforting him, uphill, telling him it was going to be just fine, everything will be just fine, you will see your family soon, this is all okay, Laura will be okay, we will take care of her, you don't have to worry anymore, you have nothing to be afraid of, we're here for you right now, we love you, it's okay, it's really okay, just rest, just rest, close your eyes, everything will be okay.

29

I WASNT EVER a bad person. I was just bad at being a person. That's what I tell myself anyway.

What you see is what you get. That's the real relief I've discovered in recovery: I might be boring as hell without alcohol, but at least I don't have to remember which lies I told. The answer really doesn't matter. In sobriety, for the first time ever, I'm just trying to be an actual person.

The funny thing is that, now, I trust recovering alcoholics

more than almost anyone else on the planet. I've learned that exceedingly artful liars become the most ardent truth-tellers. When I was drinking, I felt like my life was about making dozens of lies true at any given point in time—which is as exhausting as it sounds. I couldn't possibly keep track of all the lies I've told and, worse yet, believed. I now take all the energy I used to spend crafting excuses, and actually follow through. I'm learning to harness the simple power of doing what you say you're going to do. If we're only as sick as our secrets, I inherently trust people who actually know something about being poisoned from the inside. Alcoholics like me lived so long in the shadow of dishonesty that we've learned, the hard way, how to respect the truth.

If I'm honest about being dishonest, the truth has always been the real issue for me. Lying is, by far, my biggest character defect. For as long as I care to remember, I've been more confident and faster on my feet when dealing with the world through lies, half-truths, and omissions. Lying is a reflex. It made all my basic, passing interactions with people—acquaintances, post office clerks, airplane seatmates—light and tolerable. I just wanted to go through life without any real investment or judgment. It kept me fleeting, like a permanent background actor in other people's lives, quickly exiting the scene.

When Granddad used to ask me how I was doing, he'd joke: "And never mind the truth—just make it interesting." I took this as life advice and ran with it well into my thirties. I used to find comfort in being dishonest. Half the time, I didn't even *feel* like I was lying. The truth never sounded as good as what I made up. I figured a fictionalized version of me was always going to be better than the real me. Still, lying is the emptiest transaction you can have in life. It's counterfeit money handed to people you don't really respect. Yet, alcohol somehow made this acceptable to me. It caused consequences to dissolve in my brain, like I was always living on the *Enterprise* holodeck, where nothing was real, nothing had any weight.

Alcohol helped with that.

Lying becomes even easier. There's always been something sickeningly sweet about lies, I've learned. The way that they're imagined, crafted, then served to the unwitting like some decadent dessert. *Here. Taste this.* Lies are sugared intent. Nothing more. At first, they're elegant and complex, but that's the deceit: they're a seduction of the senses. In the end, my friends and family and random strangers and everybody in between were left with that sour sense that they've eaten too much. And I'll lie to them again and again and again—to make myself feel more secure, to make myself feel thinner, to make myself feel better. Some part of me will implode, fissure out. I'll be sad thinking about it. No one will ever believe me. Not the same way, at least. It's always there in their eyes, without fail. That flash of gray knowing, that's somewhere between pity and sadness.

As a truth-fearing alcoholic, I made up so many things on the fly that when I erased the booze, I also erased most of who I was. I have to preload the chamber with actual answers, which is downright embarrassing. I literally have to tell myself to remember that I love the director's cut of *Almost Famous* and that I find cooking therapeutic. Alcohol twisted and distorted the ugliest parts of me, destroying more relationships than I care to count. It eventually left me with a mile-long list of things to apologize and atone for. Missed deadlines, never-started projects, lies giving people false hope and expectations, stolen kisses with others' girlfriends. At this point, they feel like the actions of a complete stranger, but I can't entirely blame the booze. It all started with me.

Drinking put all my worst personality traits through an Instagram filter from hell—prettying up all my problems, making bad choices look stunning. Liquor created issues, sure, but it certainly didn't create who I was. Before alcohol, my life had *always* been unmanageable. I gossiped about friends, I overslept through my work alarm, I routinely flaked on dinner plans. I'd always been self-pitying, jealous, insecure, petty, argumentative, easily wounded, defensive, angry, afraid, and incapable of letting things go. None of this was new. Pinots, Popov, and pale ales were just gasoline on the campfire. I suddenly felt entitled to my feelings, developed an unjustified swagger and could rationalize everything with, "Well, I was drunk."

The truth is that I remembered everything.

I never thought things all the way through. I didn't consider consequences, tomorrows, or realities. It was easier to ignore things like utility bills, easier to push appointments off to later. "Later" was a magic time when things got done on their own accord. I tortured myself, especially in early sobriety, with trying to determine if I'd been a good person who did bad things or if I was a bad person who did good things. It was useless to consider, even though it haunted me. The crush-depth of my alcoholism destroyed almost every relationship, trust, and truth I had. There wasn't much further I could go. And unfortunately, no one remembers the truth the way you want them to—even if it *is* the truth. All I can do is move forward by carefully looking back and not shutting the door on it.

All things come to an end. They say time heals wounds—it's what you do with the time that's elapsed that matters. Sometimes you can apologize too early, sometimes never at all. In the end, you just have to care.

I have a newborn girl now. Her name is Mallory. Whenever she opens her eyes, she tracks and imprints every sight, sound, and smile around her. It's amazing to watch. And while I can't get that missing time back with my sons, I know this is the universe giving me another chance—a final shot at not just pretending to be a parent, but being a parent for real. In sobriety, I'm no longer acting like a child, but I'm just like my newborn daughter in so many ways. I'm looking around at life with peace, trust and, most of all, wonder.

FIVE

Stand in the place where you live.

—R.E.M.

MARCH 1991

I DIDN'T WANT to go at all. I hated hikes and pretty much being outdoors altogether. Boy Scouts had successfully ruined me on that, with its weekend-erasing tours of KOA camps with foulmouthed kids and their dads who liked to rip on me for liking *Star Trek* instead of shooting .22 rifles. One morning, my dad kind of insisted that I go hiking, down to the river beyond our house, just past the abandoned steel mill. I was about fifteen. It was late March, early 1990s. It was that time of year when winter had worn out its welcome and the sky had settled into newsprint-gray. My brand-new Nintendo had a vise-grip on my brain. Still, I somehow found myself lacing my little-worn boots with my dad and sister, wandering down the hillside toward the empty compound. There were rows and rows of unused steel I-beams scattered everywhere. A few empty machine shops surrounded the main complex, which lorded over the place with its rusted frame and shattered windows.

We walked down the railroad tracks my friends and I did a million times before—a derelict stretch of railway and long-unused trestles cutting through empty woods. I'm not even sure if the trees down there knew how to grow leaves. They were always skeleton hands. My sister and I collected iron ore pellets by the handful, flinging them down the track as my dad made casual observations about the world around us: the types of trees just by looking at the bark, the exact time of day it was based on where the sun was hanging in the sky, the weather that was heading our way simply based on the feathered clouds. My brain isn't wired to process the world that way, but my dad's is. My dad grew up in an era where the world around you mattered—not the smartphone in front of your face telling you what to think about the world around you.

The railway keeled and curled, mimicking the course of the Huron River a few hundred yards to the west—it'd go one way for a good quarter-mile before snapping back in another direction altogether. We stood on one of the trestles, looking out over the thick black wood and the rusted spikes.

That's when we first heard it.

It came in great cracks—almost like gunshots splitting the air. My sister ducked. My dad, though, did the math pretty quickly on what was happening and rushed into the woods with startling speed. That bothered me more than anything. My dad's the *jump-into-action* type, so I fully expected him to find an overturned vehicle with passengers in it that we'd have to rescue or something.

Typical.

No, it was the river. We edged our way through the woods to the frozen river. The ice was coming apart with a force greater than anything my physics teacher said was possible. There was nowhere else for the ice to go. It *had* to move. Great sections of it were colliding with winter-long pressure. This was the season of coming apart, relief, potential energy giving way.

Later in life, this was exactly how I felt about my recovery. This was precisely what it felt like to have my alcoholism coming undone. It was all breaking loose, and you couldn't get close to it. There was too much going on. You had to stand well off to the side and watch from a safe distance. All the great shards of ice, a foot thick in diameter, collected and bobbed at the river bend. If you got an ankle caught in it, you were looking at years of physical therapy.

Looking back on it, I see it as all the great lies and narratives and nonsense relationships I'd clogged my life with. Some were huge, some were tiny, all of them fighting for space. They'd all gathered to a great bottleneck where the ice simply had nowhere to go—a narrow comma in the earth—and that's where it all stopped, building and building and building.

My sister was the first to comment, sighing.

"Is that it?"

"Well, at least you were here to see that," Dad said. And he was usually right about these sorts of things.

I was convinced of the same thing. I knew that we'd borne witness to something special—probably unrepeatable in life—but Dad was suddenly not so sure. He kept watch, so we did, too.

Suddenly, his eyes narrowed.

"Watch this."

"Nothing's going to happen," I whined. I just wanted to get back to *Super Mario Bros. 3*—the one where you turn into a flying squirrel.

I remember standing there for what seemed like an hour, my wool gloves pleated with sections of crumpled snow and freezing from the wind, thinking how wrong my dad was.

And then, that's when it happened.

The ice roared. It literally *roared*.

The collected force behind the bottleneck was just too much. It all exploded, groaning as it did. Great shards of ice went in a thousand directions at once, taking down nearby trees and scouring the riverside. Snowy, thirty-foot trees went down, one by one, splintering in forty-five degree angles. Before I knew it, all the collected and broken things spread out downstream, thinning out.

I watched the carnage from above.

And now, later in life, I realize just how important this moment was. All my troubles, all my lies, all my resentments, all my failed relationships, all my doubts, and all my delusions had been similarly colliding and messily fighting for space inside me—until their collected weight was just too much to contain.

My whole life was a bottleneck.

Now, it just couldn't hold back the pressure. The problem was the solution. And that paradox wasn't lost on me. You could only go forward, no matter how much wreckage is holding you back.

When I first started entertaining sobriety, that's when the first thaw came. I wasn't sure it was happening, but it was. When I wasn't looking, though, when I wasn't thinking about why I was sitting in one AA meeting after another, that's when the real magic was taking place. Molecules were silently rearranging themselves inside me. And before I knew it, all the sludge of the past started to rush forward. The past broke apart before I had any say in the matter.

I was back on that river bend, twenty years before, watching the ice fracture and break and shatter and shift.

I also think of my father's hand on my head that night when I had the sunburn on vacation. I think of him selflessly caring for me into the night, rubbing my head, sweeping all my pain downstream. I also think of my mother silently tracing the creases of Mike's forehead, telling him to float on, assuring him everything would be okay down the line.

Ice flowed despite violently resisting itself.

These days, I feel something moving within me again—a current I'm not in control of, but one that I'm thrilled to feel all the same. It's hope and anxiety and fear and every other emotion I tried freezing out with alcohol—all of them swirling inside with an acidic nostalgia. There are always rivers beneath everything we do, quietly coursing through our lives—slowly and silently carving changes in our friendships, our online interactions, our families, our passing acquaintances, and what we tell ourselves about ourselves before we fall asleep at night. All the things we know about who we are—all the fears and insecurities that come whispering to us in the dark that suddenly flow freely. Everything about who we are is carried downriver—not by a constant current, but by the momentum of life breaking apart, coming loose, and of collected ruin.

And for the first time ever, I'm ready to see where that momentum takes me.

ACKNOWLEDGMENTS

Let's be honest here: this book wouldn't exist without my broken brain or the fine makers of Zima¨. Let's get them out of the way first. Yay! Truth be told, many people have played key roles in this book's completion as much as they have in my sobriety. (Some of them have even paid bail money.)

My parents, sister, and family put up with me when I was a disaster of a human being. They also had to learn how to live around me while I slowly learned how to re-live my life.

Without Anna David, you wouldn't be holding this book.

Without Lynn Houston, I wouldn't have found my voice.

I'd also like to thank my sponsor David,
Neal Doerner, Shawn Daley, Mike Verlie, Sean Golden,
Cole Downs, Jason Lichtenberger, Jason Rhodes,
Rikki Grace, Adam Knolls, Kerry Shea Penland,
Roger Register, Andy Ehmke, Mary Patterson Broome,
Becky Sasso, Amy Talbott, Julie Mesenburg, Jeff Plank,
Matt Hurwitz, Luke Krueger, Beth Held, Rachel Blakeman,
Mark Brown, Jennifer Hoening, Michelle Risser,
Jordan Mebane, Erik Bell, Vidas and Tracie Barzdukas,
Daniel Stephens, Tommy Rutger, Andrea Schellhause,
and Jerry Tuccille. Also: Shearwater's *Jet Plane & Oxbow*—
which I listened to non-stop while writing this thing.

Finally, Carrie: I'm sorry for everything. And thank you.

ABOUT THE AUTHOR

Paul Fuhr is an addiction recovery writer whose
work has appeared in The Fix, AfterParty Magazine,
and The Sobriety Collective, as well as *The Literary Review*
and *The Live Oak Review,* among others.

He also created and is the co-host of "Drop the Needle,"
a recovery podcast where guests share music that remind
them about specific recovery topics and personal stories.

He lives in Columbus, Ohio with his family and two cats
named Dr. No and Goldeneye.

His work can be found at www.paulfuhr.com.

90893963R00245

Made in the USA
Middletown, DE
26 September 2018